Poe and Women

PERSPECTIVES ON EDGAR ALLAN POE

General Editor: Barbara Cantalupo, Pennsylvania State University, Lehigh Valley

The Perspectives on Poe series includes books on new approaches to Edgar A. Poe, his work and influence; all perspectives—theoretical, historical, biographical, gender studies, source studies, cultural studies, global studies, etc.—are invited.

Titles in This Series

http://inpress.sites.lehigh.edu/

Poe and Women

Recognition and Revision

Edited by

Amy Branam Armiento
Travis Montgomery

LEHIGH UNIVERSITY PRESS
Bethlehem

Published by Lehigh University Press
Copublished by The Rowman & Littlefield Publishing Group, Inc.
4501 Forbes Boulevard, Suite 200, Lanham, Maryland 20706
www.rowman.com

86-90 Paul Street, London EC2A 4NE, United Kingdom

British Library Cataloguing in Publication Information Available

Library of Congress Cataloging-in-Publication Data

Names: Armiento, Amy Branam, 1976– editor. | Montgomery, Travis, 1980– editor.
Title: Poe and women: recognition and revision / edited by Amy Branam Armiento and
    Travis Montgomery.
Description: Bethlehem: Lehigh University Press; Lanham, Maryland: Rowman &
    Littlefield, [2023] | Series: Perspectives on Edgar Allan Poe | Includes index. |
    Summary: "Poe and Women presents essays by scholars who investigate the various
    ways in which women-Poe's female contemporaries, critics, writers, and artists,
    as well as women characters in Poe adaptations-have shaped Edgar Allan Poe's
    reputation and revised his depictions of gender"—Provided by publisher.
Identifiers: LCCN 2022045052 (print) | LCCN 2022045053 (ebook) | ISBN
    9781611463354 (cloth) | ISBN 9781611463361 (epub)
Subjects: LCSH: Poe, Edgar Allan, 1809–1849—Criticism and interpretation. | Poe,
    Edgar Allan, 1809–1849—Women. | Poe, Edgar Allan, 1809–1849—
    Friends and associates. | Women in literature. | Women and literature—United
    States—History—19th century. | LCGFT: Essays. | Literary criticism.
Classification: LCC PS2642.W6 P64 2023 (print) | LCC PS2642.W6 (ebook) | DDC
    818/.309—dc23/eng/20220923
LC record available at https://lccn.loc.gov/2022045052
LC ebook record available at https://lccn.loc.gov/2022045053

♾™ The paper used in this publication meets the minimum requirements of American
National Standard for Information Sciences—Permanence of Paper for Printed Library
Materials, ANSI/NISO Z39.48-1992.

Contents

List of Illustrations

Acknowledgments

During the 2017 American Literature Association Conference, we had a conversation about the work of Maureen Cobb Mabbott, a woman whose editorial work on the Mabbott edition of Edgar Allan Poe's writings has not received the attention it deserves. Our talk drifted to the many ways in which women shape our responses to Poe. We wondered whether a collection of essays about that subject might interest our colleagues. Similar collections focused on Herman Melville and Ernest Hemingway had already been published, and a volume dedicated to Poe would, we assumed, have wide appeal. After discussing the types of essays that should appear in such a book, we began to solicit contributions from colleagues, established Poe scholars as well as critics new to the field. The chapters that they wrote cover an impressive range of topics, all of which illuminate women's relationships to and with Poe. For trusting us with the honor of editing their work, we are grateful to them. Through their labors, *Poe and Women* gradually took shape, and we are proud of what all of us have accomplished together.

We would like to thank Katherine Crassons at Lehigh University Press for her excellent advice throughout the editorial process as well as Tricia Moore for her feedback during the drafting stage. We also want to recognize Scott Paul Gordon at Lehigh and Zachary Nycum at Rowman & Littlefield for assisting us with production. Ben Fisher graciously sat for an interview, and Jane Mabbott Austrian patiently answered a string of email questions about her mother and allowed us to use photographs from the Mabbott family collection. In addition, Ms. Austrian's daughter Gabrielle Albans Hirschfeld provided digital copies of those photographs. To these three people, we owe special thanks. We also express gratitude to Gareth Hinds, Candlewick Press, Denise Despeyroux, Miquel Serratosa, Leah Moore, John Reppion, Jeremy Slater, Alice Duke, and SelfMadeHero for permission to reproduce images discussed in John Edward Martin's essay.

Many of our academic associates also deserve recognition. We want to thank the members of the Poe Studies Association for the many opportunities to share research, workshop ideas, and collaborate—even during a pandemic. We do not take these exchanges for granted. To his dean, Dr. Charles Rix, as well as colleagues at Oklahoma Christian University, especially Dr. Gail Nash, who supported a course release for him, Travis expresses the deepest gratitude.

We would also like to thank our friends and family. Amy thanks Frank Armiento and John and Cyndi Branam for their willingness to listen to her talk about the successes, trials, and tribulations encountered throughout this project. For Janna Montgomery's advice and sympathetic ear, Travis is, as ever, grateful, and he is thankful to Susan Anderson, who introduced him to the delights of reading.

To the women who taught us, we owe inestimable debts. Amy is grateful to the many women who modeled what it means to be a teacher-scholar, especially Bonnie Wyss; Dr. Kathleen Sherman; Professor Jane Martin; Sister M. JoEllen Scheetz, OSF; Dr. Frances Mayhew Rippy; Dr. Maude Jennings; Dr. Margaret Reid; Dr. Angela Sorby; and Dr. Diane Long Hoeveler. Similarly grateful to exemplary women, Travis thanks Dr. Cami Agan, Dr. Peggy Gipson, Dr. Kathryn McKee, Dr. Ethel Young-Minor, and Dr. Debra Spurgeon—all of whom helped him grow as a thinker and manage the challenges of academic life.

Introduction

Amy Branam Armiento and Travis Montgomery

Publishing a volume of essays about women and Poe might seem an inauspicious undertaking. After all, Poe notoriously identified "the death . . . of a beautiful woman" as "the most poetical topic in the world," and dead, dying, or doomed women fill his writings.[1] The names Annabel Lee, Berenice, Eleonora, Morella, Lenore, Ligeia, and Madeline Usher are familiar to many readers. There are, however, additional female unfortunates depicted by Poe. Witness the sleeper Irenë, Madame L'Espanaye (and her daughter), the Marchese Montoni, Mary Rogers, Lady Rowena of Tremaine, Scheherazade, Mrs. Wyatt, and Psyche Zenobia. The list also features nameless women such as the bride of the obsessive painter mentioned in "The Oval Portrait," the wife of the homicidal narrator of "The Black Cat," and the extorted royal in "The Purloined Letter." There are, of course, others. A partial listing nevertheless reveals the frequency with which Poe portrayed women beyond help or in peril, and the implication that he fetishized such characters has not escaped critical notice. For example, Karen Weekes insists that "Poe never wrote about women at all, writing instead about a female object and ignoring dimensions of character that add depth to these repeated stereotypes of the beautiful damsel."[2] As the saying indicates, dead women tell no tales, and the persistent silencing of women in his texts suggests that Poe accepted the dominant gender ideology of the antebellum world he inhabited, a place where most Americans deemed female submission to male authority natural and desirable.

Nevertheless, many of the women in Poe's texts are, in some respects, irrepressible. Madeline Usher and Ligeia die but do not stay dead, returning to haunt the deranged men who neither control nor silence them completely. In fact, those women undermine their oppressors' power. According to Leland S. Person Jr., the uncanny reappearances of Madeline and Ligeia cause "serious disturbance[s] within the male imagination and the subversion of those reductive imaginative forms in which the male imagination would contain women."[3] Other deceased women in the Poe oeuvre—Annabel Lee, Irenë, Lenore, and Mrs. Wyatt—linger in the memories of inconsolable lovers who cannot forget them. Moreover, even female characters silenced with shocking brutality such as the wife in "The Black Cat," whose husband murders her with an ax, and Berenice, who dies of shock while a madman rips out her teeth, testify, through their appalling deaths, to the horrors of male violence against women. To be sure, gruesome images of that sort do little to advance the idea that patriarchal power is benign. In short, Poe's portrayals of women are complicated; they are not uniform in kind, and those depictions lend themselves to divergent readings.

Such interpretive elasticity may account in part for the continuing appeal of Poe's writings, and women figure prominently among the artists and critics fascinated by the writer's creative legacy. As Eliza Richards observes, "Women were among the most voluble and valuable contributors to the posthumous recuperations of Poe's literary reputation."[4] The nineteenth-century memoirs of Poe penned by Sarah Helen Whitman and Mary Gove Nichols, both of whom defended Poe's character, are familiar to scholars.[5] Women have, however, shaped Poe's reputation in more subtle ways. Consider, for example, the work of creative writers inspired by Poe's imaginative power. Women as far removed from each other in time as Harriet Prescott Spofford and Sue Grafton have taken themes explored by Poe in new directions, and creating a comprehensive list of such writers would doubtless be a daunting task. In addition, critical works produced by women have forever changed the ways scholars respond to the Poe oeuvre and think about the man himself. The research interests of these women have ranged widely, including everything from gender issues and racial matters to textual criticism and ecocritical themes.

Considering these varied interventions, a book-length work about the various ways in which women—Poe's female contemporaries, scholars, popular writers and artists, as well as women characters in Poe adaptations—have influenced perceptions of Poe is long overdue. There are, of course, models for such studies. Edited collections that highlight the various roles women have played in the lives and works of canonized American male authors have appeared in print. To illustrate, the University of Massachusetts Press published John L. Idol and Melinda Ponder's *Hawthorne and Women: Engendering and Expanding the Hawthorne Tradition* in 1999. Three years later, the University of Alabama Press brought out Gloria Holland and Lawrence R. Broer's *Hemingway and Women: Female Critics and the Female Voice*, and in 2006, the Kent State University Press released Elizabeth Schultz and Haskell Springer's *Melville and Women*. These collections, which have helped critics examine the thorny complexities of gender representations in texts written by men, opened new doors of critical inquiry.

Poe and Women should have a similar effect. Standing on the shoulders of Colin Dayan, Cynthia Jordan, J. Gerald Kennedy, Barbara Johnson, and other critics who have investigated Poe's depictions of women, many of our contributors discuss those characters, too.[6] Interpretations of that sort do not, however, account for the ways that women have influenced Poe's legacy through biography, criticism, editorial work, and creative adaptation, and *Poe and Women* offers insights into all of these subjects. This volume foregrounds how studies of Poe have been shaped by the wide-ranging contributions and forms of intervention made by women. The chapters cover a time frame that extends from the mid-nineteenth century to the twenty-first, with some contributors venturing beyond traditional literary criticism to examine Poe's unique place within popular culture. Although creative works by women are emphasized in this volume, the disruptive significance of Poe's female characters in films directed by men as well as in comics written and illustrated by artists of all genders is also explored. Some recent works in these visual media offer remarkably subversive portrayals of Poe's fictional women, revealing the ideological limits of the original characterizations while imagining new gender paradigms. Most important, these portrayals remind readers of Poe about the thematic centrality of gender in his writings, and for that reason, a consideration of such representations belongs in a book showing how women, even imaginary figures, have shaped contemporary responses to Poe and his writings. The collection also includes two surveys of Poe criticism written by women. Taken together, the following chapters demonstrate how ideologies of gender and power underlie creative and interpretive work, illuminating how female writers from the antebellum era influenced Poe's writings, how women have interpreted Poe and his texts, how the field of Poe studies is indebted to those readers and critics, and how popular adaptions of Poe material in films, fictional works, and comics represent the experiences of women. Exploring these varying areas, this volume shows how the influence of women—broadly conceived—has come to define the field of Poe studies, past and present.

Arranged by subject, the collection has two sections. The first of these, titled "Recognition," contains four essays in which contributors demonstrate how women have shaped Poe's reputation, inspired some of his writings, and interpreted his works. "'The Vast Pantheon of Speculation': Edgar Allan Poe and His Women Biographers" is the first chapter. Here, Sandra Tomc analyzes depictions of Poe in biographies written by female authors. Relationships with women inspired much of Poe's imaginative work, and writers such as Sarah Helen Whitman and Marie Bonaparte have, as Tomc argues, challenged the Griswoldian image of Poe, a figure whose lack of self-control and pecuniary prowess suggested moral corruption. Rejecting the ideals of bourgeois manhood influencing that character assessment, these women penned sympathetic accounts of Poe's life, presenting "Poe as a figure moulded and influenced by women." Far from the "failed adult man" described by Griswold, the Poe imagined by female biographers was a true genius—a tormented writer who transformed personal trauma into timeless art as well as a model for women writers whose intellectual and professional ambitions made them social outsiders.

Critics such as Eliza Richards have studied the ways that female authors from the nineteenth century inspired Poe, and in the second chapter, "Spiritual Dialogues: Lydia Maria Child, Edgar Allan Poe, and the Politics of Unity," Adam C. Bradford continues that work. In particular, he investigates the influence that *Philothea*, Child's 1836 romance of ancient Greece, wielded over Poe, who published *two* laudatory reviews of the novel. Of particular interest to him were, Bradford suggests, the philosophical ideas about cosmic unity that the book conveyed. Like her Transcendentalist associates, Child insisted that such unity was the ultimate reality while the isolate selfhood of the individual was illusory. Clearly this notion of the oneness of all things captivated Poe, who explored that concept at length through texts like "The Colloquy of Monos and Una," "Mesmeric Revelation," and *Eureka*.

The remaining chapters in section one address women's scholarship from the latter half of the twentieth century into the twenty-first. Surveying studies published since the late 1960s, Amy Branam Armiento acknowledges "women's insightful contributions to Poe studies" in her essay "Fifty Years of Women's Scholarship on Poe." These contributions cover an impressive range of subjects, some of the most investigated topics being gender and race in Poe's writings as well as nineteenth-century medicine and antebellum print culture. In addition, Armiento discusses the editorial work performed by women who have prepared editions of Poe's writings or directed the publication of Poe journals. This chapter shows not only how women have contributed to Poe studies but also how academic inclusivity enriches scholarly inquiry.

Clara Petino's chapter, "Transnational Poe and Women Scholars Abroad," complements Armiento's, indicating that international women scholars have led Poe criticism into the twenty-first century in their respective nations. Identifying studies by Japanese, Russian, Portuguese, Brazilian, and Spanish scholars, Petino observes that all of these women built on earlier investigations into the ways Poe has shaped the literary cultures of their home countries. Significantly, these critics often challenged traditional approaches to Poe's works and biography, correcting misinformation, mistranslations, and misrepresentations that derived from commentators such as Baudelaire and other male writers. This chapter honors the critical legacy of these women and indicates that their research reveals, at times, how writers outside the Anglophone world use translations and adaptations of Poe's writings to expose political tensions within their own countries. Petino also discusses the scholarship of Lois Davis Vines, an esteemed U.S. critic whose contributions to the study of Poe's literary influence in France are indispensable. To understand the transnational significance of Poe, scholars depend on the work of all the women recognized by Petino.

The second section, titled "Revision," features essays in which contributors examine contemporary representations of Poe's female characters. Conveyed through various media, including film, fiction, and the graphic novel, these portrayals not only expose the perils of patriarchal overreach but also help viewers and readers see Poe's legacy from fresh perspectives. Cinematic depictions of that sort are analyzed under a feminist psychoanalytic lens in Alexandra Reuber's "'Can You See Me?': Poe's Female Characters and the Struggle for Self-Definition on Film."[7] In this chapter, Reuber discusses three recent films, showing how they reimagine gender relationships between characters created by Poe. In so doing, she confronts the reality that most cinematic adaptations of Poe's works produced during the twentieth century were directed by men and dominated by monstrous female characters. However, three more recent Poe adaptations—*The Black Cat* (2007), *Edgar Allan Poe's "Morella"* (2008), and *Berenice* (2015)—offer surprisingly subversive depictions of women. Even though these films also had male directors, Reuber argues that they "explore the psychological impact of an autonomous female character on her male counterpart [and] challenge *his* false notions of selfhood and identity." In all of these movies, women undermine the nineteenth-century gender roles affirmed by their male counterparts, and once those repressive, social constructs become destabilized, the men feel that their identities, even their very lives, are threatened. Such psychological themes are latent in Poe's stories, but as Reuber demonstrates, the three films mentioned above bring this ideologically disruptive material to the fore. Moreover, these adaptations depict women with an agency that signals ongoing changes within the film industry itself. Featuring commentary on performances by female actors, Reuber's analyses also call attention to the collaborative nature of filmmaking, encouraging scholars to consider other ways that women influence cinematic adaptations of Poe's texts.

Like films, comics and graphic novels are often produced by teams, but in "'And She Grew Strangely': Poe, Women, and Comics," John Edward Martin indicates that many women in the comics business exercise an impressive degree of creative control over the stories they tell. Although comic adaptations of Poe have received some critical attention, Martin breaks new ground in his essay, revealing the ways in which women—in particular, Caitlin R. Kiernan, Denise Despeyroux, Leah Moore, Alice Duke, Dawn Brown, Wendy

Pini, and Rachel Pollack—as well as their collaborators have re-envisioned Poe's works, rewriting Poe's tales with female protagonists and exploring "the *communal* effects" of patriarchal violence. As he reflects on the challenges involved in adapting nineteenth-century texts for audiences whose understandings of gender differ significantly from the antebellum notions familiar to Poe, Martin argues that the alterations and interventions made by female artists ultimately appeal to a contemporary comics readership that is remarkably diverse.

In addition to creators of comics, many fiction writers have reimagined Poe's texts. In "'Sort of E. A. Poeish': Edgar Allan Poe and Female Pulp Writers," Kevin Knott traces the influence of Poe's Gothic and satiric works on stories by women writers published in *Unknown* and *Weird Tales*, two periodicals from the Golden Age of pulp magazines. Contemporaries of H. P. Lovecraft and his set, these women have not received as much scholarly attention as their male counterparts in the trade. Knott helps redress that situation. Significantly, many female pulp writers were, like Lovecraft, students of Poe, and according to Knott, Meredith Davis, Greye La Spina, Mona Farnsworth, Jane Rice, and Mary Elizabeth Counselman all pay homage to Poe. Adapting Poe's Weird fiction techniques for twentieth-century readers, these women reimagined conventions of gender *and* genre. As Knott puts it, they "cautiously subvert[ed] the more misogynistic characteristics of the pulp narratives, including the menacing of female characters to incite male characters to action, the visible display (and graphic description) of female bodies, and many other tropes."

Poe's prominence is also evident in longer fictional works by female authors published in the twenty-first century, as Melanie R. Anderson asserts in the final chapter, "Traces of Poe's House of Usher in the Work of Contemporary Women Horror Writers." For Anderson, Poe's tale of a doomed family and its ruined estate is a literary touchstone for many women producing Gothic fiction at the present time. Derived in part from the writings of his predecessors in the literature of terror, the haunted house imagined by Poe in "The Fall of the House of Usher" is a powerful symbol of the horrifying realities of violence and constraint that women can experience within the ostensibly protective walls of domesticity. Madeline Usher, who will not lie still in her tomb, resembles, in some respects, the woman who rejects inhibiting social forces. Although Poe never explored female consciousness as profoundly as he investigated the minds of troubled men, the subversive implications of his tale of the Usher family are clear to contemporary women writers such as Sarah Waters, Cherie Priest, and Silvia Moreno-Garcia, all of whom ingeniously adapt imagery and situations from "The Fall of the House of Usher" to expose the buried traumas resulting from patriarchal brutality. According to Anderson, the "vibrant and terrifying works" of these imaginative authors "address problematic parts of the Gothic tradition with an awareness of today's reading audience and contemporary social realities."

Bringing the collection to a close is an afterword in which Travis Montgomery pays tribute to Maureen Cobb Mabbott, a woman whose contributions to Poe scholarship deserve more attention. Maureen helped her husband, Thomas Ollive Mabbott, prepare *The Collected Works of Edgar Allan Poe* for publication. A homemaker for most of her adult life, Maureen nevertheless had a wealth of personal experiences and educational accomplishments that uniquely qualified her to complete what was arguably the most important editorial project in Poe studies, but her work has gone largely unrecognized. One reason for this situation is that Maureen lived on the margins of the academy, an institution dominated—especially so in her time—by men while Thomas, a scholar active within the profession, was a familiar figure. The fact remains, however, that the oft-cited Mabbott edition could not have been published without the editorial contributions and support of Maureen. Pointing out evidence of her influence on this essential textual resource, Montgomery shows that Maureen Mabbott is a woman to whom Poe scholars owe a great deal.

Comprising original interpretative essays and enlightening reviews of scholarly literature, *Poe and Women* will appeal to readers interested in Poe, his contemporaries, Poe scholarship, and the writer's omnipresence in global popular culture. As this volume makes clear, women have been vital to the establishment of Poe's reputation in the United States and abroad, and Poe-related research undertaken by women has resulted in a formidable body of scholarship that deserves more study. In addition, gender constructs prove to be a key theme in adaptations of Poe's work, and this collection highlights important texts, written and visual, that may be unfamiliar to many Poe enthusiasts. A decidedly feminist work, this collection of essays does not, however, advance a monolithic feminism; capacious in scope, the book embraces traditional approaches as well as new directions in gender studies. With no illusions that this volume exhausts all the relevant material, the editors are nevertheless confident that the following essays will prove inspirational, stimulating others to explore further the many intriguing connections between women and Poe.

NOTES

1. Edgar Allan Poe, "The Philosophy of Composition," *Essays & Reviews*, ed. G. R. Thompson (New York: Library of America, 1984), 19.

2. Karen Weekes, "Poe's Feminine Ideal," *The Cambridge Companion to Edgar Allan Poe*, ed. Kevin J. Hayes (New York: Cambridge University Press, 2002), 150.

3. Leland S. Person Jr., *Aesthetic Headaches: Women and a Masculine Poetics in Poe, Melville, & Hawthorne* (Athens: Georgia University Press, 1988), 23.

4. Eliza Richards, "Women's Place in Poe Studies," *Poe Studies* 33 (2000): 11.

5. For excerpts from these memoirs, see Benjamin F. Fisher, ed., *Poe in His Own Time* (Iowa City: Iowa University Press, 2010).

6. See Colin Dayan, "Poe's Women: A Feminist Poe?" *Poe Studies* 24, nos. 1–2 (1991): 1–12; Colin Dayan, "Amorous Bondage: Poe, Ladies and Slaves," *American Literature* 66, no. 2 (1994): 239–73; Cynthia S. Jordan, *Second Stories: The Politics of Language, Form, and Gender in Early American Fiction* (Chapel Hill: University of North Carolina Press, 1989); J. Gerald Kennedy, "Poe, 'Ligeia,' and the Problem of Dying Women," in *New Essays on Poe's Major Tales*, ed. Kenneth Silverman (Cambridge: Cambridge University Press, 1993), 113–29; and Barbara Johnson, "The Frame of Reference: Poe, Lacan, Derrida," *Yale French Studies* no. 55/56 (1977): 457–505.

7. Problematic as psychoanalysis—a practice shaped, in part, by Freudian misogyny—can be, that mode of interpretation, when shorn of sexist assumptions about gender, remains a fruitful approach for film critics and Poe scholars. See Elizabeth Young-Bruehl and Laura Wexler, "On 'Psychoanalysis and Feminism,'" *Social Research* 59, no. 2 (1992): 453–83. In this article, Young-Bruehl and Wexler acknowledge the long and complicated relationship between feminist studies and psychoanalytical inquiry. Blending those approaches is still, as Young-Bruehl and Wexler indicate, common practice in many film critiques. In particular, the notion of the "Other," despite its conceptual limitations, figures prominently in such interpretive work, and since the 1970s, that notion has been used by film critics to describe the neurotic—and often violent—responses to female sexuality (Young-Bruehl and Wexler 479). In addition, the "Other" is still an important critical tool for scholars investigating gender issues in Poe's writings. See, for example, Katherine J. Kim's "Horrifying Obsession: Reading Incest in Edgar Allan Poe's 'Ligeia'" *Sexuality & Culture* 25, no. 3 (2021): 960–80. In a similar way, Reuber makes use of the "Other" in her analyses of cinematic Poe adaptations.

Chapter One

"The Vast Pantheon of Speculation"

Edgar Allan Poe and His Women Biographers

Sandra Tomc

In Rufus Griswold's notorious biographies of Edgar Allan Poe, which appeared in 1849 and 1850, Poe is an author cursed and finally doomed by erratic paternal forces. In Griswold's telling, Poe, a child abandoned by his biological father and orphaned at the age of three, becomes the ward of John Allan, whose wealth and sophistication do not compensate for his lack of paternal judgment. As a child, Poe is already a precocious, outsized character, and his foster father's "well-meant but ill-judged indulgence" exacerbates "[t]he proud, nervous irritability of the boy's nature." In Griswold's words, "Nothing was permitted which could 'break his spirit.'"[1] At one point, when a disobedient Poe receives punishment at school, "Mr. Allan's anger" is so "aroused" by "the enormity of such an insult to his son and to himself" that he demands his money back from the school, "determined that the child should not again be subjected to such tyranny." Reflecting on this episode, Griswold wonders, "Who can estimate the effect of this puerile triumph upon the growth of that morbid self-esteem which characterized the author in afterlife?"[2] He concludes that the mixture of Poe's "irritability" and the poor paternal judgement of Allan resulted in the ill-fated writer's utter failure to absorb white male genteel standards of success and self-discipline.

Accordingly, the Poe of Griswold's imagination is notable for his failure of all nineteenth-century tests of masculinity, from self-reliance and trustworthiness to duty and success at business. Famed "for feats of hardihood, strength

1

and activity," Poe nevertheless "neglect[s] his duties and disobey[s] orders."[3] He has a chance to succeed at West Point, but his mind cannot abide "the dull routine of the camp or barracks."[4] Full of talent, Poe is taken under the wing of well-meaning editors, including T. W. White, publisher of the *Southern Literary Messenger*. Even so, Poe "[can]not bear his good fortune. On receiving a month's salary [from White] he gave himself up to . . . a condition of brutish drunkenness, and Mr. White dismissed him."[5] Many of Poe's contemporaries blamed the 1840s literary market, with its mass culture audiences and economies, for Poe's lack of success. Griswold acknowledges that "it requires considerable capital to carry on a monthly" magazine of the kind Poe dreamt of running. Yet Griswold also believes Poe could have succeeded: "I think it would not have been difficult with his well-earned fame as a magazinist, for him to have found a competent and suitable publisher." What Poe lacks is not money but "the consistency and steadiness of application indispensable to success in such pursuits."[6] He is beset by "feebleness of will."[7] Indeed, in Griswold's account, Poe is indifferent to even rudimentary self-care. At one point his friends find him "[t]hin, and pale even to ghastliness. . . . A well-worn frock coat concealed the absence of a shirt, and imperfect boots disclosed the want of hose."[8] Griswold is vaguely sympathetic: "No author of as much genius had ever in this country as much unhappiness." Nevertheless, he believes that Poe had opportunities and talents that others would have welcomed. Quoting a piece in the *Southern Literary Messenger*, Griswold concludes, "the blemishes in his life were the effects of character rather than circumstances."[9] Griswold's damning portrait of Poe, which was afterwards revealed to contain numerous inaccuracies and even outright fabrications, would be canonized in the years that followed as the sole and indisputable source of knowledge about the author. Indeed, portraits of Poe produced in the decades after his death invariably took their cue from Griswold: George Gilfillan's 1854 essay about Poe's works published in the *Edinburgh Review* harps upon Poe's lack of "self-control," "common-sense" and "sobriety," noting that while "[p]oets, as a tribe, have been rather a worthless, wicked set of people[,] . . . Edgar Poe, instead of being an exception, was probably *the* most wicked of all his fraternity."[10]

In the 1860s, defenders of Poe began to make themselves heard. Many of the most powerful in their defense of Poe were women: Sarah Helen Whitman, Elizabeth Oakes Smith, and Mary Gove Nichols.[11] Instead of simply defending Poe by disproving Griswold's accounts or disparaging Griswold for his piety and intolerance, these women writers and memorialists offered a radical rethinking of Poe's genealogy and development, shifting what in Griswold's biographies was an emphasis on father figures and the standards of genteel white masculinity to an emphasis on Poe as a figure moulded and influenced by women. In these accounts, Poe's incomprehensible conduct as a masculine subject becomes logical and transparent once he is understood as a product of feminine genealogies and energies. Whereas Griswold's biographies unfold through a series of failed paternal experiments, in which one powerful man after another tries to take Poe under his wing, the biographies of these women elaborate a sequence of maternal and domestic affiliations through which Poe emerges not as a failed adult man but as a timeless "child" of genius and imagination.

The following pages, then, relate the history of Poe's women biographers, beginning with Sarah Helen Whitman and ending with Marie Bonaparte, whose minute exploration of Poe's relationship with a lost mother represents the apotheosis of the biographical tradition launched by Poe's women contemporaries. This history of Poe's women biographers illuminates Poe's larger relationship to women writers and readers. Of course, as scholars have long understood, Poe had a complex relationship to the women writers in his New York salon circle. In part, this relationship was personal. Poe's extended flirtation with Frances Osgood, his arguments with Elizabeth Ellet, and his later engagement to Whitman made him into an object of intense gossip and scandalized interest for the women writers of his day. In addition, the relationship between Poe and these women was professional and aesthetic. In Eliza Richards's assessment, Poe as a professional author stood in a competitive relationship with women poets. Often echoing their words back to them in slightly altered, flattering, but nevertheless plagiaristic form, he sought to convert the "poetess" from "the ideal producer of poetry into an ideal consumer of his own."[12] One of the things made clear by the biographies of Poe authored by women, however, is that the Poe of the New York salons—sensitive, chivalrous, indebted to the mind and heart of the "poetess"—was in some respects the retroactive creation of women salon members, who rescued Poe not by defending him but by refiguring him as a writer shaped by and indebted to women.

In one sense, Griswold's biography itself contained an important exception to its own litany of Poe's antipaternalistic misconduct. Toward the end of his "Memoir," Griswold acknowledges that women might take exception to his portrait of Poe. He recalls a conversation he had with Frances Osgood shortly after Poe's death: "Speaking of him one day soon after his death, with the late Mrs. Osgood, . . . she said she did not doubt that my view of Mr. Poe, which she knew indeed to be the common view, was perfectly just, as it regarded him *in his relations with men*; but *to women* he was different. . . ."[13] Griswold then inserts in his biography extended passages about Poe from letters penned by Osgood, who declares, "I think no one could know him—no one *has* known him personally—certainly no woman—without feeling" an "affectionate interest in him." She goes on:

I can sincerely say, that although I have frequently *heard* of aberrations on his part from "the straight and narrow path," I have never *seen* him otherwise than gentle, generous, well-bred, and fastidiously refined. To a sensitive and delicately-nurtured woman, there was a peculiar and irresistible charm in the chivalric, graceful, and almost tender reverence with which he invariably approached all women who won his respect.

Reconfiguring Poe as a creature legible to women alone, Osgood character- izes him as a "stray child of Poetry and Passion," who became the prey of "unwomanly and slander-loving gossips."[14] Nevertheless, Griswold goes on to dismiss this view of Poe, insisting on "his shrewd and naturally unamiable character."[15] But subsequent defences of Poe suggest that these passages pro- vided a flaw in Griswold's portrait that women writers in his New York circle determined to expose.

Accordingly, the reclamation of Poe from the paternalistic history elabo- rated by Griswold animates Sarah Helen Whitman's 1860 biography, *Edgar Allan Poe and His Critics*. An intellectual and poet living in Providence, Rhode Island, Whitman was engaged to Poe briefly in 1848. The relationship had reportedly ended when Poe broke a temperance pledge he had made to her. Whitman and Poe had begun their relationship through correspondence and did not meet face-to-face more than a handful of times in the fall of 1848. It is unclear how well they actually knew each other.[16] In any case, with the publication of *Edgar Allan Poe and His Critics*, Whitman became the chief standard-bearer of Poe's rehabilitation, claiming even to have conversations with him from beyond the grave.[17] Of interest here is Whitman's reposition- ing of Poe within nineteenth-century gender landscapes and subjectivities. Whereas Osgood imagines a Poe whose true nature is only legible to a "sensitive and delicately nurtured woman," Whitman more radically rewrites Poe's literary and personal history as one inextricably woven with the lives of women relatives and women authors. Accusing Griswold of being deficient in "candor and authenticity," she presents his "Memoir" as a travesty, filled with "remorseless violations of the trust confided to him."[18] Whitman proceeds to lay out a sharply divergent history for Poe, one which focuses on his domestic life and in which women feature as his protectors and sources of inspiration.

Whereas Griswold's Poe frequents the public spaces of streets and taverns where he fails in the teleological journey of capitalist masculinity, Whitman opens her book by asking the reader to imagine a secluded indoor space, "a quiet drawing-room in ——— street, New York—a sort of fragrant and deli- cious 'clovernook' in the heart of the noisy city" where "hung, some three years ago," the portraits of famous American authors.[19] Whitman is recalling a New York literary show held in a home in the early 1850s that featured paintings of major U.S. cultural figures. Directing the reader's eye not to the authors, precisely, but to an alternative historiography enabled through the mediation of the feminized drawing room/gallery, Whitman notes that the portraits of Poe and Griswold hang on one wall side-by-side. Instead of facing a future of what Griswold called "ambition," both portraits look into the room, facing the portrait of Frances Osgood, the writer whom both Poe and Griswold reputedly loved. With this opening gesture, which transforms Griswold's linear history into a kind of intersubjective module, Whitman invites readers to see a different history of Poe, one in which Griswold, instead of acting as an objective chronicler of truth, furiously battles Poe for Osgood's devotion. In this triangulated scene, the painting of Poe takes on new meanings and resonances. Rather than memorializing a linear life journey, his portrait speaks of antic journeys that transcend life and death. His painted face is like "a beautiful and desolate shrine from which the Genius had departed" for new worlds.[20] In this revisionist history of Poe, Griswold barely deserves mention; indeed, his name goes unsaid: "Near this luminous but impassive face, with its sad and soulless eyes, was a portrait of Poe's unrelenting biographist."[21] Minimalizing Griswold allows Whitman to turn to the primacy of Osgood in the formation of both men's careers:

> In a recess opposite hung a picture of the fascinating Mrs.—, whose genius both had so fervently admired, and for whose coveted praise and friendship both had been competitors. Looking at the beautiful portrait of this lady—the face so full of enthusiasm, and dreamy, tropical sunshine—remembering the eloquent words of her praise, as expressed in the prodigal and passionate exaggerations of her verse, one ceases to wonder at the rivalries and enmities enkindled within the hearts of those who admired her genius and her grace—rivalries and enmities which the grave itself could not cancel or appease.[22]

Realigning Poe's life as one configured by Osgood, Whitman goes on to retell his history in a way that emphasizes his domestic and maternal influences. Both of Griswold's biographies end with Poe isolated and alone, his ghost looking longingly at the portals of a heaven whose gates he will never enter, wandering in a tempest, his "heart gnawed with anguish."[23] By contrast, Whitman's Poe is a fixture in the sociable realms of New York's salon world where his recitations "electrify the gay company" (22). Banishing Poe's host of male critics, including Griswold, Whitman quotes Elizabeth Barrett Browning as the supreme authority on Poe. About "The Raven," Browning, according to Whitman, wrote, "This vivid writing—this *power which is felt*—has produced a sensation here in England." Instead of situating Poe in the company of a series of father figures, Whitman puts him in the company of the salon world's women: "He delighted in the society of superior women, and had an exquisite perception of all graces of manner, and shades of expression."[24] Moreover, whereas Griswold's biography purports to chronicle Poe's failures as a professional and public figure, Whitman specifies that hers is a story produced by those with an intimate knowledge of Poe's "domestic and social life."[25]

Many of the 1840s accounts that furnished Griswold with material for his obituary and memoir depict Poe not only as an alcoholic but also as a domestic abuser. In a peculiarly vicious caricature of Poe penned by Thomas Dunn English in 1846, Poe "never gets drunk more than five days out of the seven; tells the truth sometimes by mistake; has moral courage sufficient to flog his wife, when he thinks she deserves it, and occasionally without any thought upon the subject, merely to keep his hand in."[26] In 1846, when this caricature appeared, Poe's wife Virginia was dying of tuberculosis. The idea that Poe somehow contributed to her death became part of the lurid Poe mythology generated by Griswold's memoirs. Whitman not only stamps out this rumor by asserting that Virginia died of "lingering consumption" and pointing out that even Griswold visited her and saw for himself her condition, but she also portrays Virginia as a living presence in Poe's life as an artist.[27] She brings Virginia in to sit in the company of the salon women who redeem Poe's reputation: "Sometimes his fair young wife was seen with him at these weekly assemblages in Waverley Place. She seldom took part in the conversation, but the memory of her sweet and girlish face, always animated and vivacious, repels the assertion, afterwards so cruelly and recklessly made, that she died a victim to the neglect and unkindness of her husband."[28]

In the 1860s, more reminiscences of Poe emerged from the women writers with whom he had socialized. Most significant, perhaps, were the reminiscences published by Elizabeth Oakes Smith. In fact, Smith had published a defense of Poe in 1857, before Whitman's biography had appeared. The defense was noncommittal on the question of Poe's morality, largely reproducing Griswold's characterization of Poe as a person with numerous "vices" and "radical defect[s] of character."[29] Nevertheless, Smith here began a tentative redemption of Poe which she would later expand. Describing Poe as "a white-winged angel trailing his beautiful wings through the filth and mire of the highway," Smith allowed herself to wonder what could make someone behave in so self-destructive a way.[30] She decides that Poe, far from being responsible for his own flaws and ungrateful to helpful fathers, suffered from a dark paternal legacy.

In one sense, Smith recapitulates Griswold's idea of Allan as someone who overindulged Poe during childhood, an overindulgence responsible for Poe's later lack of self-discipline, but unlike Griswold, for whom Allan is little more than a misguided parent, Smith sees Allan as a darkly sinister figure who has committed a "grievous crime." "Mr. Allen [*sic*]," she argues, "was childless and wealthy." She goes on, "When [Allan] had once assumed the responsibility of this boy, it was his duty to carry it through, and to see how the world went with him. After he had denuded him by his indulgence, it was the hight [*sic*] of cruelty for him to cast him defenseless as he was upon the hard bosses of the world."[31] In this passage, Smith blames not just Allan but the larger ideology of masculine aggression—encapsulated by the term "hard bosses"—that, in her mind, Poe had imbibed. She adds, "[I]t must be borne in mind that the young Edgar was living in a society in which spirit is ranked as the test of manliness, where coercion is reserved, like the whip, for the slave only, and where the assertion that 'he who ruleth himself is greater than him who taketh a city,' is a musty old fogy view, unbecoming a gentleman."[32] In Smith's view, Poe is the victim of a social orthodoxy that celebrates violent, transgressive behaviors in men.

Smith's next defense of Poe, published in 1867 after Whitman's book had given fuel to Poe's defenders, was considerably more vociferous, not only in its reclamation of Poe but also in its insistence that Poe had been wronged by male authority and belonged, not in a history of fathers whose trust he had betrayed, but in a history of nurturing poetic women. Whereas Smith's first article begins with images of men "drunk in the gutter" and mentions Poe's "gross appetites," her second begins by denouncing Allan.[33] Referencing the title of her piece, "Autobiographic Notes: Edgar Allan Poe," Smith says, "I give the Allan in this name because it is generally so written; but I think the middle one should be at once and forever dropped."[34] Smith informs readers that the name "Allan"

is that of a man who had befriended the poet—protected and educated him, but who finally abandoned him to his fate, leaving him to battle with the world as best he could, he, totally unable to compete with the world, with no understandable weapons for the contest, born with vast, gloomy premonitions, shadowy intimations of grandeur, stupendous day-dreams, which had no visible relation to what was passing around him—weird, unearthly visions which shut out the real—gorgeous idealisms overmastering the actual; a *demonized* man, in the fullest sense; and when his guardian—this wealthy, conventional, every-day man—assumed the responsibility of taking such a boy in charge, he had no right to abandon him.[35]

Although Smith concedes that some of Poe's friends were repulsed by his errors, she also insists that any person's mistakes, even Poe's, will be forgiven by friends of true noble sentiment. Encompassing in her condemnation not only Allan but also, by implication, Griswold and Poe's other false male friends, Smith repositions Poe in a different group of friends, "persons of noble penetration, who could worthily estimate him," substituting Sarah

Helen Whitman for Griswold in the ranks of Poe's biographers and once again relocating Poe from the street to the salon of Anne Lynch.[36]

Similar attempts to reclaim and relocate Poe are made by Mary Gove Nichols. Like Smith and Whitman, Nichols moves Poe from the derelict scenes of failed white masculinity—the gutter, the tavern, the stormy street— to the scenes of household and family over which women preside. In her 1863 article, "Reminiscences of Edgar Poe," Nichols recounts a "little excursion" she took with literary friends to Fordham to see Poe.[37] There they find Poe not reeling in a tavern or muttering incantations but living in a "little cottage at the top of a hill" with "grand old cherry-trees in the yard."[38] Whereas Griswold's Poe is a wild, uncontrolled character constantly trespassing upon the sober dictates of genteel masculinity, Nichols's Poe is a figure of determined, almost touching, self-discipline. During her visit, Nichols discovers that Poe keeps a bird he caught, "a full-grown bob-a-link," locked up in a cage on the porch. "The poor bird," says Nichols, "was as unfit to live in a cage as his captor was to live in the world. He was as restless as his jailer, and sprang continually in a fierce, frightened way, from one side of the cage to the other. I pitied him, but Poe was bent on training him."[39] The wild bird represents, of course, Poe's wild disobedient side, the side that writes his otherworldly masterpieces and that is implicitly kept in check in the little cottage in the countryside.

Unlike Smith, who dwells on the mistakes made by Allan, Nichols focuses on the affirming atmosphere created by Poe's domestic life with his wife Virginia and mother-in-law, Maria Clemm or "Muddy." Ignoring the erratic or indulgent father, Nichols focuses instead on Virginia and Muddy as sources of gentle inspiration and protective discipline. The one a veritable angel, so pale she seemed "almost a disrobed spirit," the other "hale and strong," "a sort of universal Providence for her strange children," these women tend to Poe and keep his wild spirit in check.[40] For Griswold, Poe's grimy dishabille—the holes in his pants, the sockless feet—is the sign of his personal failure as a masculine subject. Nichols offers a Poe whose struggles with dress are the result of poverty. Like Griswold's Poe, Nichols's Poe loves to engage in competitive feats like long jumping. In Nichols's account, however, Poe's efforts to show off his manly skills are not ruined by his refusal to be successful and ambitious. They are fruitless in the face of recalcitrant poverty. The poignant result of Poe's manly feats is that he defeats his opponents at the expense of his gaiters, which, because of his poverty, he cannot afford to replace. The fact that Poe laughs off this moment, scorning to feel shame at his exposed legs, tugs at Nichols's heart: "I had pitied the poor bob-o'-link in his hard and hopeless imprisonment, but I pitied Poe more now."[41]

Written in the 1860s, these biographies of Poe by his women friends would shortly become part of a much larger Poe mythology. Their influence over this mythology is not insubstantial. In her introduction to *Gender and the Poetics of Reception in Poe's Circle*, Eliza Richards argues that to understand Poe we need to go to "the scene of Poe's creation, the literary salons and ephemeral publications of New York City where he publicly staged his performance of tortured isolation in collaboration with prominent women poets."[42] But one of the things that becomes clear in a comparison of these women writers' reminiscences and the record of Poe's time in the New York salon world is the fact that the two do not readily match. Most of Poe's major works were already written by the time he entered the salon world. More important, he was there for very little time. Having spent most of his career writing in relative obscurity in Baltimore, Richmond, and Philadelphia, Poe moved to New York in the middle of 1844, living in the suburbs and largely isolated from the New York literary scene. "The Raven" was published in January 1845 and was such a success that Poe suddenly found himself the toast of the town. It was at this point that he began to frequent the weekly literary salons of Anne Charlotte Lynch, where he met not only Osgood, Smith, and Nichols but also Elizabeth Ellet and Margaret Fuller, among many others.[43] Yet Poe's intimacy with salon culture was short-lived, barely lasting out the year. In March 1845, Poe became intimate with Osgood and began his romantic relationship with her. By the end of 1845, their relationship had cooled, and Poe seems to have become involved in another flirtation with Elizabeth Ellet. In January of 1846, a little over a year after Poe's entry into salon culture, he fell out with Ellet over some indiscreet letters he had exchanged with Osgood. The explosive arguments that followed, which included a run-in with Ellet's brother and a brawl with English, ensured that Poe was permanently removed from Lynch's guest list.[44] He was never to recover from this disgrace and would not be part of the salon scene again.

Far from acting as the "scene of Poe's creation," the New York salon backdrop seems to have formed a fleeting, if flashy, episode in Poe's twenty-year career as a professional writer. In fact, the salon world and its tortured genius figures were very much formulated for Poe after his death, partly through Griswold's agency and partly through the agency of the women writers who sought to dispute Griswold's account. Precisely to the extent that Griswold emphasized a scene of masculinist achievement, ambition, and self-control, against which Poe could be made to seem a failure, Poe's women biographers emphasized the nurturing, feminized environment of the salons, against which Poe could be made to seem a tragic victim of masculinist ideology.[45] In this sense, Richards's contention that Poe was the romantic individualist male author who divided himself from his mass market woman contemporaries is not strictly accurate. Rather, these women writers were central to the creation of Poe as a victim of the harsh world of professional authorship, a victim who was not only defeated by men like John Allan and Griswold but who also relied on the care and nurturance of women writers. Whitman, in particular, though she had known Poe for barely three months, became an important source for late nineteenth-century Poe biographers. Apparently intent on wresting Poe from the clutches not just of Griswold but of a host of later nineteenth-century biographers, Whitman founded an entire alternative genealogy for Poe, deciding that they were descended from a common ancestor.[46] Whitman thus traced Poe's kinship with women poets through a dynastic chain.

In the early twentieth century, the traditions established by Whitman wound their way through the mythology of Poe, texturing the influential biographies penned by Susan Archer Weiss and Mary E. Phillips. Titled *The Home Life of Poe*, Weiss's 1907 account features portraits of the late writer filtered through his intimate associations and abodes. Weiss herself knew Poe as a distant acquaintance, and her mother had been a neighbor on the street in Norfolk where the Poe family lived for a short time. The book opens in Poe's babyhood with a series of maternal figures: "It may be regarded as a somewhat curious coincidence that the first glimpse afforded us of Edgar Poe," says Weiss, "is on the authority of my own mother." Living close to the Poe family, Weiss's mother remembers meeting the Poe children in a neighbor's playroom and recalls (inaccurately, it turns out) how they were cared for by their grandmother, Elizabeth Poe's mother, "a very nice old woman, plump, rosy and good-natured," in "a huge white cap with flaring frills," who was "devoted to the children."[47] The rest of the book owes its information to a series of "old ladies" who provide Weiss with anecdotes relating not to Poe's professional and public life but to his private life: his loves, his marriage, his domestic habitations.

Mary E. Phillips's monumental biography, *Edgar Allan Poe—The Man*, published in 1926, repeats these maternal themes, particularly in its account of Poe's early life. Still implicitly grappling with Griswold's legacy, Phillips spends significant time disputing accounts of Poe as an alcoholic, arguing that Poe struggled not with drinking but with his own acutely sensitive spirit: "It was his inherited nerve exhaustion, not a toper's taste of liquor, that Edgar Allan Poe—child, youth, and man—fought with an heroic strength of will wholly unknown to most of his harshest critics."[48] In Phillips's account, it is Poe's upbringing, in particular Allan's harshness and "practicality," that lead to Poe's later misery. Even as a child, Poe contains a "romantic 'mystery'" that "the practical Mr. Allan could not understand," a mystery that enrages Allan and makes him feel as if Poe is "ungrateful."[49] Instead, little Edgar thrives under the tutelage of women, in particular a series of mother figures. Phillips describes the "devoted" Mrs. Allan, who cherishes Poe "in the pure joy of her mother-love," doing by him "precisely what she would have done by a like boy of her own blood."[50] At one point, Phillips describes the little Edgar living in the Allan household in Richmond surrounded entirely by mothers—in this case, Frances Allan, plus the Allan family nurse, an enslaved woman, and the spirit of Edgar's mother, the dead Elizabeth Poe, whose grave was nearby. Here there is no judgemental patriarchal eye to arrest Poe's development:

> When the spring days came of 1812, Mammy would take her charge to the dancing lights and shadows under the tall trees in the 'Old Church on the Hill'—not far away; where others, of her like and his, held their sunny holidays over the green turf, beneath which, 'close to the Eastern Wall,' slept little Edgar's young mother. There he played about until her spirit in the twilight sent him to the other lovely mother awaiting his coming to her earthly home.[51]

These early maternal influences, according to Phillips, form the armature for Poe's unearthly imagination later on.

Nowhere was this reading of Poe as the subject of networks of feminine and maternal agency more spectacularly realized than in the biography of Poe written by Marie Bonaparte, *The Life and Works of Edgar Allan Poe*, which appeared in 1933. *The Life and Works*, which is part biography and part literary criticism, represents a kind of apotheosis of the work begun by Whitman.[52] Missing from its detailed, 200-page biographical essay is any trace at all of Griswold beyond the briefest mention of his post at *Graham's*. Indeed, the biography is remarkable for virtually erasing not just Griswold but also David Poe, John Allan, T. W. White, John Pendleton Kennedy, James Russell Lowell, Nathaniel Parker Willis, Thomas Dunn English, Louis Godey, and any of the other dozens of professional writers, editors, and publishers with whom Poe was centrally involved. Instead, Bonaparte focuses *exclusively* on the details of Poe's relationships with women both in his life and work. Yet Bonaparte does not simply recapitulate the domesticated Poe produced by the nineteenth-century women writers who moved in his social world. On the contrary, Bonaparte, a disciple and patient of Sigmund Freud who would herself become a psychoanalyst, elaborates Poe as Freudian subject, a person whose whole being in its deepest recesses is formed not by his friends and lovers, but rather by his traumatic relationship with his dead mother.[53] In this sense, Bonaparte both built upon and revised the Poe imagined by Whitman and Smith, a Poe whose lack of subservience to paternal authority culminates, for Bonaparte, in the utter absence of father figures from his psychic life.

The Poe described by Whitman, Smith, Nichols, and others, is a soul full of brilliance and potential damaged by nineteenth-century masculinist culture, victimized first by Allan and then by Griswold. In his disabled state, their Poe looks to a series of motherly figures such as Frances Allan, Jane Stannard,

Muddy, Virginia, Frances Osgood, and Sarah Helen Whitman for strength and comfort. To Whitman and Smith, Poe is a kind of tragic "child," a child of genius crushed by the remorseless standards of U.S. capitalist masculinity. Bonaparte's Poe is equally damaged and equally innocent, but instead of being brutalized by failed father figures, he is a subject tragically galvanized by his mother's death when he was three. Retelling Poe's history, Bonaparte hypothesizes that his mother's untimely demise cast a dark and imperious shadow across the rest of his existence, crippling his relationships with both men and women, driving him to seek out the self-loss of opium and alcohol, and setting him on the road to self-annihilation. Trivialized and even effaced in earlier biographies, Poe's mother, Elizabeth Arnold Poe, here becomes a kind of vast and tragically inescapable power while functioning as the source of Poe's visionary talents.

Bonaparte begins her biography with an unusual rhetorical move: a poignant account of Poe's mother as she was in 1811, struggling to keep her family together while enduring the terminal stages of pulmonary tuberculosis. Either deserted or left a widow by her husband David Poe the year before, Elizabeth Poe arrives with the Virginia Players in Richmond with two-year-old Edgar and newborn baby Rosalie in tow. Sick and exhausted, she is desperate to keep up her acting career, her sole source of income. She has no strength left, however. In a tiny garret room above a millinery shop, impoverished and helpless, she suffers through her final weeks of life: "No doctor is known to have entered that room. There, drearily alone, through the shortening November and December days, the heartsick, dying woman, would have lain and listened to her Rosalie's wails, or to customers in the shop below, or to Edgar pattering on the narrow stairs."[54] Bonaparte draws this description of Elizabeth Poe's final days principally from Hervey Allen's 1926 biography *Israfel*. Allen trivializes the events surrounding Elizabeth's death, presumably minimizing Poe's parentage to highlight the unprecedented, seemingly unearthly genius of Poe himself. Allen says of Elizabeth's death, "the tragedies of the little doll actress were over"; "her small world" had played its last "tragi-comedy."[55] For Bonaparte, on the other hand, this scene is momentous: "Doubtless, Edgar was taken for a last look at his 'sleeping' mother, a picture which was never to fade from his memory." Even though lost to his conscious memory, the picture would stay "in that other deeper memory which, unknown to us in ourselves, survives to form our natures, and our fates." Poe's "unconscious memories of his loved mother's long months of illness and decline" would stamp themselves indelibly in his psyche and form the pattern for his life from then on.[56]

Here again, as in the accounts of other women writers, Bonaparte gives us a feminized Poe who "preferred girls to boys."[57] In this case, however, feminine or maternal psychic energy plays a role very different from the roles played by Poe's women friends and lovers in the earlier biographies. In the reminiscences by Osgood, Whitman, and Smith, the various mother figures in Poe's life shelter his bruised mind and body, soothing him with the balm of friendship and affection. In Bonaparte's biography, Poe is not just influenced or soothed by women but structured entirely through his primary relationship with his mother, his professional and personal future written in the scene of his mother's death. Thus, for Bonaparte, Poe's famous female characters, with their unnaturally white faces and black hair, their orb-like eyes and phantom voices, their burials, deaths, and ghostly reappearances, rehearse in faithful repetition Poe's primal loss: "Elizabeth Arnold's diaphanous beauty and the mysterious malady by which she was slowly consumed, were later to be immortalised by her son's genius in the forms of Berenice, Morella, Madeline, Eleonora and Ligeia."[58] The image of Elizabeth Arnold—"worn and etherealized by disease, but still beautiful and young as, when a child, he saw her on her death-bed,"—that image "was to live on unchanged in his unconscious and issue therefrom endlessly repeated."[59]

This tragic, Freudian "repetition compulsion" structures Poe's intimate life with women. In Bonaparte's mind, Poe unconsciously senses and is fatally attracted to women who display a tubercular pathology: "The inno-cent Virginia, small, consumptive, part-angel and soon dying, came nearest to his sexual ideal and provided the nearest illusion to his having found his lost love."[60] Osgood, with whom Poe possibly carried on an affair in 1845, would, Bonaparte points out, soon die of tuberculosis. Bonaparte argues that she must have born telltale traces of the disease well before its positive mani-festation: descriptions of her suggest her unearthly pallor. Not only a "child of genius" but also an "eternal orphan," Poe puts himself in situations where he reexperiences his mother's loss, whether by loving women about to die or by sabotaging relationships that threaten to issue in typical adult sexual rela-tions, which he did, in Bonaparte's account, with Whitman, among others. Thus "he clung to the robe of every mother-phantom that entered his life" while fleeing in terror his "dire sado-necrophilist sexuality."[61] For Bonaparte, "the 'lost one' of the poems and tales is no one woman but the synthesis of many: Elizabeth, Helen, Frances, and Virginia, whose features, though super-imposed, nevertheless remain those of his mother."[62]

It is in this context that Bonaparte situates Poe's relationships to men. Subordinated to the "lost mother," the male figures populating Poe's life are, in Bonaparte's account, vague flickering presences who offer tenuous and temporary havens from "the acute depressive attacks" driven by Poe's compulsion to repeat the death of his mother.[63] The only function men serve in Poe's life is to encourage him to drink. In Bonaparte's analysis, Poe drinks and takes opium to forestall the dreadful, giddy extremes of his "hypomania" and depression. John Sartain, George Lippard, Henry Beck Hirst, and others

are mentioned briefly in Bonaparte's account not because they are writers
and professional compatriots but because they take Poe to hotels and taverns,
where "drink, in the safety of men, permitted the release of his repressions
and diverted his aggressive instincts into other channels."[64] Bonaparte's book
thus represents the opposite extreme of the Poe envisioned by Griswold.
In both cases, the unfortunate author is a helpless, anarchic figure, but in
Griswold's account, Poe endlessly broods over and recklessly defies the
sober ideals of Victorian masculinity, rejecting one kindly father figure after
another. But in Bonaparte's biography, these figures are of no account; their
puny, merely local claims on Poe's time and the temporary relief they offer
from turmoil are in the end no match for the vast, ineradicable power of
the lost mother. Recognizing that power, Bonaparte asserts, "Drink would
give him the illusion of feeling male and powerful until, racked by pain and
remorse, he returned to Mrs. Clemm's care with never-maintained resolutions
of abandoning drink forever."[65] Drink, opium, and ink (i.e., the writing of
poems and stories) step in to hush the clamorous horrors in Poe's head.

     Published in 1933, Bonaparte's work would be immortalized in the 1960s
and 1970s as the site of a contestation between two giants of poststructuralist
theory, Jacques Lacan and Jacques Derrida.[66] Lacan's famous "Seminar on
the Purloined Letter" took Bonaparte to task for her conceptualization of the
unconscious as something linked to repressed childhood experiences. Derrida,
with both derision and humor, then accused Lacan of being traumatized by
Bonaparte and of repressing her arguments in his own glittery performance
of psychoanalytic truth. But, as Scott Peeples reminds us, partly because of
its embroilment in the central philosophical debates of the mid-twentieth
century, Bonaparte's biography and critical readings wielded considerable
influence over Poe studies. For Peeples, Bonaparte's book is "one of the great
achievements of Poe scholarship." She was "the first critic to write extensively on the Poe canon" while also being "a close reader of the first order."[67]
Her vision of a Poe haunted by a lost mother not only inspired the rich pano-
ply of psychoanalytic studies of Poe that flourished between 1960 and 2000,
but it also inspired important Poe biographies, including, most prominently,
Kenneth Silverman's *Mournful and Never-ending Remembrance*, in which
loss and mourning are the organizing tropes of Poe's existence.

     It is useful to note, by way of conclusion, that Poe was perhaps an unlikely
candidate for the kind of redemption engineered by his women friends and
devotees in the second half of the nineteenth century. Indeed, in many ways,
this redemption, which became internal to Poe myth and biography, chimes
poorly with the realities of Poe's reputation and writing practices. Poe's
contemporaries, for example, do not seem to have regarded Poe as in any
way a feminized, maternalized, or nonheteronormative writer. Such writers certainly abounded in the period. N. P. Willis, for example, was openly

understood as a purveyor of moody poetry and saccharine albums aimed at women consumers. Poe, by contrast, was known for his violence and spite as a critic and for the gruesomeness of his tales. Neither his tales nor most of the poems cater to what were understood in the 1830s and 1840s to be feminine tastes. On the contrary, as Jonathan Elmer and others have argued, Poe's tales owed more to the cheap, true-crime sensationalism of the penny press than to the genteel album and poetry culture of the salon world's women writers.[68] One explanation for Poe's posthumous reclamation by women writers is that they felt a certain amount of guilt for his exile from polite literary society and a certain guilt for his death. Certainly, Poe's exile from Lynch's circle, which occurred just as Virginia was dying, did not make his final years easier. Whitman especially, who was part of this circle and abruptly broke off her engagement with Poe, might have been filled with self-blame when he died so soon afterwards. In this reading, Osgood, Whitman, Smith, Nichols, and others rewrote Poe's history as a redemption not of Poe but of themselves, recasting what was originally their cruelty as kindness and affection.

But it is also the case that Poe functioned both before and after his death as a peculiarly powerful example of the stereotypical tortured genius of romantic myth, a myth which dominated U.S. literary culture throughout most of the nineteenth century. Although scholars typically see this authorial postulate as male, in fact, in the 1850s and 1860s the tortured genius became an ideal of self-postulation for women writers as well.[69] It is possible that by appropriating and reimagining Poe as a figure formed by women, the women writers who survived him sought to remake him as one of their own company, a kind of avatar in whose eerie, powerful form they could themselves stride out before the world as figures of genius. Certainly, this picture of Poe as a muse for women writers appears in the fiction of the period. In her 1859 novel, *Beulah*, Augusta Jane Evans tells the story of a young woman birthed as a writer by her first reading of Poe. Her male guardian and future husband Dr. Hartwell warns Beulah, who is at this point no more than twelve, to keep away from his volume of Poe, as if his works harbor forbidden information. Beulah is curious, however, and one day, when her guardian is away, she furtively takes the Poe volume from the shelf. She reads it all in one sitting. She is astonished, transformed: "The spell of this incomparable sorcerer was upon her imagination."[70] Giving "herself up to the guidance of one who, like the 'Ancient Mariner,' holds his listener fascinated and breathless," she reads "with the eagerness of a child clutching at its own shadow in a glassy lake."[71] She is "[m]ystified, shocked, and yet admiring." She takes the book to her guardian, eager to discuss its "seemingly infallible reasoning." Instead of assisting her, Dr. Hartwell takes the book away, saying: "You must not play with such sharp tools just yet. Go and practise your music lesson." Right then, Beulah decides to become an author on the model of Poe. "This study of Poe," says Evans, electrifies Beulah's intellect and creativity, becoming "the portal through which she entered the vast Pantheon of Speculation."[72]

NOTES

1. Rufus Griswold, "Memoir of the Author," in *Poe in His Own Time: A Biographical Chronicle of His Life, Drawn from Recollections, Interviews, and Memoirs by Family, Friends, and Associates*, ed. Benjamin F. Fisher (Iowa City: University of Iowa Press, 2010), 109. The "Memoir" of Poe offered here was a revision of the famous obituary Griswold had published upon Poe's death in 1849. See [Rufus Wilmot Griswold], "Death of Edgar Allan Poe," *New York Daily Tribune*, October 9, 1849, in *Edgar Allan Poe: The Critical Heritage*, ed. I. M. Walker (London: Routledge and Kegan Paul, 1986), 294–302.

2. Griswold, 109.

3. Ibid., 112, 113.

4. Ibid., 114.

5. Ibid., 117.

6. Ibid., 122.

7. Ibid., 128.

8. Ibid., 115.

9. Ibid., 139. Griswold in a footnote attributes this phrase to an 1850 article in the *Southern Literary Messenger*, then edited by John Moncure Daniel, which vilifies and condemns Poe as a person of no talent. Griswold misquotes the source.

10. George Gilfillan, "Authors and Books. Edgar Poe," in *Poe in His Own Time*, 175.

11. In *Poe's Helen Remembers* (Charlottesville: University of Virginia Press, 1979), John Carl Miller speculates that Whitman and other women writers were afraid of Griswold's power as an editor and waited until his death in 1857 to write extended defenses of Poe (xxvii).

12. Eliza Richards, *Gender and the Poetics of Reception in Poe's Circle* (Cambridge: Cambridge University Press, 2004), 54.

13. Griswold, 146, emphasis added.

14. Ibid., 147.

15. Ibid., 151.

16. Whitman and Poe began writing to each other in September 1848, after which Poe visited her in Providence. He proposed marriage almost immediately. They had not met until that point and seem to have seen each other only a handful of times afterwards. In December 1848 their engagement was abruptly broken off by Whitman for reasons that remain unclear, though most biographers believe she heard rumors of a drinking binge.

17. See pp. 109–27 of Richards's *Gender and the Poetics of Reception in Poe's Circle* for an excellent account of the odd relationship that Whitman developed with the posthumous Poe, which included visitations by his ghost.

18. Sarah Helen Whitman, *Edgar Allan Poe and His Critics* (New York: Rudd & Carleton, 1860), 14.

19. Ibid., 19.

20. Ibid., 19.

21. Ibid., 20.

22. Ibid., 19–20.

23. Griswold, 151.

24. Whitman, 23.

25. Ibid., 25.

26. Thomas Dunn English, *1844, or, The Power of the "S.F.": A Tale* (New York: Burgess, Stringer & Co., 1847), 123.

27. Whitman, 27.

28. Ibid., 26.

29. Elizabeth Oakes Smith, "Edgar A. Poe," *United States Magazine* 4, no. 3 (March 1857): 262.

30. Ibid., 262.

31. Ibid., 263, 264.

32. Ibid., 263.

33. Ibid., 262, 263.

34. Elizabeth Oakes Smith, "Autobiographic Notes: Edgar Allan Poe," *Beadle's Monthly Magazine of Today* 3 (February 1867): 147.

35. Ibid., 147.

36. Ibid., 147.

37. Mary Gove Nichols, "Reminiscences of Edgar Poe," *Sixpenny Magazine* 4, no. 20 (February 1, 1863): 471.

38. Ibid., 471.

39. Ibid., 471.

40. Ibid., 472.

41. Ibid., 472.

42. Richards, 2.

43. For accounts of Poe's entry into Anne Lynch's circle, see Kenneth Silverman, *Edgar A. Poe: Mournful and Never-ending Remembrance* (New York: HarperCollins, 1991), 278; and Dwight Thomas and David K. Jackson, *The Poe Log: A Documentary Life of Edgar Allan Poe, 1809–1849* (Boston: G. K. Hall, 1987), 484.

44. Accounts of Poe's exile from salon society are available in Silverman, *Mournful*, 282–91, and *Poe Log*, 623. See also "That Was New York: Anne Lynch's Salon," *New Yorker* (September 19, 1936): 67, which confirms that in January 1846 Poe stopped being a guest at Lynch's events.

45. For general accounts of the mid-century scene of women's poetry, see Anne E. Boyd, *Writing For Immortality: Women and the Emergence of High Literary Culture in America* (Baltimore: Johns Hopkins University Press, 2004); Mary Loeffelholz, *From School to Salon: Reading Nineteenth-Century American Women's Poetry* (Princeton: Princeton University Press, 2004); Susan S. Williams, *Reclaiming Authorship: Literary Women in America, 1850–1900* (Philadelphia: University of Pennsylvania Press, 2006).

46. Miller, 182–83.

47. Susan Archer Weiss, *The Home Life of Poe* (New York: Broadway Publishing, 1907), 1.

48. Mary E. Phillips, *Edgar Allan Poe—The Man*, vol. 1 of 2 (Chicago: John C. Winston, 1926), 31.

49. Ibid., 107.

50. Ibid., 107.

51. Ibid., 110.

52. In addition to drawing on Whitman, Bonaparte derived some ideas from an article-length psychoanalytic analysis of Poe published by U.S. feminist and author Lorine Pruette in 1920. See Pruette's "A Psycho-Analytical Study of Edgar Allan Poe," *The American Journal of Psychology* 31 (1920): 370–402. Pruette's analysis is comparatively crude, but it suggests the unbroken continuity of interest among readers in Poe's relationships to women.

53. For an account of Bonaparte's relationship to Freud, see Lisa Appignanesi and John Forrester, *Freud's Women* (London: Weidenfeld and Nicolson, 1992), 329–51.

54. Marie Bonaparte, *The Life and Works of Edgar Allan Poe: A Psycho-Analytic Interpretation*, trans. John Rodker (London: Imago Publishing, 1949), 6.

55. Hervey Allen, *Israfel: The Life and Times of Edgar Allan Poe* (New York: Farrar & Rinehart), 39.

56. Bonaparte, 7.

57. Ibid., 10.

58. Ibid., 7.

59. Ibid., 60.

60. Ibid., 83.

61. Ibid., 172, 87.

62. Ibid., 60.

63. Ibid., 87.

64. Ibid., 87.

65. Ibid., 87.

66. These famous essays and the controversies surrounding them are gathered together in *The Purloined Poe: Lacan, Derrida, and Psychoanalytic Reading*, ed. John P. Muller and William J. Richardson (Baltimore: Johns Hopkins University Press, 1987). However, Derrida's essay, "The Purveyor of Truth," is significantly abridged in this volume. To understand his attack on Lacan's repression of Bonaparte's text, see Jacques Derrida, Willis Domingo, James Hulbert, Moshe Ron, and M.-R. L., "The Purveyor of Truth," *Yale French Studies* 52 (1975): 31–113.

67. Scott Peeples, *The Afterlife of Edgar Allan Poe* (Rochester: Camden House, 2004), 38.

68. See Jonathan Elmer, *Reading at the Social Limit* (Stanford: Stanford University Press, 1995), especially chapter 4. See chapter 3 of Sandra Tomc, *Industry and the Creative Mind: The Eccentric Writer in American Literature and Entertainment, 1790–1860* (Ann Arbor: University of Michigan Press, 2012).

69. As Gustavus Stadler notes in *Troubling Minds: The Cultural Politics of Genius in the United States, 1840–1890* (Minneapolis: University of Minnesota Press, 2006),

equations of women's artistic virtuosity with "Genius" were a feature of 1850s literary and entertainment culture. For a discussion of women writers' relationship to figures of romantic genius, both male and female, see chapter 5 of Tomc, *Industry*. See also chapter 1 of Victoria Olwell, *The Genius of Democracy: Fictions of Gender and Citizenship in the United States, 1860–1945* (Philadelphia: University of Pennsylvania Press, 2011).

70. Augusta Jane Evans, *Beulah* (New York: Derby and Jackson, 1859), 146.
71. Ibid., 147
72. Ibid., 148.

Chapter Two

Spiritual Dialogues

Lydia Maria Child, Edgar Allan Poe, and the Politics of Unity

Adam C. Bradford

On September 24, 1836, not long after the appearance of Lydia Maria Child's *Philothea: A Grecian Romance*, a review of her work appeared in the *Southern Literary Messenger*. The *Messenger's* principal critic at this time was none other than Edgar Allan Poe, whose preference for melancholic poetry and macabre tales might lead one to think he would have little encouraging to say about Child's newest work, a philosophical romance set in ancient Greece, and yet this was not the case. In his opening paragraph, Poe sang Child's praises, claiming that "the work before us is of a character very distinct . . . and places the fair writer in a new and most favorable light." To be sure, he esteemed the work so highly that he ultimately found himself "turn[ing] . . . these pure and quiet pages with that species of gasping satisfaction with which a drowning man clutches the shore."[1] Poe's enthusiasm for Child's work has received little critical attention, and his fascination certainly seems, in some respects, peculiar. Child was best known for her abolitionist advocacy that certainly would not have attracted Poe, given his own thoughts on the subject.[2] Moreover, Child's reputation was, as a result of such advocacy, at its nadir at the time Poe reviewed her novel, and the effusive praise he offered her seems an unlikely means of garnering literary favor or securing entrance into literary conversations and coteries that were increasingly shut to Child herself; so it appears unlikely that his response was simply an attempt to navigate the literary marketplace to his advantage. Rather, it seems that Poe's admiration for *Philothea* was genuine.[3]

This puzzling situation invites scrutiny. The investigation that follows illuminates the significance of the *Philothea* review vis-à-vis Poe's other writings and helps readers better understand some of the cultural challenges that antebellum writers of progressive literature faced. Poe's admiration for Child's work derives from his appreciation for Transcendental discourses concerning unity that mark her narrative. They are discourses that Poe, who had little overtly positive to say about the Transcendentalists themselves, would nevertheless employ throughout his career, ultimately embedding them in "The Colloquy of Monos and Una" and "Mesmeric Revelation," as well as in the center of the text that he felt was his masterpiece, namely the 1848 prose-poem *Eureka*. In particular, both Poe and Child affirm a spiritualist discourse that inspires an important reconceptualization of the self—one with the potential to reformulate democratic identity and politics. Poe's appreciation of Child's work is attributable to the way in which she seeks to draw her readers to a greater understanding of their social responsibilities to one another through what is, in essence, an affective spiritualism. Much of the ideology, if not the language, of this approach is reflected in Poe's prose-poem. Committed, like Child, to affective spiritualism, Poe is, however, wary of its subversive implications, particularly the idea that cosmic unity exposes social divisions as artificial. Thus in his writings, Poe avoids the perils that authors with Child's political allegiances faced while proclaiming the equality of all people before an antebellum mass audience skeptical about social reform.

PHILOTHEA'S *POLITICAL PHILOSOPHY*

Brief synopses of both works are warranted, as each occupies a less than prominent role in its author's canon. *Philothea* is essentially the story of two women, Philothea and Eudora, who must navigate the xenophobic political atmosphere of Periclean Athens. Both women face significant challenges while preparing for their prospective marriages, but Philothea's struggles are the most relevant to this essay. Philothea is the beloved of Paralus, son of Pericles, but when she is impoverished by the city's new anti-immigrant laws, Pericles deems her an unsuitable match for his son. Her losses mount when she faces exile with her grandfather Anaxagoras, who is condemned for failing to properly honor the Olympians. Her exile causes Paralus to lose his mind until the lovers are eventually reunited and Paralus undergoes a mystic, therapeutic intervention at the hands of the Ethiopian Tithonus—a process that restores his sanity but leads to his quick demise. Published over a decade after *Philothea*, Poe's *Eureka* appears to be a text altogether different from Child's. It is, among other things, a cosmological treatise that proposes a model of the universe based on the radical, impending collapse into unity of all matter—a big crunch, one might say. It charts this model by revising previous scientific conceptualizations of the universe as well as philosophical notions relating to epistemic and metaphysical truth offered by Bacon, Aristotle, Kant, and others.

As these summaries suggest, these works bear little superficial resemblance to each other. A nonfictional text, *Eureka* features neither a plot nor characters as *Philothea* does, and Poe's prose-poem certainly is not historically and topically oriented like Child's book. However, their shared commitment to ideas of affective and spiritual unity brings these texts into conversation with one another—and goes a long way toward explaining Poe's appreciation of Child's work.

As mentioned earlier, the politics that complicate Philothea's experience in Athens are fraught, but they are also the locus for much of Child's exploration of affective and spiritual unity. At the novel's beginning a rather strident nativism has gripped Athens, and, as a result, laws have been put in place that disrupt what had been, up to that point, a relatively cohesive and pluralistic social body unified in its appreciation of Athenian culture. Philothea's greatest loss from that upheaval is not so much the loss of property or economic independence (both of which are stripped away by the new legal frameworks) but her ability to marry Paralus. Her grief over this turn of affairs is notable for the way in which it leads her to characterize the nature of their relationship. In her words, they enjoy a union so complete that "before I can speak my thoughts, he utters my very words," and yet solemnizing that union through marriage would make her "the means of bringing degradation and losses upon him" and is, therefore, impossible.[4] According to the novel, Philothea's grief over this situation results from the fact that "the gods have united human beings by some mysterious principle, like the according notes of music. . . . [S]ouls originally one, have been divided, and each seeks the half it has lost"—a half she has apparently found but with which she cannot reunite due to unnatural legal impediments.[5] The idea that human beings are halves of a whole that experience restoration through partnering of the type described by Philothea tallies with the notion forwarded by Aristophanes in Plato's "Symposium." Discoursing with Socrates and company, Aristophanes narrates Zeus's creation of the sexes by splitting an otherwise whole and unified being into two halves—a creature half-man, half-woman into man and woman: "He spoke and cut men in two. . . . After the division the two parts of man, each desiring his other half, came together, and throwing their arms about one another, entwined in mutual embraces, longing to grow into one." Such a longing, he goes on to say, is a reflection of "our original nature," and the "making one of two" equates with "healing the state of man."[6] Philothea's lament, then, is rooted not only in the injustice done to her because of her status as an immigrant but also in her deep sense of loss over being denied what seems like a natural right, a frustration of her divinely sanctioned desire for (re)union. In a universe where spiritual unity with another is one's true state, the legal prohibition of such unions suggests that contemporary political and legal arrangements undermining the natural order are unjust.[7]

Child's interest in artificial prohibitions that might prevent two individuals from partnering should come as no surprise to those familiar with the political positions she had staked out in other works. In *Hobomok*, her first and arguably her most famous novel, Child tells the story of Mary Conant, who defies her Puritan father by marrying a Wampanoag native with whom she has a child. Progressive by early nineteenth-century standards, the work challenges popular gender and racial stereotypes as well as antebellum fears about miscegenation. Mounting such challenges was, in the words of Carolyn L. Karcher, the hallmark of her writing, "the central theme of *Hobomok* and indeed of [Child's] entire life as a reformer and writer," with "interracial marriage . . . symbolizing both the natural alliance between white women and people of color, and the natural resolution of America's racial and sexual contradictions."[8] As progressive as *Hobomok* and other works challenging prohibitions against interracial marriage were, the unions that Child chronicles are rarely, if ever, the kind that Paralus and Philothea experience. Child's "The Indian Wife" (1828) and "A Legend of the Falls of St. Anthony" (1846) express conflicting attitudes about the idea that such a marriage could represent affective and spiritual communion, just as *Hobomok* does. Mary Conant does not desire to wed Hobomok because of a deep and abiding connection of spirit and mind, such as Paralus and Philothea enjoy, but rather because, after receiving news that her English lover is presumed dead at sea, she is overcome with "a broken and confused mass" of thoughts and feelings, "in which a sense of sudden bereavement, deep and bitter reproaches against her father, and a blind belief in fatality were alone conspicuous."[9] Lost in this "whirlwind of thoughts and passions," she offers herself to Hobomok, saying, "I will be your wife, Hobomok, if you love me"—a gesture made out of a desire to be loved, out of spite toward her father, or in hopes of escaping from an overwhelming grief, but certainly not because of a deep "longing to grow into one."[10]

The spiritual unity central to Paralus's and Philothea's marital longings is unique in Child's larger oeuvre, which may account not only for Poe's appreciation of the romance but also for his relative lack of interest in the rest of her writings. In fact, the only other text that Poe comments on at any length in his public acknowledgements of Child's work is a piece of poetry, "Marius Amid the Ruins of Carthage." Like *Philothea*, this poem has a classical theme, but Poe devotes a mere two sentences to that piece, which, in his estimation, exhibits Child's "intense appreciation of genius in others," "the force of her poetic expression," and her "fervid and fanciful nature."[11]

Poe's reticence to engage with the *rest* of Child's work likely derives from his regressive racial sensibilities, which made him less than predisposed to take up Child's banner, let alone to celebrate her cause. In fact, one can easily imagine him eschewing any commentary on the miscegenation that Child dramatized while "implicitly conceptualizing questions of sovereignty and entitlement in . . . familial relations . . . and the terrain of white women's rights" because such work was at the political and social margins of respectability.[12] Needless to say, directly engaging controversial topics could professionally injure a writer trying to navigate the publishing market and some of the literary salons of the period. Favorable commentary on those transgressive unions might have been as damaging to Poe as the fictional creation of them was, at times, to Child. Poe's strategy, as Maurice Lee has described it, was "to remain culturally, morally, and philosophically distant" from many of the social and political causes that Child was attracted to when producing his own literature.[13] His "average racism," to quote Terence Whalen, displayed in his own writing was a reflection of both the social and economic pressures with which he contended, and that struggle certainly kept him out of alignment with the causes and concerns of Child's larger body of work.[14] Nevertheless, Philothea's desire to marry Paralus, which involves an instance of miscegenation within the nativist cultural and legal frameworks described in the novel, was sufficiently removed from contemporary American (racial) contexts for Poe to appreciate that amatory bond, even though, in many ways, it was a reflection of the same political commitments that mark Child's other subversive works.[15]

If Poe was drawn to the discourses on spiritual unity in *Philothea*, he did not have to satisfy himself solely with the descriptions of the relationship between Paralus and Philothea, for Child was preoccupied with similar ideas throughout the text. A prime example is an extensive conversation between Plato, Anaxagoras, and Phidias, in which Anaxagoras gives voice to a series of ideas that, while drawn from the real Anaxagoras's philosophical positions, are expressed through language that seems almost Emersonian. He says, "[T]he sight of that glorious orb, [the sun], leads the contemplative soul to the belief in one . . . Universal Mind, which in manifesting itself produces order in the material world, and [simultaneously] preserves the unconfused distinction of infinite varieties."[16] Anaxagoras's discourse suggests that nature stands as a hieroglyphic, to borrow from Emerson, disclosing the truth that there is one "Universal Mind" that "manifests itself" (or becomes visible and appreciable) through the physical matter of the universe and is, in fact, responsible for the "infinite varieties" of apparently spiritually infused material objects that constitute it.[17] Plato, in the same conversation, clarifies this concept when he says, "The soul, in its present condition, is an exile from the orb of light" (i.e., his conceptualization of Anaxagoras's "Universal Mind"), "and whatever we can perceive of truth, or imagine of beauty, is but a reminiscence of our former more glorious state of being."[18] Both philosophers imagine the individual person as integrally bound to the "Universal Mind," the "orb of light." In this cosmological view of the nature of humanity, the longing for two souls to be one is less an effect of Zeus's splitting one man into halves and more a symptom of the solitary soul's longing to exist not in an individuated state but in the collective whole where that soul existed originally and whence it has been drawn.

Other references to the innate need and desire for union/reunion appear scattered throughout the novel. A refrain from a hymn that is sung, heard, and recited at various moments in the novel reveals the character of the lovers' relationship as well as the broader relationship between the personal and the universal. The declaration "Come hither, kindred spirits come! Hail to the mystic two in one!" recurs throughout the final chapters, constantly reinforcing the notion that all souls are two things simultaneously: entities granting individual identity to discrete beings and parts of a universal spiritual essence with which separate souls will eventually be reunited.[19] The central idea in this oft-repeated refrain is the overt subject of another portion of dialogue between Plato and Anaxagoras, in which the latter exclaims, "Marvelous, indeed, is the mystery of our being," to which Plato replies, "It involves the highest of all mysteries," namely that the self "contain[s] within himself a type of all that is—from the highest to the lowest plane of existence,—[otherwise] he could not enter the human form."[20] The individual, in such a conceptualization, is merely a reflection or a "type" of "all that is"—the Universal Mind—without which that person "could not enter human form" and to which the singular self is apparently destined to return.

In her discourses on marriage and the Universal Mind, Child's writing reverberates with philosophical ideas drawn from Anaxagoras and Plato, and in many ways, it resonates with concepts that would become part of Emerson's Transcendentalism as articulated in *Nature*, a work published the very same year as *Philothea*. However, Child's narrative weds the notes of this discourse to a second register, an affective one, which depends upon the notion of a common spiritual heritage and destiny that undergirds a political order wherein social reform is possible. *Philothea* is, among other things, a sentimental novel that liberally features tropes similar to those Child used elsewhere to encourage such reform.[21] In *Philothea*, affective traction is gained in several highly charged emotional moments narrated in such a way that readers empathize with the novel's characters. Initially, many of these scenes center on Philothea's and Paralus's anguish as they suffer the dramatic consequences of their thwarted union, inviting readers to "feel" along with the characters the effects of their situation. Readers witness Philothea's "tears start[ing] from fountains long sealed, and rest[ing] like dew-drops on her dark lashes," and imagine the depths of the grief that would inspire such an emotional response in a woman who otherwise demonstrates significant resilience.[22] Equally significant is Paralus's passing, in which his "suffering . . . became more and more intense . . . [until] bodily pain seemed at times too powerful for endurance" before mercifully, "after an acute spasm of pain had subsided[,] . . . he smiled faintly, . . . imprinted a kiss upon her lip[,] . . . [and] departed to return to earth no more."[23] Over and over, the text grants intimate access to the characters' grief and pain and invites readers to experience that trauma, to "feel" it. These invitations to "feel" with the characters, if effective for a reader, create, in essence, a shared experience of injustice and a sense of the bitterness and sorrow that accompany it. Adam Smith describes this phenomenon in his *Theory of Moral Sentiments*, claiming that through "the imagination we place ourselves in [another's] situation" and that in doing so "we endure all the same torments . . . and become in some measure the same person with him, and thence form some idea of his sensations, and even feel something which, though weaker in degree, is not altogether unlike them." Out of this emotional experience emerges a concert of thought, Smith goes on to say, as "[t]he man whose sympathy keeps time to my grief, cannot but admit the reasonableness of my sorrow."[24] Imaginatively sharing experience, affect, and thought in such a way leads to a peculiar communion described by Emma Brinkema as "the self as a potentially expanded and composite feeling being" wherein "the imagination [not only] forms an impression of the sensations of the other" but also, through "sympathy," achieves "the material commingling of affects . . . [as people keep] time to each other in a slow, locked embrace."[25] If nineteenth-century readers like Poe experienced reading *Philothea* in such a way, then the book locked reader and characters together in an affective experience of injustice, sorrow, and longing. The text invited those readers to approximate the characters' pain and to yearn with them for a just social and legal system that would more closely resemble the state of nature.

Child's attempt to blend Transcendental insights with affective experience in order to disclose the need for social reform has little to do with ancient Athens, of course. In fact, the pattern of blending idealist philosophy with emotional appeals in the service of contemporary U.S. social reform was, as hinted earlier, the keynote of Child's writing. Denominating this mixture "sentimental transcendentalism," Jeffrey Steele identifies strains of it throughout her career, from the publication of *Hobomok* in 1824 to the 1842 appearance of *Letters from New York*.[26] Given the correspondences between the antimiscegenation laws that Child took aim at in *An Appeal in Favor of That Class of Americans Called Africans* (1833) and the social and legal prohibitions that prevent Philothea and Paralus from marrying, one begins to see how the romance, which never overtly addresses the American taboo, might nevertheless challenge the principles at its heart, so to speak.[27]

Poe certainly seems interested in moments from the novel in which the theme of spiritual unity *and* affective appeals are present. In fact, the passages that Poe quotes from or paraphrases in his review of *Philothea* are invested in both of these. These two particular passages take up a significant portion of his review, their presence testifying to Poe's attraction to "sentimental transcendentalism." The first consists of almost the entirety of Chapter 11. In that passage, Plato arrives at the place where Anaxagoras and Philothea live in exile after being cast out of Athens. He brings news of the heartbroken and nearly catatonic Paralus as well as an invitation from Pericles to Philothea to return to Athens, offered in the hope that her homecoming will mend Paralus's broken mind. Philothea, wounded to hear that Paralus seems now almost beyond reason, queries Plato whether or not the troubled Paralus remembers her or, indeed, any of his friends and family. Plato responds, "The name of Philothea was too deeply engraven to be washed away by the waters of oblivion. . . . [Y]ou are ever in his visions. . . . What I have told you proves that your souls were one, before it wandered from the divine home; and it gives hope that they will be re-united, when they return thither after their weary exile in the world of shadows."[28] This conversation draws tears from Philothea while Child seemingly invites the reader to feel in some measure the title character's anxiety, her grief, and her longing for the removal of barriers to her union. Poe's quoting and paraphrasing of this chapter seems significant because the section focuses on the need for a reunification of Philothea and Paralus to take place in order for Paralus and, so it seems, the natural order itself to be restored. After dwelling on Chapter 11 at length, Poe characterized it thus: "Many long passages about this portion of the narrative are of a lofty and original beauty. The dreamy, distraught, yet unembittered existence of the husband, reveling in visions of Platonic philosophy . . . with the uncompromising devotion and soothing attentions of the wife—are pictures whose merit will not fail to be appreciated."[29] Curiously, Poe hints that the "lofty and original beauty" of this particular chapter might be located most powerfully not only in the "visions of Platonic philosophy" Paralus seems to experience but also in the persistent dedication ("uncompromising devotion") exhibited by Philothea in her desire to be with and nurture him. It is a devotion signaled through her deep grief, a pain to which Child allows readers intimate access to catalyze a sense of sympathy and an awareness of injustice. Both Paralus's Platonic visions and Philothea's affects therefore focus on or enact (re)union, inviting readers to desire it on the lovers' behalf.

The second of the two passages discussed by Poe constitutes most of Chapter 15, in which Tithonus, an Ethiopian healer, tries to restore Paralus to sanity. Tithonus explains that he cannot do so without drawing Paralus's soul out of his body and putting it back with the aid of a spirit wand. Tithonus performs the first part of this mystic ritual successfully, whispering an incantation and touching his wand to Paralus's temple, which leaves Paralus's body apparently lifeless on the couch next to Philothea. This provokes Philothea into an almost frantic state where she "shudder[s]" in fear and pleads with Tithonus "in tones of agonized entreaty," "Oh, restore him! Restore him!" Tithonus, with "respectful tenderness," recalls Paralus's spirit into his body using another set of incantations and wand movements. Paralus then narrates his experience to Philothea as she kneels "by the couch" while holding his hand and "bath[ing] it in tears."[30] Interestingly, Paralus describes a curious merger with the universe followed by a return to individuated existence. Before his soul was withdrawn, Paralus claims that he thought "a thick vapor enveloped [him,] . . . a dark cloud; and a stunning noise in [his] head."[31] But once his soul left its material prison with a touch of Tithonus's wand, "the darkness began to clear away. But there was strange confusion. All things seemed rapidly to interchange their colors and their forms—the sound of a storm was in mine ears—the elements and the stars seemed to crowd upon me and my breath was taken away."[32] Reunited with the "Universal Mind," Paralus experienced an existence in which there were no distinctions between what previously had appeared as discrete objects. "[A]ll things . . . interchange[d] their colors and their forms," and he seemingly became one with "the elements and the stars" that "crowd[ed] upon" him and left him breathless. The reunion of his spirit with the "Universal Mind" apparently permeating and constituting the entirety of the universe was marked by Tithonus, who exclaimed, "The soul seeketh to ascend!"[33] This merger was shortly undone, and Paralus's individuated soul called back into his body; but before his return to mundane existence, he spoke with "a voice above [his] head" that, upon his query as to whether or not this is "the divine home, whence I departed into the body," told him, "It is the divine home. Man never leaves it. He ceases to perceive."[34] The notion forwarded here has rather compelling implications for people thinking about the nature of their relationship to the "Universal Mind" that forms the universe. The voice essentially testified that individuals, in truly Emersonian fashion, are integral parts of the "Universal Mind" permeating and constituting all things but that in their bodily form they simply fail to recognize themselves as such. Still, as the narrative above attests, the Ur-state of humankind, the state to which all are destined to return, is one in which the individual is melded to the universe. This section, which Poe quotes almost in its entirety, is thus, once again, a section that not only conceptualizes the self as part of a larger universal spiritual unity but also weds that idea to affective expressions of the desire for such union.

Passages such as these ultimately led Poe to judge the text not only "an honor to our country" but also "a signal triumph for our country-women."[35] In

Poe's final estimation, Child had created a text whose "purity of thought and lofty morality are unexceptionable," and despite his resistance to didacticism, Poe felt that *Philothea* "might be introduced advantageously into our female academies."[36] As his review attested, the spiritual themes of the novel merited praise for Child and promised illumination for its readers, especially those in the nation's "female academies."[37] Poe's suggestion that the text might contribute in meaningful ways to the education of women indexes his awareness of the powerful political potential of the work, for the "female academies" of the early nineteenth century were places that prepared women to contribute to the growth and stability of the young republic primarily by intellectually, spiritually, and culturally enriching the domestic space and tempering the "minds of the husbands, suitors, brothers, or sons" who dwelled there.[38] Cultivating such "republican womanhood," or "republican motherhood," as the case may be, was the mission of most of the female academies of the period—at least according to the men who frequently wrote about or talked about such academies (Poe included, apparently).[39] According to Benjamin Rush, a revolutionary-era proponent for public education, women should be "taught the principles of liberty and government; and the obligations of patriotism should be inculcated upon them. The opinions and conduct of men are often regulated by the women in the most arduous enterprises of life . . . [, and] the first impressions upon the minds of children are generally derived from the women. Of how much consequence, therefore, is it in a republic, that they should think justly upon the great subjects of liberty and government!"[40] Poe's belief that Child's book would be of benefit to the "female academies" thus indicates that he considered an understanding of the individual's fundamental nature as part of the divine "Universal Mind" as well as the inculcation of a social order reflecting that spiritual truth essential to the education of citizens in a democratic republic.

POLITICS IN POE'S POSTMORTEM VISIONS

Poe's own commitments to bringing individuals to a sense of their nature as part of the Universal Mind and to the political transformation associated with that process would find clearest and most compelling articulation in *Eureka*, but his earlier works anticipated those commitments. It is well known that throughout his career Poe demonstrated a persistent interest in questions related to the spiritual nature of humankind. That theme is evident in tales such as "Shadow—A Parable," "The Conversation of Eiros and Charmion," "The Colloquy of Monos and Una," "Mesmeric Revelation," "The Facts in the Case of M. Valdemar," "Ligeia," "Eleonora," and "Morella," as well as in the poems "Sonnet—Silence," "Israfel," "Al Aaraaf," and "The Raven," among others. These works do not necessarily approach the question of humanity's spiritual nature from the same perspective. For instance, the Gothic overtones of works such as "Silence—A Fable," "Shadow—A Parable," "Morella," and "Ligeia" do not draw readers to think of spirit and spirituality in the highly mystical way that "Mesmeric Revelation" and "The Colloquy of Monos and Una" do.[41] However, *all* of these tales demonstrate Poe's career-long interest in questioning the nature of the relationship of life to afterlife, the corporeal to the spiritual, the finite to the infinite, and the human to the divine. A nuanced reading of each of these texts would be worthwhile, but one can discern the compelling sense of Poe's progressive working and reworking of ideas related to spiritual unity through an examination of three works: "The Colloquy of Monos and Una," "Mesmeric Revelation," and *Eureka*. Taken together, these texts evince a sophisticated conceptualization of such unity, a vision that not only resembles Child's but also affectively brings readers to a sense of their deep interconnectedness as integral parts of a larger universal whole.

"The Colloquy of Monos and Una" first appeared in *Graham's Magazine* in 1841, shortly after Poe began working for that Philadelphia publication and approximately five years after he had reviewed Child's *Philothea*. Poe biographer Arthur Hobson Quinn considered the 1841 text "one of the preliminary steps to 'Eureka'" precisely because of the way that it interrogates both the relationship of life to afterlife and the idea of spiritual unity.[42] The tale is essentially a conversation between two deceased lovers, Monos and Una, who exist in an afterlife, the nature of which is the subject of their dialogue. The description of that afterlife begins with Una's request of Monos "to know the incidents of your own passage through the dark Valley and Shadow."[43] Monos then offers Una a long description of the beginnings of postmortem existence not unlike Paralus's narration of the same process to Philothea in a scene that Poe quoted extensively in his *Messenger* review. According to Monos, Death is simply a "breathless and motionless torpor" that nevertheless "did not deprive me of my sentience."[44] Like Paralus hearing the voice of Tithonus, Monos is capable of hearing those around him, feeling their touch and their ministrations to his corpse and even seeing their forms flit about in front of his eyes. However, those sensory experiences were, Monos suggests, unusual. "[T]aste and smell were inextricably confounded, and became one sentiment, abnormal and intense"; "the rays which fell upon the external retina I appreciated . . . only as sound—sound sweet or discordant as the matters presenting themselves at my side were light or dark in shade"; "hearing[,] . . . although excited in degree, was not irregular in action"; and touch was "tardily received, but pertinaciously retained, and resulted always in the highest physical pleasure."[45] These changes in perception are coeval with the development of "a sixth sense" of sorts, a "self-existing sentiment of duration [or time] . . . existing (as man could not possibly have conceived it to exist) independently of any succession of events."[46] This emergent sense is a consequence of his now ongoing reintegration into the broader universe, "the first obvious and certain step of the intemporal soul upon the threshold of the temporal Eternity."[47] This sixth sense apparently becomes his primary means of experiencing reality, a way of being marked solely by an awareness of time passing endlessly. Monos first experienced that peculiar existence not with terror and horror, but in a mode of disinterested observation while "the soul watched narrowly each second as it flew, and, without effort, took record of its flight—without effort and without object."[48] Finally, individuated identity became meaningless, grew "more indistinct," and Monos experienced himself as a locale, not as an individuated self: "the idea of entity . . . merged in that of place. The narrow space immediately surrounding what had been the body, was now growing to be the body itself"—as he became, in essence, one with his very surroundings both physically and spiritually.[49] Eventually, Una died, and her coffin was placed atop that of Monos in the grave where they both moldered until "dust had returned to dust" and "the sense of being had at length utterly departed"—leaving Monos existing only as *"Place and Time*," the final experience of the dead, Una included, so it seems.[50]

In their final disposition, then, Monos and Una reconnect themselves inextricably to the universe. They cease to be individuals and become what their names literally mean: "One." At one with the Universe, they experience what the tale suggests is characteristic of the universal, location (place) and duration (time), but nothing more. They are reunified with the universe and thus with each other as well.[51] According to G. R. Thompson, "the 'union' of true lovers" in the tale is effected by their physical "rotting away," which joins them in "'unity' with the essence of the universe."[52] Their reunification is not, however, without complication, and that cosmic merging differs significantly from the reunion longed for in *Philothea*. It is true that Poe presents the tale without a hint of horror. Neither Una nor Monos seem at all bothered by their loss of identity, their entombment, their decay at the hand of "worms," and their ultimate loss of any sense of individuality. However, the tale is very much at odds with itself, for, like Child's work, "The Colloquy of Monos and Una" presents the experience of losing personal identity through a conversation between two beings despite the fact that they should not exist as separate selves any longer, according to the process as Monos relates it. The structure of the dialogue is thus at odds with the assertions of the tale itself, a text that celebrates the loss of individual identity while curiously sustaining it. It is a contradiction that Poe would try to resolve when he wrote "Mesmeric Revelation" a few years later but would not work out until he abandoned the dialogic narrative structure inherent in both tales—something he did for *Eureka*.[53]

"Mesmeric Revelation" first appeared in *The Columbian* magazine in 1844, approximately three years after "The Colloquy of Monos and Una." Described by Quinn as "a prelude to 'Eureka,'" the work conveys Poe's belief that the ideas grappled with in "The Colloquy of Monos and Una" needed further development.[54] In "Mesmeric Revelation," Poe maintained the dialogic structure of his previous work, although the 1844 tale features a mesmerist and a "patient" suffering from tuberculosis instead of two lovers. In addition, unlike Monos and Una, both characters are still alive, at least until the end of the tale. Mr. Vankirk, the sufferer, sends for the narrator at the beginning of the work "not so much to administer to my bodily ailment, as to satisfy me concerning certain psychic impressions which, of late, have occasioned me much anxiety and surprise," impressions related specifically to "the soul's immortality."[55] His hope is that by entering the mesmeric state and being questioned about the nature of the soul and its ultimate disposition his intuitions might be either confirmed or checked, as mesmeric practice, the tale asserts, allows for "perception . . . through channels supposed unknown, [into] matters beyond the scope of the physical organs"—even matters spiritual.[56] After he mesmerizes Mr. Vankirk, the narrator begins interrogating his patient about the relationship between the material and the spiritual, between the human and the divine. Directed by Vankirk to ask him about God, the narrator poses the following queries: "Is not God a spirit? . . . Is not God immaterial?" Vankirk answers:

> There is no immateriality—it is a mere word. . . . That which is not matter, is not at all. . . . [T]here are gradations of matter of which man knows nothing; the grosser impelling the finer, the finer pervading the grosser. . . . These gradations of matter increase in rarity or fineness, until we arrive at a matter unparticled— without particles—indivisible—one. . . . The ultimate, or unparticled matter, not only permeates all things but impels all things—and thus is all things within itself. This matter is God. . . . God, with all the powers attributed to spirit, is but the perfection of matter.[57]

The implications of the notion that there is no spiritual/material divide and that all things conceptualized by humans as spiritual are a species of the material (or, stated another way, that all things material are grosser manifestations of the spiritual) are then explored through a series of questions and answers that rewrite conventional understandings of human and divine as well as of life and afterlife. In a moment that resonates with the language of *Philothea*, the narrator asks, "You assert, then, that the unparticled matter, in motion, is thought?," to which Vankirk replies, "In general, this motion is the universal thought of the *universal mind*. This thought creates. All created things are but the thoughts of God."[58] Much like the cosmic entity described in *Philothea*, the universal mind of Poe's "Mesmeric Revelation" bears an intimate relationship to the creation and existence of all things in the universe, and the similarity deepens as the discourse continues. As Vankirk goes on to say, "[M]ind, existing unincorporate, is merely God. To create individual, thinking beings, it was necessary to incarnate portions of the divine mind. Thus man is individualized."[59] In such a conceptualization, individual human beings are, in essence, bits or pieces of the divine universal mind (God) integrated with other forms of grosser matter and existing as discrete individuated beings and elements of the divine at the same time. Much like the Platonic notions in *Philothea* that human souls are apparently drawn out of the "Universal Mind" or the "orb of light," the soul as conceptualized in "Mesmeric Revelation" has a divine origin while Poe, unlike Child, insists that the soul is as much a material element as a spiritual one.[60] The philosophical resonances between *Philothea* and "Mesmeric Revelation," brokered through mutual investments in a line of mystical thought that runs at least from Plato forward to Mesmer, Swedenborg, and even Emerson, are notable, but important distinctions between Poe's ideas and Child's must be addressed. In "Mesmeric Revelation," Poe thwarts the idea of reunification with the divine—a key idea articulated in *Philothea*—when Vankirk says, "Divested of corporate investiture, [man would be] God—would be unindividualized. But he can never be thus divested—at least never *will be*—else we must imagine an action of God returning upon itself—a purposeless and futile action. Man is a creature. Creatures are thoughts of God. It is the nature of thought to be irrevocable."[61] This passage suggests that the reunification of the individuated soul with the divine source is impossible. Once the soul is individuated that individuation is perpetual, so it seems. Such a principle is at odds with the desire for reunification as articulated in *Philothea*, in which Philothea and Paralus conceptualize themselves as individuated souls in need of being reconstituted as a whole entity—an entity that may very well have an ultimate destiny of reunification with the Universal Mind itself, a return to the "orb of light" whence, it seems, all soul(s) were drawn.

"Mesmeric Revelation" thus signals another step for Poe in his conceptualization of the relationship between the human and the divine at the same time that it reverses some of the thought regarding unity that marked "The Colloquy of Monos and Una." His articulations of the origins of the individuated soul in "Mesmeric Revelation" approximate more closely Child's work than ideas expressed in "The Colloquy of Monos and Una," but by moving away from the possibility of reunification, Poe distinguishes his thinking from Child's.[62] Still, Poe's return to the subject of spiritual unity through "Mesmeric Revelation" in 1844 might also explain his curious return to his 1836 review of *Philothea*, which he recycled with minor variations in

The Broadway Journal in 1845, approximately six months after "Mesmeric Revelation" appeared in *The Columbian*. Poe's reasons for returning to Child's work were varied. Since his relocation to New York in 1844, Poe had certainly come into contact with Child, who was also living there at the time. Child was frequently in the company of Margaret Fuller, and the two attended Anne Lynch's literary salons, as did Poe. Moreover, on February 15, 1845, Child secured publication in *The Broadway Journal* of a review of Fuller's *Woman in the Nineteenth-Century* after having provided an advance copy of the work. The review itself appeared only one week prior to Poe assuming editorial duties at the *Journal*, and before that time, Poe had been reading and contributing religiously to the publication. As prominent New York literati, the two undoubtedly crossed paths at various points during the mid-1840s while living in the area. Such encounters not only gave Poe the personal connection necessary to describe Child in his 1846 "The Literati of New York" (hereafter "Literati") but may have spurred him to revisit Child's text and to recirculate, with minor changes, the aforementioned review. In his "Literati" description of Child and her work, Poe specifically mentions *Philothea*, which he describes as a book "written with great vigor . . . [and a] style [that] is a model for purity, chastity and ease."[63] Poe adds that "we turn with a species of gasping satisfaction . . . to the pure and quiet pages of *Philothea*," characterizing the novel as "not only the best work of its author but the best work of a class in which are to be ranked *Telemachus* of Fenelon and the *Anacharsis* of Barthelemi."[64] This reference to *Telemachus* and *Anacharsis* is important, for both of these narratives explore the legacy of Greek democracy and egalitarianism as well as questions of good governance and citizenship. Both works also contributed significantly to the "new cult of the antique" that drove renewed interest in the history, culture, and politics of classical Greece since the Enlightenment.[65] Poe ends his review by proposing that *Philothea* "might be introduced, with advantage, into our female academies" because the narrative's "purity of thought and elevation of tone are admirably adapted to scholastic purposes," once again forwarding the notion that the value of the text was tied to the political work of the domestic sphere as understood within a nineteenth-century context.[66]

"Mesmeric Revelation," along with Poe's publication of the second review as well as "Literati," suggests that Child and her work continued to register in his literary consciousness during the period leading up to the publication of *Eureka*, a book that arguably stands as his ultimate word on the subject of spiritual unity, the relationship between the human and the divine, and the important social and political implications that might grow out of a correct understanding of these.[67] Poe spends a considerable amount of the first section of *Eureka* locating the philosophical discourses that he wishes to sustain.

Somewhat playfully, he mentions theories forwarded by Aristotle, Bacon, Newton, Kepler, and others before moving on to challenge more fundamental ideas such as ways of knowing (e.g., empirical inquiry and intuition) and distinctions between matter and spirit. While discussing the latter, he repeats some of his claims from "The Colloquy of Monos and Una" and "Mesmeric Revelation" about there being no such distinctions. Poe's own discourse on spirituality in *Eureka* bears a striking resemblance in many ways to Child's, even though the contexts in which these discourses are presented differ radically. Once again, Poe, like Child, envisions human beings as drawn from a collective spiritual whole and having a common destiny. To support this conception, Poe argues as follows:

> The utter impossibility of any one's soul feeling itself inferior to another; the intense, overwhelming dissatisfaction and rebellion at the thought; these, [along] with the omniprevalent aspirations at perfection, are but the spiritual, coincident with the material, struggles towards the original Unity—are, to my mind at least, a species of proof . . . that each soul is, in part, its own God, its own Creator: in a word, that God the material and spiritual God now exists solely in the diffused Matter and Spirit of the Universe.[68]

Not unlike Child, who invokes the "Universal Mind" that "manifest[s]" itself in the "natural" world, Poe suggests that humans' resistance to imagining anyone or anything superior to themselves is a result of their latent recognition of themselves as component parts of that deity, the Universal Mind, or "God"—to invoke Poe's moniker—now "diffused" throughout the universe as matter and spirit. Moreover, Poe suggests that the intuitive recognition of this supposed truth is tied up with an affective experience. He cites "the intense, overwhelming dissatisfaction and rebellion" that people experience when they try to contravene the truth of their own spiritual nature and believe that there is something greater than themselves in the universe. Thus, an assertion that contravenes the natural order produces pain for the one subject to it, a situation not unlike that in *Philothea,* wherein legal assertions contradicting the natural order produce emotional pain.

In a final ecstatic and poetic vision of the universe, Poe moves even more decisively to tie the recognition of people's spiritual natures to affective experience. He reiterates the idea that humans are diffuse elements of the divine longing to unite with one another and to re-form an otherwise dissipated being. He imagines "an epoch in the Night of Time, when a still-existent Being existed." This being, seeking

> joy [in] his Existence . . . [devised a way to spend] his Eternity in perpetual variation of Concentrated Self and almost Infinite Self-Diffusion. What you call The Universe is but his present expansive existence. He now feels his life through

an infinity of imperfect pleasures—the partial and pain-intertangled pleasures of those inconceivably numerous things which you designate as his creatures, but which are really but infinite individualizations of Himself. . . . [T]he general sum of their sensations is precisely that amount of Happiness which appertains by right to the Divine Being when concentrated within Himself.[69]

Here Poe asks readers not only to conceptualize all matter as spiritual and material diffusions of a Divine Being but also to understand that the purpose for this diffusion is to allow him to experience the myriad emotions of the creatures that his diffusion has produced. Thus, the universe exists, in a sense, largely to facilitate the ability of this Divine Being "to feel" in ways that would otherwise be impossible. In Child's work, individuals longed for reunification with other individuals, and all were ultimately drawn from the Universal Mind although destined to return to it—a dual layer of reunification that produced "joy" in the process. Like Child, Poe similarly sees the coalescence of individuals into the Divine Being not only as a natural occurrence but also as an event increasing the "joy" of all involved.[70]

The feelings that the Divine Being experiences through self-diffusion are not the only ones Poe concerns himself with, nor are they the most important. Readers also have their sentiments targeted by Poe when he invites them to imagine the existence of this being that longs for joy not immediately available. It is true that, unlike Child's work, *Eureka* does not call readers to witness the sentimental tear or the longing and languid sigh of a lover thwarted from obtaining the beloved. However, readers are invited to imagine this Divine Being's apparent loneliness, to conceptualize it as extreme enough to justify him literally tearing himself into pieces. In doing so, the text calls forth readers' sympathy, but at the same time, it suggests that they are parts of that lonely being now surrounded by a vast collection of other similar parts. Thus, they are left to imagine themselves as bound to every other person (or thing) in the universe in a radical affective endeavor, and they are asked to understand that their desire for unity is not only natural but necessary if joy is the ultimate result.

In envisioning themselves as integral parts of a diffused, divine whole seeking affective communion, readers of both *Eureka* and *Philothea* can see their relationship to others in a new light. In *Eureka*, individuals are something akin to siblings, and in *Philothea*, lovers; but in both texts, people are integral parts of one another. Certainly, in that conceptualization, the boundaries between selves begin to break down, and one can only see oneself in a radically intersubjective way, even while experiencing existence from a singular and otherwise unique subject position. This state of interbeing marks Child's politics—and Poe's. Bound together as co-constitutive pieces of the Divine, people are inseparable, and the categories of difference routinely invoked to stratify and segregate human beings are unnatural. In such a situation, how does any one person's experience take precedence over another's? As constituent parts of the Divine, how does any one individual have any less worth or importance than any other? How can people esteem laws, social strictures, or cultural prohibitions that run counter to the order of things? Such behavior seems difficult to justify if one grants Poe's and Child's assertion that though humans are many they are also one.

This mantra is, of course, the fundamental idea at the heart of American democracy, a paradox enshrined not only in the period's *de facto* national motto "E Pluribus Unum" ("out of many, one") but also in the Constitution's attempt to balance federal power, states' rights, and even the status of enslaved people (the latter of which, it clearly failed miserably to do).[71] Poe's politics were rarely local or overly topical—unlike Child's, which, with the exception of *Philothea*, almost always were both. Still, Poe was concerned throughout his career with the fundamental principles at the heart of democratic society and with how these principles might be challenged or subverted.[72] Moreover, given that cosmology is a subject often invoked by writers who advanced their own ideas about appropriate governance—think Paine's *Common Sense* or Whitman's *Democratic Vistas,* for two examples—it seems fitting to conceptualize Poe's discourse on unity in *Eureka* as a literary reflection on "E Pluribus Unum," a rearticulation of the refrain from Child's *Philothea*: "Hail to the mystic two in one!" In a sense, both Poe's *Eureka* and Child's *Philothea* become what W. C. Harris has called a supplement to "the operative documents of state formation," one in which "the abstract philosophical problem of the one and the many [is imagined] . . . in a concrete, particular form," that is, in the imaginative construction of a spiritual and material universe in which people may act as if they are many but must never forget that they are also one.[73]

Significantly, although the nation's founding documents sought to meld the many into one through legal prescription, Poe and Child try to do the same by leading readers to a sense of shared affect and spiritual kinship. In short, Poe's work in *Eureka* and Child's in *Philothea* spiritualize and affectively charge the prevailing political idea "Out of many, one," but—and this point is crucial—neither writer ever really goes beyond helping readers conceive that expanded sense of self. Rather than overtly exploring how this new understanding of the self might translate into contemporary political reform, Poe and Child are both content to lead readers to reimagine their collective coalescence into the divine. Poe's reason for entertaining such a radically intersubjective view of human beings only as a general, abstracted principle (in terms that largely elide anything related to his immediate political moment) derives from the fact that his own personal experience and prejudices made the types of political and social reforms that a monistic conception of the universe might call for simply unpalatable. Like Child, Poe was drawn to see humanity as a *category* of beings, as iterations of the divine, but unlike Child in much of the rest of her work, he shied away from seeing the divine in every individual despite apparent differences of race, gender, and class. Postulating the idea of collective divinity was one thing, but allowing it the currency in contemporary politics to sweep away something like antimiscegenation laws was quite another.

This disconnect between theory and practice is, in fact, what allows one to account for Poe's high praise, his ability to respond to Child's text with a sense of "gasping satisfaction."[74] To be sure, the novel was less overtly topical than much of her other reformist works. Poe was therefore able to appreciate her celebration of radical unity and to imagine the affective bonds that accompany a sense of such unity without having to make the practical leap Child would require of her readers in virtually every other text in her oeuvre other than *Philothea*: redefining contemporary social values and politics based on such a cosmic realization. Existing largely in the abstract, the ideas posited by Child could win Poe's respect without his feeling obliged to face their immediate, contemporary political implications—a situation that Poe would replicate when writing *Eureka*. Child's abstraction of these ideas explains why *Philothea* went a long way toward rehabilitating Child's reputation as a literary figure after her controversial publication of *An Appeal in Favor of That Class of Americans Called Africans*, which championed abolition, defended interracial marriage, and argued for equal rights for all Americans regardless of race or gender. Given that Child's novel was welcomed by reviewers as having "nothing in common with . . . the 'Appeal'" and was deemed by many, like Poe, the best work of her career in part because it veiled its reformist impulses, *Philothea* provides a window into understanding the nature of the challenges progressive writers like Child encountered in antebellum America.[75] To be embraced by the reading public and to navigate successfully the literary marketplace in the 1830s and 1840s typically involved sublimating, if not abstracting, one's progressive politics.[76] Thus, an understanding of Poe's appreciation of *Philothea* points both toward the subtle but persistent influence that Child's work likely had on his thinking as he conceived and wrote pieces like "The Colloquy of Monos and Una," "Mesmeric Revelation," and *Eureka* as well as toward the fraught political ground that would have to be traversed if the nation and its people were to re-form, in approximation of Poe's Divine Being or Child's Universal Mind, into a more perfect union.

NOTES

1. Edgar Allan Poe, "Critical Notices: *Philothea,*" *Southern Literary Messenger* 2, no. 10 (September 1836): 659, The Edgar Allan Poe Society of Baltimore, https://www.eapoe.org/works/criticsm/slm36090.htm.

2. A discussion of Child's abolitionist work will follow, but suffice it to say that Poe's stance toward abolitionism was anything but sympathetic. He actively tied abolitionism to the work of Henry Wadsworth Longfellow, who he lamented was part of a "small coterie of abolitionists, transcendentalists, and fanatics in general" that made his work condemnable. See Poe's review titled "Longfellow's Poems" in *Aristidean* (April 1845): 130, The Edgar Allan Poe Society of Baltimore, https://www.eapoe.org/works/criticsm/ar45101.htm. He cast similar aspersions at James Russell Lowell, whose "prejudices on the topic of slavery" made him, according to Poe, incapable of "speak[ing] well, in the literary sense, of any man who is not a ranting abolitionist." See Poe's "Review of *Fable for the Critics*" in *Southern Literary Messenger* 15, no. 3 (March 1849): 189, The Edgar Allan Poe Society of Baltimore, tghhttps://www.eapoe.org/works/criticsm/slm49101.htm. Critics have mined Poe's relationship to the abolitionist movement rather extensively. See Paul Christian Jones, "Poe's 'Hop-Frog' and the Abolitionist Rhetoric of Pathos," *Journal of American Studies* 35, no. 2 (August 2001): 239–54. See also Terence Whalen's "Average Racism: Poe, Slavery, and the Wages of Literary Nationalism"; Betsy Erkkila's "The Poetics of Whiteness"; and Elsie LeMire's "'The Murders in the Rue Morgue': Amalgamation Discourses and the Race Riots of 1838 in Poe's Philadelphia," all of which appear in *Romancing the Shadow: Poe and Race*, ed. J. Gerald Kennedy and Liliane Weissberg (Oxford: Oxford University Press, 2001). Poe's disdain for abolitionism should not be equated with a full-throated endorsement of slavery. Many critics argue that Poe was troubled by its horrors, even as he expressed ambivalence toward social movements calling for its end. For more on challenges to slavery found in Poe's work, see Matt Sandler, "Poe's Survival Stories as Dying Colonialisms," in *The Oxford Handbook of Edgar Allan Poe*," ed. J. Gerald Kennedy and Scott Peeples (New York: Oxford University Press, 2019); Maurice Lee, "Absolute Poe: His System of Transcendental Racism," *American Literature* 75, no. 4 (December 2003): 751–81; and Dana Nelson, "Economies of Morality and Power: Reading Race in Two Colonial Texts," in *A Mixed Race: Ethnicity in Early America,* ed. Frank Shuffelton (New York: Oxford University Press, 1993).

3. For those unfamiliar with the Child oeuvre, it is probably worth noting that *Philothea* was written in 1836, three years after her publication of *An Appeal in Favor of That Class of Americans Called Africans*—an abolitionist text that prompted several less progressive admirers to abandon any public support of Child, if not to condemn her outright. In the words of Child's biographer, Carolyn Karcher, "What most scandalized Child's public in this monumental indictment of slavery—the first major study of the institution to advocate immediate emancipation and an end to all forms of racial discrimination—was its argument for racial equality and integration, which culminated in an attack on anti-miscegenation laws," a call and an attack that was a bridge too far for many of even her more progressive fans. See Carolyn L. Karcher,

"Lydia Maria Child," in *Dictionary of Literary Biography: American Short-Story Writers Before 1880,* ed. Bobby Ellen Kimbel and William E. Grant (Detroit: Gale, 1988), n.p.

4. Lydia Maria Child, *Philothea: A Romance* (Boston: Otis, Broaders and Co., 1836), 14.

5. Ibid.

6. Plato, "Symposium," in *The Portable Plato,* ed. Scott Buchanan (New York: Penguin, 1976), 145–46.

7. It is important to note that while this characterization of the creation of the sexes focuses largely on heterosexual unions, Aristophanes did not limit natural unions to suit a binary notion of gender. In his estimation, there were three different types of human beings that existed prior to their splitting: men-men, women-women, and men-women. The splitting of these three distinct types of beings into separate entities meant that they would seek reunification with partners that recreated their original unions. Thus, same-sex (re)unions were just as natural in his estimation as others.

8. Carolyn L. Karcher, "Introduction" in *Hobomok and Other Writings on Indians* (London: Rutgers University Press, 1986), xx.

9. Lydia Maria Child, *Hobomok and Other Writing on Indians* (London: Rutgers University Press, 1986), 121.

10. Child, *Hobomok,* 121; Plato, 145.

11. Edgar Allan Poe, "The Literati of New York City," *Godey's Ladies Book* 33 (September 1846): 129, The Edgar Allan Poe Society of Baltimore, https://www.eapoe.org/works/misc/litratb5.htm. In this piece, Poe also mentions *Hobomok* as well as Child's *The History of the Condition of Women.* Poe's *Southern Literary Messenger* review contains references to the following works by Child: *Hobomok, The American Frugal Housewife, The Mother's Book,* and an edited collection titled *The Juvenile Miscellany.* However, in neither critical text does Poe allude to Child's abolitionist writings.

12. Melissa Ryan, "Republican Mothers and Indian Wives: Lydia Maria Child's Indian Stories." *ESQ: A Journal of the American Renaissance* 56, no. 1 (2010): 34.

13. Maurice Lee, "Absolute Poe: His System of Transcendental Racism," *American Literature* 75, no. 4 (2003): 774.

14. See Terence Whalen, "Average Racism: Poe, Slavery, and the Wages of Literary Nationalism," in *Romancing the Shadow: Poe and Race,* 3–40.

15. Philothea was Ionian, and Paralus, Athenian. While both Athenians and Ionians were "Greeks," the radical nativism that characterizes Athenian self-conceptions in this text marks any foreigner as an "other" posing a threat to the state. Thus, other "Greek" peoples are subjected to some of the same nativist laws and provisions that individuals of different races and from vastly different locales are subject to. In short, their foreignness becomes the basis upon which they are deemed socially unacceptable in a way not entirely dissimilar to the social ostracism depicted in other works by Child.

16. Child, *Philothea,* 46.

17. The resemblance between such language and that of Emerson is remarkable, given that Emerson described humans as essentially drawn from a well of "Oversoul"

and "[e]mbosomed for a season in nature" with a destiny to reunite with and contribute to the constitution of that Oversoul when such embosoming ended in death (1). See Ralph Waldo Emerson, Nature: *A Facsimile of the First Edition with an Introduction by Jaroslav Pelikan* (Boston: Beacon Press, 1985), 1. Child knew Emerson not only by reputation (both navigated Boston's progressive social circles) but also through Margaret Fuller, one of Child's closest friends and confidantes. Child was an integral part of the "Conversations" circle that Fuller had hosted since at least 1825, and the two were lifelong friends. Given the depths of their friendship, it may be appropriate to say that Child's Transcendental gleanings are more attributable to Fuller than to Emerson.

18. Child, *Philothea*, 48.

19. Ibid., 201, *passim*.

20. Ibid., 143.

21. See Laura L. Meilke, "Sentiment and Space in Lydia Maria Child's Native American Writings, 1824–1870," *Legacy* 21, no. 2 (2004): 172–92. According to Meilke, Child's fiction was clearly sentimental, with "moving domestic scenes such as the separation of families, the abuse of slaves at the hands of both masters and mistresses, . . . and the creation of forced and improper sexual relationships," all of which signaled a "challenge to the progressive narrative of history and prevailing racial hierarchy, based on sympathy and using sentimental rhetoric" (173).

22. Child, *Philothea*, 142.

23. Ibid., 205.

24. Adam Smith, *The Theory of Moral Sentiments* (Dublin: Beatty and Jackson, 1777), 15, Google Books, https://www.google.com/books/edition/_/SxEvAAAAYAAJ?hl=en&gbpv=1.

25. Eugenia Brinkema, *The Forms of the Affects* (Durham: Duke University Press, 2014), 16.

26. Jeffrey Steele, "Sentimental Transcendentalism and Political Affect: Child and Fuller in New York," *Toward a Female Genealogy of Transcendentalism*, ed. Jana Argersinger and Phyllis Cole (Athens: University of Georgia Press, 2014), 207–26. Scholarship on *Philothea,* which is much less copious than scholarship on the rest of the Child canon, has a few significant preoccupations, one of which, as Steele's work indicates, is the resonances between the 1836 book and contemporary Transcendentalism. The other major vein of criticism was New Critical, focusing primarily on stylistic matters. See William S. Osborne, *Lydia Maria Child* (Boston: Twayne, 1980). He offers a representative example when he describes *Philothea* as "simple, the structure is tight, the style is rich, the background is carefully sketched in, the characters are substantial, and the themes are artfully worked out" (90).

27. This fact also suggests that critical characterizations of *Philothea* as "a renunciation of her [earlier] ambition" or a retreat from public abolitionist advocacy in the wake of the broad resistance to *An Appeal in Favor of That Class of Americans Called Africans* are only partly accurate. See Carolyn L. Karcher, *The First Woman in the Republic: A Cultural Biography of Lydia Maria Child* (Durham: Duke University Press, 1994), 236.

28. Child, *Philothea*, 141–42.

29. Poe, "Critical Notices," 661.

30. Child, *Philothea*, 195.

31. Ibid.

32. Ibid.

33. Ibid.

34. Ibid., 196.

35. Poe, *"Critical Notices,"* 662.

36. Ibid.

37. Ibid.

38. Margaret Nash, "Rethinking Republican Motherhood: Benjamin Rush and the Young Ladies' Academy of Philadelphia," *Journal of the Early Republic* 17, no. 2 (1997): 175.

39. Linda Kerber, *Women of the Republic: Ideology and Intellect in Revolutionary America* (New York: Norton, 1986), 11. Kerber was the first scholar to limn the contours of what she called "republican motherhood," a discursive construct in which childrearing and democratic politics were connected, the idea being that as children were exposed to the homespace, and a mother's influence in particular, those young people learned to play their appropriate roles within a democratic republic. Margaret Nash revised Kerber's thesis by demonstrating that prevailing antebellum gender discourses were focused on the influence that women wielded not only over their children but also over their husbands, suitors, brothers, etc. Curiously enough, there are few records indicating that faculty members within these academies actually spoke or wrote frequently about either "republican motherhood" or "republican womanhood," contrary to the many men who wrote about such academies in the popular press, suggesting, according to Doris Malkmus, it might be appropriate to wonder just how powerfully present the ideology of republican motherhood was in the lives of young women of the period, despite the fact that republican motherhood was the primary reason why some men supported women's education. For more information, see Doris Jeanne Malkmus, "Female Academies in the Early Republic" (MA Thesis, University of Oregon, 1993).

40. Benjamin Rush, *Essays Literary, Moral and Philosophical by Benjamin Rush, M.D., and Professor of the Institutes of Medicine and Clinical Practice in the University of Pennsylvania* (Philadelphia: Thomas and Samuel Bradford, 1798), 19, *Early American Imprints Series* 1, no. 34495.

41. Featuring a postmortem conversation between two lovers, "The Colloquy of Monos and Una" belongs to a group of texts that scholars often call "angelic dialogues." For two recent studies of those works, see the following: Betsy Erkkila, "Perverting the American Renaissance: Poe, Democracy, Critical Theory," in *Poe and the Remapping of Antebellum Print Culture*, ed. J Gerald Kennedy and Jerome McGann (Baton Rouge: Louisiana State University Press, 2012), 65–100; and Jeffrey Andrew Weinstock, "Before and After: Anticipatory Anxiety and Experience Claimed in Poe's Angelic Dialogues," *Poe Studies* 52 (2019): 91–109.

42. Arthur Hobson Quinn, *Edgar Allan Poe: A Critical Biography* (New York: D. Appleton-Century Co., 1941), 325, The Edgar Allan Poe Society of Baltimore, https://www.eapoe.org/papers/misc1921/quinn00c.htm.

43. Edgar Allan Poe, "The Colloquy of Monos and Una," *Collected Works of Edgar Allan Poe,* ed. Thomas Ollive Mabbott, vol. 2 (Cambridge: Harvard University Press, 1968), 607, The Edgar Allan Poe Society of Baltimore, https://www.eapoe.org/works/mabbott/tom2t000.htm.

44. Ibid., 612.

45. Ibid., 613.

46. Ibid., 614–15.

47. Ibid., 615.

48. Ibid., 616.

49. Ibid.

50. Ibid., 617.

51. This situation indicates the extent to which Poe indulges in anything resembling sentimentality in the tale. There are some affectively charged moments in "The Colloquy of Monos and Una," but they are subtle and do not perform the kind of political work that Child may have been performing when she filled *Philothea* with moments that seemingly invite readers to grieve over the unjust and unnatural thwarting of (re)union.

52. G. R. Thompson, *Poe's Fiction: Romantic Irony in the Gothic Tales* (Madison: University of Wisconsin Press, 1973), 187.

53. It is probably worth noting here that the narrative structure also sustains a corresponding ambiguity related to the affective registers of the tale. Consider that the dialogue itself suggests an ongoing affective connection in one respect (i.e., the lovers are engaged in an intimate dialogue about their experiences), and their conversation suggests that they will share some form of unified existence throughout eternity. Nevertheless, given that Monos narrates an end to individuated sentience, it is hard to fathom how such an affective bond can be sustained. If two are truly one, then there is no "other" to whom one can address one's attentions. It will not be until the writing of *Eureka* that Poe truly grapples with questions of affect.

54. Quinn, 419.

55. Edgar Allan Poe, "Mesmeric Revelation," *Collected Works of Edgar Allan Poe,* ed. Thomas Ollive Mabbott, vol. 3 (Cambridge: Harvard University Press, 1968), 1031, The Edgar Allan Poe Society of Baltimore, https://www.eapoe.org/works/mabbott/tom3t000.htm.

56. Ibid., 1030.

57. Ibid., 1034.

58. Ibid., 1036, emphasis mine.

59. Ibid.

60. Poe's ability to stand at the crossroads of scientific materialism and dualism was by no means unique to him—rather, it was a phenomenon made possible by the state of scientific thinking at the time. Scholars such as Justine Murison, John Tresch, and Matthew Taylor have commented extensively on Poe's enthusiasm for a scientific materialism melded, at times, with a seeming mysticism. See John Tresch, "'Matter No More': Edgar Allan Poe and the Paradoxes of Materialism," *Critical Inquiry* 42, no. 4 (Summer 2016): 865–98. According to Tresch, "In Poe's cosmic narratives—cryptic, fragmentary, arabesque—opposed pairs walk hand in hand: rationalization

and enchantment, observation and imagination, spirit and matter, thought and concrete medium. In so doing, each term veers in and out of its specificity; matter, encompassing all, becomes matter no more, absolute nihility" (896). See also chapter 2 of Justine Murison, *The Politics of Anxiety in Nineteenth-Century American Literature* (Cambridge: Cambridge University Press, 2011), 47–75; and Matthew Taylor, "Edgar Allan Poe's (Meta)physics: A Pre-History of the Post-Human," *Nineteenth-Century Literature* 62, no. 2 (September 2007): 193–221.

61. Poe, "Mesmeric Revelation," 1037.

62. It is worth noting that whatever subtle moments of sentimentality marked "The Colloquy of Monos and Una" are essentially scrubbed from "Mesmeric Revelation." Child, it seems, felt it important to wed notions of spiritual unity to affective discourses that demonstrated the imperative for appropriate social and political arrangements. Poe, in "Mesmeric Revelation," seems entirely consumed with simply laying out his conceptualization of the spiritual nature of humankind and doing so with little to no affective charge.

63. Edgar Allan Poe, "The Literati of New York," *The Works of the Late Edgar Allan Poe,* ed. Rufus Griswold (New York: J. S. Redfield, 1850), 99, The Edgar Allan Poe Society of Baltimore, https://www.eapoe.org/works/misc/litratd5.htm#childlym.

64. Ibid. In his 1836 review, Poe had indicated that *Philothea* was "of that class of works of which *Telemachus* . . . and the *Anacharsis* . . . are the most favorable specimens," but he did not give that claim pride of place, suggesting that the merits of *Philothea* had grown increasingly apparent to him in the interim ("Critical Notices," 659).

65. Matthew R. Poteat, *Henry Toole Clark: Civil War Governor of North Carolina* (Jefferson: McFarland, 2009), 192, Appendix A, note 8. Fénelon's work, *Les Aventures de Télémaque,* is essentially the story of the education of Telemachus by Mentor. The Archbishop of Cambrai, Fénelon was the appointed tutor of the grandson of Louis XIV. The text is generally seen as a rebuke of Louis's absolutist rule and an attempt to promote a new, more parliamentary style of governance in France. As a testament to its early articulation of democratic principles, Thomas Jefferson not only included the text in his library at Monticello but apparently read it with some regularity. For more information, see Kevin J. Hayes, *The Road to Monticello: The Life and Mind of Thomas Jefferson* (New York: Oxford University Press, 2008), 227. Barthélemy's work, formally titled *Voyage de Juene Anachrasis en Grece,* narrates the travels of Anachrasis the Younger throughout Greece during the Greek classical period and spends copious amounts of time talking about and praising governmental structures and the citizenry.

66. Edgar Allan Poe, "Literary: Mrs. Child's *Philothea,*" *Broadway Journal* 1, no. 2 (May 31, 1845): 344, The Edgar Allan Poe Society of Baltimore, https://www.eapoe.org/works/criticsm/bj45095.htm.

67. *Eureka* has enjoyed a considerable amount of attention since its publication, and critical engagements usually run within a few primary veins of inquiry. Some critics view the text primarily as an aesthetic exercise. See Edward Wagenknecht's *Edgar Allan Poe: The Man Behind the Legend* (London: Oxford University Press, 1963) and Jerome McGann's *The Poet Edgar Allan Poe: Alien Angel* (Cambridge: Harvard

University Press, 2014). McGann insisted that Poe's book "should be understood in poetical rather than philosophical or scientific terms" (102). There is also a long line of studies in which scholars have investigated the intersection of *Eureka* with or contributions to scientific thinking, ranging from William Browne's 1869 article in the *New Eclectic Magazine* to Frederick Conner's 1949 "Poe and John Nichol: Notes on the Source of 'Eureka'" to William Schiek's 1992 "An Intrinsic Luminosity: Poe's Use of Platonic and Newtonian Optics." Other relevant studies are Allan Halline's "Moral and Religious Concepts in Poe," *Bucknell University Studies* 2, no. 3 (1951): 126–50; David Ketterer's *New World for Old: The Apocalyptic Imagination, Science Fiction, and American Literature* (Garden City, NY: Doubleday, 1974); and Susan Manning's "Poe's 'Eureka' and American Creative Nihilism," *Journal of American Studies* 23, no. 2 (1989): 235–51. In these texts, scholars have investigated *Eureka* primarily as a philosophical treatise, usually as an "application of Aristotelian philosophy . . . to aesthetics" (Manning 249). I am deeply indebted in this essay to the work of W. C. Harris, one of the few critics to examine the political dimensions of *Eureka* and arguably the first to recognize that the work was "getting at the mechanism of American social formation by addressing the terms of its foundation." See W. C. Harris, "Edgar Allan Poe's 'Eureka' and the Poetics of Constitution," *American Literary History* 12, no. 1/2 (2000): 2.

68. Edgar Allan Poe, *Eureka,* ed. Susan Levine and Stuart Levine (Chicago: University of Illinois Press, 2004), 104.

69. Ibid., 105.

70. It is worth noting that Poe unquestionably conceptualizes his divine, universal being as male—referring to it as "him" and, following in the Judeo-Christian tradition, referencing it as "Jehovah." Such conceptualizations of the "Universal Mind" are absent in Child's work, where she refrains from assigning gendered nomenclature or characteristics to it. This marks another appreciable distinction between the work of the two authors and stands as a subtle corrective by Poe to Child's attempt to forward a more progressive agenda than he was ultimately comfortable with.

71. W. C. Harris is the one who initially makes this connection between Poe's work and the traditional national motto of the United States, a dynamic he describes in further detail when he says "the topos that preoccupies Poe in his cosmology is the same that preoccupied authors of the operative documents of [American] state formation: the abstract philosophical problem of the *one and the many,* realized in a concrete particular form . . . the problem of unifying disparates without violating the identity (that is, the difference) of its constituents" (3).

72. There is a rather significant critical history documenting the way in which Poe's work sustained an ongoing commentary on democracy, arguably beginning with Ernest Marchand's seminal essay "Poe as Social Critic," *American Literature* 6 (1934): 28–43. One of the more relevant and enlightening examples to recently appear is Reiner Smolinski and Jeff Rumiano's "Poe's Party Politics in the Age of Jackson," in *Poe Writing/Writing Poe*, ed. Richard Kopley and Jana Argersinger (New York: AMS Press, 2013), 57–76. For more examples, see Rick Rodriguez, "Sovereign Authority and the Democratic Subject in Poe," *Poe Studies* 44, no. 1 (2011): 39–56; Theron Britt, "The Common Property of the Mob: Democracy and Identity in

Poe's 'William Wilson,'" *Mississippi Quarterly* 48, no. 2 (1995): 197–210; Katrina Bachinger, "Tit for Tat: The Political Poe's Ripostes to Nineteenth Century American Culture and Society," *Romantic Reassessment* 87, no. 4 (1981): 46–90; and Burton R. Pollin, "Politics and History in Poe's 'Mellonta Tauta': Two Allusions Explained," *Studies in Short Fiction* 8 (1971): 627–31.

73. Harris, 3.

74. Poe, "Critical Notices," 659.

75. Sarah Josepha Hale, *"Philothea," American Ladies' Magazine* 9 (1836): 480–81. Hale was not alone in showing appreciation for *Philothea* by drawing distinctions between it and *An Appeal in Favor of That Class of Americans Called Africans.* According to Carolyn Karcher, "reviewers of *Philothea* welcomed [Child] back into the literary fold and intimated they would gladly regard the *Appeal* as an aberration, provided she would put abolitionism behind her" (*First* 236). See Chapter 10 of Karcher's *The First Woman in the Republic* for more information.

76. This state of affairs would change dramatically by the early 1850s, when more overtly political works like *Uncle Tom's Cabin* would enjoy widespread acclaim and bring literary fame to their authors.

Chapter Three

Fifty Years of Women's Scholarship on Poe

Amy Branam Armiento

In October 1968, the second issue of the *Poe Newsletter* included a brief piece titled "Faulkner and 'Helen'—A Further Note" by Aretta J. Stevens.[1] Many readers may not have noticed that this three-sentence note was the newsletter's first contribution by a woman scholar. The next year Margaret J. Yonce published the first feature article by a woman: "The Spiritual Descent into the Maelström: A Debt to the 'The Rime of the Ancient Mariner.'"[2] Nancy Niblack Baxter's and Iola S. Haverstick's notes appeared in the same number.[3] Throughout the 1970s, women contributed articles and notes regularly, and in 1973, the year the *Poe Studies Association Newsletter* premiered, women scholars published there, too. Yet many of their names and contributions are unfamiliar to Poe critics today.

Although women have published on Poe for decades, few scholarly studies have focused on their critical contributions. That is not, however, the case for some other canonical male writers. Charlene Avallone's chapter "Women Reading Melville/Melville Reading Women" from *Melville and Women* and select essays in *Hawthorne and Women: Engendering and Expanding the Hawthorne Tradition* such as those by Claudia Durst Johnson, Margaret B. Moore, and Rita K. Gollin highlight nineteenth-century women's reception of these authors' works.[4] However, Jamie Barlowe's chapter, "Re-Reading Women II: The Example of Brett, Hadley, Duff, and Women's Scholarship," in *Hemingway and Women: Female Critics and the Female Voice* and Elizabeth Schultz and Haskell Springer's introduction, "Melville Writing Women/Women Writing Melville," in *Melville and Women* are more in line with the material this chapter presents.[5] Barlowe, Schultz, and Springer investigate the relatively recent work of women scholars in their respective author studies. The closest work of that kind devoted to Poe is *The Afterlife of Edgar Allan Poe*, in which Scott Peeples presents "a general survey of Poe studies from Griswold's obituary to the year 2002."[6] In this critical overview, he devotes a section to female characters in Poe's works and uses pronouns to signal the gender identities of the scholars analyzing those characters, but highlighting women's contributions to Poe studies was not the express purpose of his project.

A supplement to Peeples's study but more limited in scope, this chapter illuminates not only specific contributions by individual women critics but also the key scholarly conversations in which they have participated. Some of the work covered by Peeples is mentioned here, but this chapter features critics omitted from *The Afterlife of Edgar Allan Poe* and accounts for a number of scholarly works published between 2002 and 2018, referencing articles (primarily those appearing in the two Poe newsletters/journals), edited collections, biographies, editions of Poe's writings, and monographs.[7] In addition, this chapter deals almost exclusively with publications by U.S. women scholars as well as a few works by critics born abroad but employed by U.S. colleges and universities. Significantly, all this material is presented as a bibliographic essay, not an annotated bibliography. The latter is, of course, a mere alphabetical arrangement of resources, but this essay features a topical organization allowing readers to see how scholarly conversations have developed around key subjects. This approach has clear benefits. Instead of discussing critical works in isolation, the writer of a bibliographic essay can draw attention to the relationships between critics, showing how they respond to each other directly, and even when scholars are not in direct conversation with each other, a bibliographic essayist can show how their ideas on specific subjects align and diverge. Those features are evident in this chapter, which foregrounds important trends in Poe scholarship produced by women. In addition to shedding light on the relationships between critics, a bibliographic essay can reveal relationships between the various subjects of scholarly inquiry themselves. For example, this chapter opens with an account of feminist readings of Poe texts, some of which rely on psychoanalytic ideas. Those ideas, in turn, surface in criticism that women have produced about gender in general as it relates to the Poe oeuvre, and these explorations are relevant to other identity-based interventions in Poe criticism such as women's investigations of Poe's treatments of racial matters. This essay actually addresses several other topics that have received scrutiny from female critics, including print culture, genre studies, disability studies, ecocriticism, and editing, to name only five. In addition to recognizing the topical breadth of women's contributions to Poe studies, readers of this bibliographic essay should be able to appreciate those contributions in context, to see them as part of ongoing critical conversations that have taken place over the past fifty years.

Poe's controversial depictions of female characters might seem a tantalizing subject for feminist scholars. However, during the 1980s and 1990s, few critics pursued such readings. Peeples has speculated that, "because a feminist response . . . seems too obvious," this topic "has received less attention" than others, but he recognizes scholars who proposed deconstructionist readings suggesting that Poe had feminist sympathies.[8] Published after Peeples's 2004 book, articles by Monika Elbert and Kristen Renzi are two recent examples in this vein. In "Poe and Hawthorne as Women's Amanuenses," Elbert takes the position that these writers' female characters represent actual women, concluding that these portrayals evince earnest attempts "to empower the hushed woman."[9] Similarly implying that Poe's texts may be more feminist-friendly than they appear, Renzi submits that Egaeus, in "Berenice," illustrates Poe's nuanced understanding of "gendered miscommunications and gendered violence."[10] However, in 1984, Beth Ann Bassein, a critic not mentioned in Peeples's book, had soundly rejected the notion that Poe's depictions of women were feminist. She insisted that Poe's "death woman" trope cannot be defended, taking issue with Poe apologists who rely upon Baudelaire's view that Poe held chivalric attitudes toward women, exposing the antifeminist underpinnings of chivalric ideals.[11] Bassein's position persists as a challenge to readings such as Elbert's and Renzi's. Although they may disagree about Poe's attitudes toward women, all of these critics extend feminist readings of Poe's texts to pronouncements about his personal beliefs.

Many scholars take a different tack to make works by Poe palatable to feminists. They "complicate the equation of Poe with his misogynistic narrators and even make the case that he defamiliarizes, and in so doing reveals, the ugly implications of his characters' misogyny."[12] In effect, these critics refuse, directly or indirectly, to conflate a story's narrator or a poem's speaker with Poe. In "'Not a Woman': The Murdered Muse in 'Ligeia,'" Catherine Carter posits that the eponymous character represents "the creative aspect of the mind," eschewing the assumption that the narrator's treatment of Ligeia reflects Poe's attitudes toward women.[13] Categorizing creativity as "feminine," she invokes the masculine–feminine fusion associated with romantic androgyny, a topic discussed at length by Diane Long Hoeveler.[14] Depicting a woman as symbol/object rather than person/subject does, of course, raise additional concerns about Poe's own estimation of women, but Carter does not speculate on this matter. Like her, other scholars have formulated feminist readings that avoid the intentional fallacy. For instance, Dawn Keetley limits her discussion to certain male narrators who view each woman not as a "'real' mother" but as "a projection."[15] She argues that Melanie Klein's psychoanalytic theory of envy explains why the narrators consider women's reproductive potential a threat. Interpreting these men as child figures, Keetley insists that they feel compelled to destroy their figurative mothers when those women do not fulfill infantile desires.[16] To discourage readers from confusing Poe with his narrators, she generalizes this tendency to a societal expectation "that the mother be there entirely for the child."[17]

Other scholars focus not on female characters in Poe's texts but on women in Poe's life, drawing attention to neglected influences on his creative work and opening new lines of biographical inquiry. In 2000, Eliza Richards published a call-to-action in *Poe Studies*, urging scholars to take seriously the numerous ways in which American women writers have shaped the Poe oeuvre, a subject that few critics had explored. Richards points out the irony of this omission, stating, "This dismissal is especially notable since Poe himself responded at length to [women's] work: much of his practical criticism, especially in his later years, was devoted to women writers from both sides of the Atlantic."[18] Noelle Baker and Mary De Jong had, in part, addressed this matter before Richards delivered her reproach. Baker studied Sarah Helen Whitman's career and uncovered ways in which Poe took advantage of her "regional reputation" by forming a connection to her when "he struggled with his own career in the late 1840s."[19] Taking a different approach, De Jong investigated how Frances Osgood viewed Poe's role in her life, emphasizing that Poe's dubious personal reputation posed problems for poetesses known to consort with him. In effect, she argues that their attachments to Poe enhanced their own notoriety "at the risk of infamy."[20] Building on the work of Baker and De Jong, Richards published *Gender and the Poetics of Reception in Poe's Circle* in 2004, a book that provided unequivocal proof of Poe's indebtedness to professional women writers.[21] Richards shifted the discussion of women in his life, insisting that they were not minor influences on Poe but, in many cases, role models for him. One of the consequences of this research is that many nineteenth-century women writers have been recovered, and these authors were, independent of their connections to Poe, formidable writers themselves. Kirsten Silva Gruesz's study of Maria Gowen Brooks illustrates that fact.[22] Ascertaining the significant contributions that such women have made to U.S. literature has, of course, long been at the heart of feminist studies.

Other Poe scholars are drawn to Poe's representations of or connections to men. For instance, Jacqueline Bradley frames "The Cask of the Amontillado," "Berenice," and "The Tell-Tale Heart" as crises of masculinity. Focusing on the narrators' (mis)perceptions of their relationships with women, she reveals the symbolic ways in which the murders expose relations of power, arguing that the "physical and figurative barriers" between characters are "penetrated" by Montresor, Egaeus, and the unnamed narrator of "The Tell-Tale Heart" and associating their actions with patriarchal violence.[23] Working alongside Clark

Moreland, Karime Rodriguez turns to the construction of masculinity in "The Black Cat," which she views as an imaginative piece inspired by Fuseli's *The Nightmare* (1781). By pairing an interpretation of the painting with the tale, she concludes that that the protagonist fears becoming feminine.[24] Likewise, Alexandra Reuber uses a psychoanalytic approach to spotlight the male ego and its desire for preservation in "The Fall of the House of Usher." She shifts the reader's attention from Usher's traumatic experience to the narrator's, reading the text as the narrator's nightmare of confronting "his fear of death."[25] Barbara Johnson moves the spotlight from male characters to Poe's relationship to another (male) Romantic writer—William Wordsworth—in "Strange Fits: Poe and Wordsworth on the Nature of Poetic Language." A titan of the Romantic movement, Wordsworth was surely known to Poe, and Johnson asks how the two writers' poetical theories and practices were related. She begins by acknowledging that their approaches seem opposed, yet she concludes that their ideas about poetic language are "symmetrically inverse stories."[26] She points to their shared interests in diction as well as personification and determines that the two men have remarkably similar notions about writing. In addition, she observes that both writers' works manifest "repetition compulsion and the death instinct."[27] For Johnson, Wordsworth and Poe exhibit in their commentaries and productions the conviction that "the poetic function" is a "correlative . . . of loss."[28] All of the readings mentioned in this paragraph fit under the umbrella of psychoanalytic treatments of Poe and his works, a critical category that includes earlier articles by Roberta Reeder, Julia Mazow, and Renata Mautner Wasserman.[29]

Women have also applied critical race theory to Poe's texts.[30] In "Rethinking Race and Slavery in Poe Studies," Teresa Goddu urged Poe scholars to focus not on determining whether Poe himself was racist or pro-abolitionist but on "situat[ing] his texts within a larger sociocultural field and at the nexus of multiple cultural discourses."[31] Goddu, along with Toni Morrison and others, transformed how scholars talk about Poe and race, abandoning futile attempts to pin down Poe's personal views and directing critical attention to the ways that his writings treat racial matters.[32] For example, Marcia Nichols and Charlene Waters have explained how minstrelsy conventions inform Poe's tales. Nichols points out the irony of Poe's use of an Egyptian in "Some Words with a Mummy" to subvert white male power. She observes that the white characters in that tale control all other bodies, analyzing this power dynamic by drawing parallels between these men's actions and those of anatomists and medical students who perform dissection. Moreover, she demonstrates how the men's interactions with Allamistakeo evoke minstrelsy, a tradition that simultaneously pokes fun at the white elite only to reinforce its power by making persons of color "the butt of the joke."[33] Similarly, Waters links Fortunato and the skeleton in "The Cask of Amontillado" to the dandy and Mr. Bones, two stock characters in minstrel shows. To establish the parallels, she identifies Poe's inclusion of similar conventions such as homonymic wordplay and repetition. She contends that Poe's appropriation of the minstrel form adds another layer to the inversion of power dynamics in this particular tale.[34]

Some critics have identified ways that Poe addressed racial themes in more understated ways. Cindy Weinstein compares Poe's treatment of time in *Pym* to rhetoric used to describe race relations.[35] Christina Zwarg employs affect theory to re-frame Poe's storytelling and use of mesmerism in "A Tale of the Ragged Mountains" as a response to the nation's participation in "slavery and racism driving imperialism."[36] Amy C. Branam [Armiento], who analyzes "Politian," and Erin Forbes, who devotes separate articles to "The Premature Burial" and "Dream-Land," decipher references to slavery encoded in these Poe texts.[37] Armiento explains how Poe appropriates a Gothic sixteenth-century Roman setting to speak obliquely about the American South, moving beyond the Sharp–Beauchamp feud that inspired "Politian" to discuss the play's subtle commentary on race. Forbes also takes a closer look at Poe's use of Gothic devices, interpreting interment in "The Premature Burial" as a symbol of "social death" and likening that tale to the narrative of the freedom seeker Henry "Box" Brown. In a similar way, she detects in "Dream-Land" allusions to the maroon community, a group of African Americans living near Virginia's Dismal Swamp and seeking refuge from enslavement.

Other scholars have examined what Poe reveals about U.S. imperialism and its effects. Whereas many critics have expounded upon what "black" signifies in Poe's texts, Maria Karafilis asks readers to interrogate Poe's use of the word "red," which she says represents Native Americans, the violence against them, and the practice of miscegenation. Pairing Poe with Hawthorne, she posits that they critique "expansionist rhetoric and Indian removal policies."[38] Karafilis concludes that both writers predict that the extinction of the "Red Man" will result in the annihilation of the "White Man" as well. She deems "The Masque of the Red Death" the "story . . . that brings this idea to its fullest development."[39] Heather Chacón deals with antebellum anxiety about national identity formation in "The Man That Was Used Up." Referencing political statements from prominent men of the time, she argues that Poe expresses the fear that the United States sacrifices its founding ideals of liberty, freedom, and equality by following the Old World paradigm of conquest and expansion. In effect, the tale serves as a warning that the United States must avoid reproducing the type of government that it revolted against.[40]

Articles on how race, gender, and sexuality intersect in Poe's writings have also appeared. According to Courtney Novosat, the epigraph in "The Murders in the Rue Morgue" encourages readers to notice gaps in the text, lacunae related to issues of sexuality and race that other scholars have isolated but not fully investigated. She asserts that Dupin's superficial reading of clues invites readers to delve deeper into "euphemistic or symbolic meanings."[41] In particular, Novosat lays out evidence for sexual relationships between the narrator and Dupin as well as between Madame and Mademoiselle L'Espanaye. Additionally, she emphasizes how the orangutan invites a reading of Poe's views on race, for the text implies that "the guilty ape" is "the simian stand-in for the nonwhite other."[42] In effect, the tale upholds whiteness as superior because it is not implicated in the crime. Novosat's exploration of the nexus of race, gender, and sexuality in "The Murders in the Rue Morgue" offers fresh insights into this tale. Along the same lines, Suzanne Ashworth looks at these intersections in the character of M. Valdemar. She writes, "[Valdemar] is sexually perplexing and physically strange, and he lives the queer subject's raw exposure to the machinations of disgust and death."[43] She views his body as nonnormative, and following Poe's textual clues, she identifies him as an immigrant, possibly of mixed race.[44] Fusing various interpretative approaches, Novosat and Ashworth show how readings of race informed by gender studies and queer theory affirm the richness and relevance of Poe's works for today's readers.

In addition to these context-centered interpretations, women who study Poe have shed new light on "Book History [and] the romantic institution of lyric poetry."[45] Connections between Poe's writing and the domestic print culture of his era have intrigued many scholars. Alexandra Urakova examines Poe's works in relation to the other matter running in the magazines and gift books in which his works appeared, and she considers how Poe responded creatively to readers' expectations, using "The Purloined Letter," "The Cask of Amontillado," "The Thousand-and-Second Tale of Scheherazade," and "The Literati of New York" as case studies.[46] In "The Gift (Book) That Keeps on Giving: Poe's 'The Purloined Letter,' Rereading, Reprinting, and Detective Fiction," Gila Ashtor also discusses "The Purloined Letter," examining three printings of the tale in relation to other items from the collections and periodicals in which those versions of Poe's detective tale appeared.[47] For example, she treats "The Purloined Letter" as a companion piece to the poems published alongside it in *The Gift* (1845), speculating that antebellum readers may have read the story as a cautionary tale about leaving home or as a warning against neglecting one's spouse, among other interpretative possibilities.[48] Continuing this interpretive trend, Kathryn K. Shinn describes the role of gift books in the antebellum publishing market and how the genre played an instrumental part in furthering Poe's career. The relationship between Poe and those professional opportunities was, Shinn points out, symbiotic, for the inclusion of works by Poe, a writer of enduring fame, saved many gift books from obscurity.[49]

Like Urakova, Ashtor, and Shinn, many scholars have studied how Poe's publications fared in the literary marketplace.[50] In "Poe's Moon Shot: 'Hans Phaall' and the Art and Science of Antebellum Print Culture," Marcy J. Dinius defines "hoax" for both Poe and Richard Adams Locke (the author of "Great Astronomical Discoveries Lately Made") as the misrepresentation of imaginative works as scientific texts. By blurring the line between the two types of writing, hoaxers could compete in a periodical market that treated "the arts and science as rivals for popular attention and that allowed the free circulation of texts without concern for their authorship or authenticity."[51] The relationship between Poe and U.S. print culture was also the subject of two monographs published in 2012: Laura Langer Cohen's *The Fabrication of American Literature: Fraudulence and Antebellum Print Culture* and Sandra Tomc's *Industry and the Creative Mind: The Eccentric Writer in American Literature and Entertainment, 1790–1860.*[52] Both of these studies, like Meredith McGill's *American Literature and the Culture of Reprinting, 1834–1853* (2007), present extensive analyses of the publishing milieu in which Poe toiled.[53]

Many other studies related to the literary marketplace feature global perspectives. For instance, Joan D. Grossman looks at how Poe influenced Russian writers, and her book was the first critical work by a woman reviewed in *Poe Studies.*[54] In addition, special issues of *The Edgar Allan Poe Review* deal with Poe's literary legacies in Spain, Portugal, and Romania, and each issue includes contributions from women.[55] These international scholars address many subjects about Poe as well as topics related to their respective nations, including Poe's influence on the Spanish short film, evaluations of translations of his works, and assessments of how his writings have been received within each nation.[56] To give one more example, Jana Argersinger credits Lois Davis Vines's edited collection of essays, *Poe Abroad: Influence, Reputation, Affinities*, with moving the study of Poe "beyond a Eurocentric focus."[57]

Scholarship on lyric poetry by Poe is an additional field of inquiry. Virginia Jackson revisits excerpts from Poe's Longfellow reviews to substantiate her claim that Poe's concern is not so much about the originality of Longfellow's poetry itself but about a reality Poe struggled to acknowledge: all poets were plagiarists because anything that a poet might want to express had been expressed before.[58] Monica Peláez illuminates a similar conflict between accepting or rejecting antebellum writing conventions. She characterizes Poe's death poems as attempts to align himself with the sentimental tradition, pointing out that the original version of *Tamerlane* departs from that tradition while his 1845 revision conforms to it.[59] She concludes that Poe had to use subtle techniques to distinguish his poetry from popular consolatory verse, for the sentimental treatment of death had a grip on the nation's reading public.[60]

From a feminist perspective, Eve Célia Morisi examines Poe's employment of the lyric form, discussing how he presents women in his poems. She challenges the scholars who read Poe's "love lyrics" as objectifications of women and reminds readers that he composed a variety of such poems, many of which were "flirtations" or expressions of "gratitude" to real women.[61]

Poe's prose works also exhibit deliberate design, as many critics have observed. Grace Farrell Lee and Kathleen Sands present Jungian readings of *Pym*.[62] Lee reads Pym's adventures as mirroring the mythological trope of "the descent into Hell" while Sands sees the work as depicting "a rite of passage" reminiscent of "the formation of the mythic hero."[63] Rachel Boccio unravels the competing notions of time, cyclical and linear, in "The Fall of the House of Usher."[64] Barbara Cantalupo submits a close reading of *Eureka*, positing that Poe uses an "overload of scientific detail" to convince readers of the accuracy of his observations on the universe.[65] Women have also looked at narration in Poe's stories, using structuralist techniques to explicate his skillful handling of point of view. Maura Grace Harrington uses this approach to determine the focalizer in "Hop-Frog." She argues that the narrator is someone connected to Hop-Frog but not necessarily an alter ego, or double, as others have suggested. Harrington never identifies a specific person, but she notes that the teller must "sympathize with Hop-Frog's plight or . . . in a situation analogous to" him, for the narrator seems to support his course of action.[66] In her reading of "The Man That Was Used Up," Joan Tyler Mead asserts that the narrator is disingenuous when he alleges that he does not understand the mystique of General Smith, for his own descriptions of the man reveal that he is enthralled by Smith's mechanical movements and artificial appearance.[67] In addition, Alissa Burger examines how Lovecraft and King rely upon Poe's model of the unreliable narrator.[68]

Poe's close attention to form has inspired some scholars to investigate his handling of genre. An example of this approach is "Poe's Genre Crossing: From Domesticity to Detection," by Bonita Rhoads, who disrupts traditional thinking about C. Auguste Dupin by comparing him to "the domestic woman."[69] In effect, she makes the case that the detective story exists as distinct from yet reliant on "household," or domestic, fiction.[70] Similarly, Susan Amper dubs "The Assignation" a murder mystery *and* deems it a critique of Thomas Moore's Byron biography.[71] Book-length studies such as Karen Roggenkamp's *Narrating the News: New Journalism and Literary Genre in Late Nineteenth-Century American Newspapers and Fiction* and Dorothea E. von Mücke's *The Seduction of the Occult and the Rise of the Fantastic Tale* also tackle these labeling difficulties presented by some of Poe's texts.[72]

Just as scholars have uncovered how Poe can complicate genre, they have also discussed how he merges literature with music and other fine arts. Carmen Trammell Skaggs shows how Poe's writing is infused with musical terms in *Overtones of Opera in American Literature from Whitman to Wharton.*[73] Charity McAdams explores the role of the ballad in Poe's creation of Roderick Usher.[74] Besides Poe's preoccupation with sound, his fondness for vivid visual imagery has been observed. Cantalupo's *Poe and the Visual Arts* is a culmination of her earlier work on the influence of painting, drawing, and optical illusions in Poe's works, a subject that Judith Saunders, Laura Saltz, and Elvira Osipova have examined as well.[75] To an extent, these studies broaden previous arguments about how to interpret visual symbols in Poe's works such as analyses by Cordelia Candelaria and Gayle Denington Anderson.[76] Susan Elizabeth Sweeney, Susan Williams, and Lauren Curtright explain how emerging technologies related to the visual arts functioned in some of Poe's tales and affected his life. Specifically, they investigate the influence of the daguerreotype on Poe, his writings, and his historical moment.[77] Cantalupo, Saltz, and Sweeney have received awards from the Poe Studies Association for their research into Poe's fascination with visual media.[78]

Another popular interdisciplinary approach is examining Poe's mingling of literature with religion and philosophy. The second issue of the *Poe Newsletter* included an article in which Margaret J. Yonce juxtaposes Poe's "A Descent into the Maelstrom" and Coleridge's "The Rime of the Ancient Mariner" to prove that both writers convey "account[s] of spiritual rebirth and self-transcendence."[79] Branam [Armiento] reads Poe's inclusion of "Catholic Hymn" in "Morella" as illustrative of the latent presence of the mother goddess in Christian religion. Despite Poe's allusion to the Virgin Mary in this invocation, she argues that the author seems unaware of the residual references to Mary's divine predecessor(s) and their accretive power.[80] Elizabeth Vincelette explains how *Eureka* is the religious culmination of Poe's poetics. She highlights the ways in which *Eureka* aligns with and breaks from Transcendentalist philosophy, stating that Poe's intent is to "re-mythologiz[e] [religion] with the poem."[81]

When, in 2001, Elvira Osipova urged scholars "to use a philosophical approach to Poe since Poe, himself, was very philosophical," some women in the United States had already made forays into that field.[82] Playing on René Descartes' famous pronouncement "I think; therefore, I am," Nancy Berkowitz Bate suggests that William Wilson is not a real person but his doppelgänger's "dream persona." Once the narrator realizes that he is Wilson's dream version of himself, his strange relationship with the actual Wilson becomes apparent to him, and this revelation leads to the narrator's existential crisis.[83] Bate believes that this tale is designed to mock Descartes' philosophy, as indicated by her title—"I Think, but Am Not."[84]

Many scholars have directly commented upon the entanglement of religio-philosophy and science in Poe's works, too. Christina Murphy's explication of "A Descent into the Maelstrom" stresses how he uses the forces of attraction and repulsion to bring the narrator to a humble understanding of his relationship to God.[85] For Ruth M. Harrison, Poe's interest in math and science is avid, and his writings anticipate many discoveries in these fields. She asserts that his fascination with "the strange loop," i.e., the Möbius strip, "is not surprising," arguing that many of his works demonstrate an intricacy of design and a preoccupation with aids such as the strange loop "in decoding the secrets of the universe."[86] Although Harrison includes multiple works in her analysis, she gravitates toward *Eureka*, a philosophical text that encourages scientific speculation. Harriet Holman also looks at *Eureka*. She explains how the Epicurean method in *Eureka* serves as a metaphor for Poe's disdain of Transcendentalist philosophy. She admires Poe's use of this "discredited theory of physics" to mock the Transcendentalists, noting that they were like the atoms in Epicurus's theory that were "attracted to each other," resulting in "larger bodies" that "shone brighter than any individual among them."[87] Demonstrating yet again how the two areas overlap, Sara Brio looks at the relationship between religion and science in her reading of the satirical text "Some Words with Mummy." She states, Allamistakeo "mocks the extremities inherent in each topic of debate which says that it must be *either* science or religion that holds the key truth and purposefully muddles the two."[88]

Medicine, a subcategory of science, has long interested women studying Poe. Margaret Alterton discovered evidence that Poe drew upon medical periodicals such as the *Chirurgical Journal of Leipsic* and the *London Lancet* when he formulated his theory that dying women were the most poetical of subjects.[89] Published in 1974, Wendy Flory's "Usher's Fear and the Flaw in Poe's Theories of the Metamorphosis of the Senses" was another forerunner to recent analyses of medicine and literature. Flory asserts that Poe was fascinated by sensory perception in "The Fall of the House of Usher," particularly the question of whether the senses ceased at or persisted after death.[90] Although she does not tie her discussion to specific medical concepts, Flory describes a hypothesis devised by Poe to account for psychological conditions and biological processes described in this tale. In this way, she helps to establish Poe's interest in medical advancements. As scholars have placed more emphasis on Poe's relationship to his time and place, the articles on Poe and medicine have become more extensive. Justine Murison investigates how Poe employs an 1830s theory, the physiology of the reflex arc, in his satires.[91] J. Alexandra McGhee, Vicki Hester, Emily Segir, and Suzanne Ashworth establish Poe's awareness of and interest in mesmerism, dissection, mental health, and medical ethics.[92] Related studies filled the 2017 issue of *Poe Studies* (titled "Edgar Allan Poe and Nineteenth-Century Medicine"), which featured an introduction by Dana Medoro and included three articles by women.[93] Psychology often touches on medical issues, and in addition to the previously mentioned psychoanalytic studies that address the mental states of Poe's characters, Lynne Piper Shackelford presents "The Fall of the House of Usher" as a dramatization of a "shared psychotic disorder" to explain the narrator's (mis)perceptions.[94]

Whereas studies about philosophical and scientific matters have been part and parcel of Poe scholarship for decades, specialists in disability studies have only recently taken up Poe's works. Vanessa Warne's "'If You Should Ever Want an Arm': Disability and Dependency in Edgar Allan Poe's 'The Man That Was Used Up'" is a notable example, for this article builds upon work in critical race theory and masculinity studies to turn readers' attention to Poe's treatment of characters and their (dis)abilities. She does not sidestep a discussion of the Brevet Brigadier General A. B. C. Smith's literal disabled body as do many other critics who favor symbolic and figurative readings of his condition. For Warne, "The Man That Was Used Up" is a story that underscores the secret nature of disability and dependency on others in the antebellum United States, pointing out the irony that the seemingly heroic General Smith depends on an enslaved person. This situation undermines, Warne suggests, conventional notions of ability that shore up the power of enslavers.[95]

Another nascent trend in Poe studies is the publication of scholarship informed by animal studies. In "'A Series of Mere Household Events': Poe's 'The Black Cat,' Domesticity, and Pet-Keeping in Nineteenth-Century America," Heidi Hanrahan emphasizes the central role that the feline plays and stresses its presence as literal rather than figurative.[96] Similarly, Colleen Glenney Boggs deconstructs language (and, therefore, relationships) in "The Black Cat" and "The Murders in the Rue Morgue" to determine who achieves human status and therefore wields power, noting that these Poe stories expose the human/animal binary as artificial.[97] For example, she believes that, in the latter tale, Poe's emphasis on the criminality of an apparently human but essentially animal figure undermines the idea of a clear demarcation between species.

Geospatial and ecocritical studies have garnered more attention in recent years, too. In the 1970s, two important, yet pithy, essays about these subjects were published: "The Cabin by the Lake: Pastoral Landscapes of Poe, Cooper, Hawthorne, and Thoreau" by Rosemary Franklin and "The Writer in the Crowd: Poe's Urban Vision" by Linda Miller.[98] Longer studies of Poe and place were published by Whitney May and Katherine Bowers in 2017.[99] In 2018, Philip E. Phillips's edited collection featured numerous essays on this subject, with women scholars describing Poe's connections to Boston, Philadelphia, Germany, Russia, and Egypt.[100] Sara Crosby's "A Weird Tonic for the Anthropocene: Poe's Use of Gardenesque Landscapes as Nature Cure" should be mentioned here as well. Her discussion of Poe's works, although primarily medical in nature, touches on the human destruction of the environment and exposes the paucity of ecocritical research on Poe.

Besides theoretical approaches, pedagogical research is another dynamic area of Poe scholarship in which women have been active. In American middle, high school, and college classrooms, Poe's Gothic tales and poems tend to be the most studied, and women educators have exchanged ideas about how to teach "Annabel Lee," "The Fall of the House of Usher," "The Raven," and many other works.[101] In addition, the detective stories are popular in the classroom, as many female scholars have indicated.[102] Occasionally, Poe's other fictional works appeal to teachers, and responding to that interest, Marcy J. Dinius shares an experience about teaching the science fiction story "The Unparalleled Adventure of One Hans Pfaall."[103] Moving beyond traditional discussions devoted to Poe's works, Eliza Richards and Lois Davis Vines encourage teachers to show students how domestic and international authors relate to Poe.[104]

Locating Poe's source material is another way that women have advanced Poe scholarship. Numerous notes in the *Poe Newsletter* and *Poe Studies*, including multiple ones authored by Adeline Tintner and E. Kate Stewart, appeared in the 1960s and 1970s.[105] More recently, Dorothy Z. Baker links Poe to Cotton Mather and John Winthrop's notion of American exceptionalism in a book-length study.[106] Bonnie Shannon McMullen draws parallels between stories by the Scottish writer John Howison published in *Blackwood's* and Poe's sea stories.[107] Her article complements other comparative studies of tales from nineteenth-century periodicals and Poe's stories such as Hoeveler's "Reading Poe Reading Blackwood's: The Palimpsestic Subtext in 'The Fall of the House of Usher.'"[108] All but one of the feature articles in the autumn 2018 issue of *The Edgar Allan Poe Review* are about influences on Poe, and half the authors are women. Some of these critics make explicit connections between Poe and established writers. Other scholars identify less familiar Poe sources. To illustrate, Gina Claywell considers how the cadets at West Point influenced Poe's poetry. Another example is Ellen M. Bayer's exploration of the effects of landscape architect Andrew Jackson Downing's design theory on "The Domain of Arnheim" and "Landor's Cottage."[109]

Inspired by writers throughout the world, Poe has himself inspired authors around the globe, and that legacy has been traced in several studies by women. Judy Osowski's two-part "Fugitive Poe References" tracks Poe allusions by various authors.[110] Numerous notes written by women in "Marginalia," a feature in *Poe Studies*, establish connections between the works of Poe and various literary texts, including Richard Wright's *Native Son*, Henry James's "Glasses," William Faulkner's "A Rose for Emily," and Herman Melville's *Omoo*.[111] Poe's influence on other writers is not confined to the United States, as research by Ana Hernández del Castillo, Erika Hulpke, and Lois Davis Vines demonstrates. Cantalupo's edited collection *Poe's Pervasive Influence* represents this transnational interest as well.[112]

Poe biography is yet another field in which women have made significant contributions. Not only nineteenth-century female contemporaries of Poe but also twentieth-century biographers such as Mary E. Phillips, Marie Bonaparte, and Frances Winwar have recounted his life.[113][113] Agnes Bondurant reconstructs Poe's Richmond in an effort to shed new light on his upbringing.[114] Barbara Moore's *The Fever Called Living* is a creative nonfiction piece combining Poe biography and imaginative content.[115] Bettina Knapp's *Edgar Allan Poe* begins with a lengthy chapter on Poe's life, and the subsequent chapters weave together biographical details, Poe's literary theory, close reading techniques, and sociohistorical interpretation. Like many Poe biographers before and after her, she emphasizes how the poems and tales expose Poe's own "psychological and emotional needs," stating that "Poe is a phenomenon unique in literature."[116] Similarly, Liliane Weissberg's biography, composed in German, includes a biographical sketch that follows an overview of nineteenth-century America.[117] Like Knapp, Weissberg organizes her discussion thematically. Unlike Knapp, she devotes chapters to Poe's work as a critic and his influence on other national literary traditions. Her final section references items related to print culture, including information on publication history, manuscripts, and editions. Dawn B. Sova's *Critical Companion to Edgar Allan Poe: A Literary Reference to His Life and Work* provides basic information on Poe's life, writings, and popular culture subjects related to Poe.[118] Keeping Poe in the popular culture spotlight has become a noteworthy part of Jill Lepore's career. Her work for *The New Yorker* draws attention to Poe's skills as a writer of detective and horror fiction while, sometimes irreverently, reminding readers of his foibles.[119]

One more area of Poe's studies that has benefited from women's time and talent is editing. Susan Levine coedited four volumes with her spouse, and Maureen Cobb Mabbott finished her husband's Poe editions for Harvard University Press.[120] Gothic specialist Diane Long Hoeveler (with Frederick Frank) produced the 2010 Broadview Press edition of *The Narrative of Arthur Gordon Pym of Nantucket*. In addition to annotations, the edition features supplemental materials such as maps, reviews, and excerpts from other writers' works that allude to *Pym*.[121] Women have also held editorial positions for the two Poe-centered academic journals. In 1990, twenty-two years after the first issue of G. R. Thompson's *Poe Newsletter* appeared, Jana Argersinger, a professional editor, joined the staff of *Poe Studies*. However, she was not the first woman to hold an editorial position. From 1971–1988, Kathleen McLean served as the associate editor, and in 1997, Cantalupo became the first woman appointed to the editorial board.[122] Ten years prior, Cantalupo had become the second woman to join the editorial staff of the *PSA Newsletter*, the precursor to *The Edgar Allan Poe Review*, assuming the editorial assistant position previously occupied by Barbara White. In 1989, Susan R. Delaney joined Cantalupo for one issue. Cantalupo then took a hiatus until 1997, which is the year that she became the editor. In 2000, the *PSA Newsletter* transformed into *The Edgar Allan Poe Review,* and Cantalupo edited that periodical until 2004.[123] In 2007, she returned. For several years thereafter, the two major Poe journals were edited by women, Argersinger as co-editor of *Poe Studies* and Cantalupo as the editor of *The Edgar Allan Poe Review*. Both women have extensive experience in the field, and under their leadership, the journals have promoted contemporary literary trends as well as older critical approaches. These editors have championed inquiries into Poe's life and works that have kept Poe studies in step with cutting-edge critical theory.

As this survey shows, many women have seized the opportunity to take Poe research in new directions. To be sure, this chapter is, despite the wide range of publications it references, only a partial account of women's scholarship on Poe. The work of women who have published on Poe in *ESQ, Criticism, ATQ, Nineteenth Century Studies, Texas Studies in Literature and Language,* and many other literary journals also merits investigation.[124] Additional areas of women's scholarship such as studies devoted to women of color, queer women, women creative writers, as well as the ways women's criticism on Poe differs from men's could be explored in greater depth. More work can be done to bring the women scholars cited by Peeples into conversation with critics who have published since 2002, many of whom are named here. Furthermore, scholars may want to review gender parity in recent edited collections on Poe.[125] It may be valuable to extend this type of analysis to editions of Poe's writings, which often have been collaborations between men and women, and/or to the editorial review boards, past and present, of both Poe journals. Although this overview is by no means an exhaustive account of women's scholarship on Poe, it documents women's insightful contributions to Poe studies and acknowledges the rich tradition of women's writing on Poe. Those who study Poe have spent countless hours building the case that "our" author is relevant to multiple audiences for reasons that transcend time and place. Within this group, women have been and continue to be a vital constituency, and it is imperative to ensure that those who "help build the frame" of Poe studies represent as inclusive a group as possible so his work retains that relevance for years to come.[126]

NOTES

1. Aretta J. Stevens, "Faulkner and 'Helen'—A Further Note," *Poe Newsletter* 1 (1968): 31.

2. Margaret J. Yonce, "The Spiritual Descent into the Maelström: A Debt to the 'The Rime of the Ancient Mariner,'" *Poe Newsletter* 2, no. 2 (1969): 26–29.

3. Nancy Niblack Baxter, "Thomas Moore's Influence on 'Tamerlane,'" *Poe Newsletter* 2, no. 2 (1969): 37; Iola S. Haverstick, "A Note on Poe and *Pym* in Melville's *Omoo*," *Poe Newsletter* 2, no. 2 (1969): 37.

4. Charlene Avallone, "Women Reading Melville/Melville Reading Women," in *Melville and Women*, ed. Elizabeth Schultz and Haskell Springer (Kent: Kent State University Press, 2006), 41–59; John Idol and Melinda Ponder, eds., *Hawthorne and Women: Engendering and Expanding the Hawthorne Tradition* (Amherst: University of Massachusetts Press, 1999).

5. Jamie Barlowe, "Re-Reading Women II: The Example of Brett, Hadley, Duff, and Women's Scholarship," in *Hemingway and Women: Female Critics and the Female Voice*, ed. Lawrence Broer and Gloria Holland (Tuscaloosa: University of Alabama Press, 2002), 23–32; Elizabeth Schultz and Haskell Springer, "Melville Writing Women/Women Writing Melville," in *Melville and Women*, ed. Elizabeth Schultz and Haskell Springer (Kent: Kent State University Press, 2006), 3–14.

6. Scott Peeples, *The Afterlife of Edgar Allan Poe* (New York: Camden House, 2004), ix.

7. The year 2018 marked the fiftieth anniversary of the *Poe Newsletter*, which evolved into *Poe Studies/Dark Romanticism*. Hereafter, all references to *Poe Studies*, *Poe Studies/Dark Romanticism*, and *Poe Studies: History, Theory, Interpretation* will be designated "*Poe Studies*."

8. Peeples, *Afterlife*, 108.

9. Monika Elbert, "Poe and Hawthorne as Women's Amanuenses," *Poe Studies* 37 (2004): 21.

10. Kristen Renzi, "Hysteric Vocalizations of the Female Body in Edgar Allan Poe's 'Berenice,'" *ESQ* 58, no. 4 (2012): 601.

11. Beth Ann Bassein, *Women and Death: Linkages in Western Thought and Literature* (Westport: Greenwood Press, 1984), 44, 49.

12. Peeples, *Afterlife*, 110.

13. Catherine Carter, "'Not a Woman': The Murdered Muse in 'Ligeia,'" *Poe Studies* 36 (2003): 45.

14. Diane Long Hoeveler, *Romantic Androgyny: The Women Within* (University Park: Pennsylvania State University Press, 1990).

15. Dawn Keetley, "Pregnant Women and Envious Men in 'Morella,' 'Berenice,' 'Ligeia,' and 'The Fall of the House of Usher,'" *Poe Studies* 38 (2005): 2.

16. Ibid., 9.

17. Ibid., 2.

18. Eliza Richards, "Women's Place in Poe Studies," *Poe Studies/Dark Romanticism: History, Theory, Interpretation* 33, nos. 1–2 (2000): 1–12.

19. Noelle Baker, "'This Slender Foundation . . . Made Me Immortal': Sarah Helen Whitman vs. Poe's Helen," *Poe Studies* 32 (1999): 8.

20. Mary De Jong, "'Read Here Thy Name Concealed': Frances Osgood's Poems on Parting with Edgar Allan Poe," *Poe Studies* 32 (1999): 36.

21. Eliza Richards, *Gender and the Poetics of Reception in Poe's Circle* (Cambridge: Cambridge University Press, 2004).

22. Kirsten Silva Gruesz, "Maria Gowen Brooks, In and Out of the Poe Circle," *ESQ* 54 (2008): 75–110.

23. Jacqueline Bradley, "Character Doubles and Barrier Imagery in Poe's Work," *The Edgar Allan Poe Review* 9, no. 2 (2008): 55.

24. Clark Moreland and Karime Rodriguez, "'Never Bet the Devil Your Head': Fuseli's *The Nightmare* and Collapsing Masculinity in Poe's 'The Black Cat,'" *The Edgar Allan Poe Review* 16, no. 2 (2015): 205.

25. Alexandra Reuber, "Narcissistic Love and the Fear of Death: Poe's 'Fall of the House of Usher' Re-Evaluated," *Nineteenth-Century Literature in English* 14, no. 2 (2010): 179. In this essay, Reuber references Leila May's article on the sibling relationship between Madeline and Roderick to offer insight into the nineteenth century's attitude toward family. See Leila May, "'Sympathies of a Scarcely Intelligible Nature': The Brother–Sister Bond in Poe's 'Fall of the House of Usher,'" *Studies in Short Fiction* 30, no. 3 (1993): 387–96.

26. Barbara Johnson, "Strange Fits: Poe and Wordsworth on the Nature of Poetic Language," in *A World of Difference* (Baltimore: Johns Hopkins University Press, 1989), 99.

27. Ibid., 90.

28. Ibid., 98.

29. Roberta Reeder, "'The Black Cat' as a Study in Repression," *Poe Studies* 7 (1974): 20–22; Julia Mazow, "The Undivided Consciousness of the Narrator in *Eureka*," *American Transcendental Quarterly* 26 (1975): 55–60; Renata Mautner Wasserman, "The Self, the Mirror, the Other: 'The Fall of the House of Usher,'" *Poe Studies* 10 (1977): 33–35.

30. Peeples acknowledges Poe scholars' debt to Colin Dayan for identifying the significance of the intersection of gender and race in Poe. See Peeples, *Afterlife*, 111–12.

31. Teresa Goddu, "Rethinking Race and Slavery in Poe Studies," *Poe Studies* 33 (2000): 15.

32. Toni Morrison, "Black Matters," in *Playing in the Dark: Whiteness in the American Literary Imagination* (New York: Vintage, 1992): 1–28. J. Gerald Kennedy and Liliane Weissberg's edited collection is a seminal text. See *Romancing the Shadow: Poe and Race* (New York: Oxford University Press, 2001).

33. Marcia Nichols, "Poe's 'Some Words with a Mummy' and Blackface Anatomy," *Poe Studies* 48 (2015): 13. She acknowledges her debt to Dana D. Nelson in constructing her argument. See Nelson's "The Haunting of White Manhood: Poe, Fraternal Ritual, and Polygensis," *American Literature* 69, no. 3 (1997): 515–46.

34. Charlene Waters, "The Color of Amontillado: The Influence of Blackface Minstrelsy in 'The Cask of Amontillado,'" *The Edgar Allan Poe Review* 19, no. 1 (2018): 47.

35. Cindy Weinstein, "When Is Now?: Poe's Aesthetics of Temporality," *Poe Studies* 41 (2008): 81–107; Cindy Weinstein, "When Is Now? Poe's *Pym*," in *Time, Tense, and American Literature: When Is Now?* (New York: Cambridge University Press, 2015), 39–63. Her *Poe Studies* essay received the 2008 James W. Gargano Award for an outstanding article on Poe.

36. Christina Zwarg, "Vigorous Currents, Painful Archives: The Production of Affect and History in Poe's 'Tale of the Ragged Mountains,'" *Poe Studies* 43 (2010): 7. Suzanne Ashworth incorporates affect theory as part of her analysis of "The Facts in the Case of M. Valdemar." See "Cadaverous Intimacies: Disgust, Desire, and the Corpse in Edgar Allan Poe's 'Valdemar,'" *Criticism* 58, no. 4 (2016): 565–92.

37. Amy C. Branam [Armiento], "Gothic Displacements: Poe's South in *Politian*," in *Edgar Allan Poe: Beyond Gothicism*, ed. James M. Hutchisson (Newark: University of Delaware Press, 2011), 69–88. Erin Forbes, "From Prison Cell to Slave Ship: Social Death in 'The Premature Burial,'" *Poe Studies* 46 (2013): 32–58; Erin Forbes, "Edgar Allan Poe and the Great Dismal Swamp: Reading Race and Environment after the Aesthetic Turn," *Modern Philology* 114, no. 2 (2016): 359–87.

38. Maria Karafilis, "American Racial Dystopia: Expansion and Extinction in Poe and Hawthorne," *Poe Studies* 48 (2015): 19.

39. Ibid., 20.

40. Heather Chacón, "Prosthetic Colonialism: Indian Removal, European Imperialism, and International Trade in Poe's 'The Man That Was Used Up,'" *Poe Studies* 50 (2017): 46–68.

41. Courtney Novosat, "Outside Dupin's Closet of Reason: (Homo)sexual Repression and Racialized Terror in Poe's 'The Murders in the Rue Morgue,'" *Poe Studies* 45 (2012): 82.

42. Ibid., 91.

43. Ashworth, "Cadaverous Intimacies," 575.

44. Ibid., 578.

45. Jana Argersinger, "From an Editor's Easy Chair: A Partial View of Prospects in Poe Studies," *The Edgar Allan Poe Review* 4, no. 1 (2003): 49, n. 3, 43.

46. Alexander Urakova, "'The Purloined Letter' in the Gift Book: Reading Poe in a Contemporary Context," *Nineteenth-Century Literature* 64, no. 3 (2009): 323–46; Alexandra Urakova, "Poe, Fashion, and Godey's Lady's Book," *The Edgar Allan Poe Review* 15, no. 1 (2014): 37–46.

47. Gila Ashtor, "The Gift (Book) That Keeps on Giving: Poe's 'The Purloined Letter,' Rereading, Reprinting, and Detective Fiction," *Poe Studies* 45 (2012): 59.

48. Ibid., 64.

49. Kathryn K. Shinn, "Gift Books," in *Edgar Allan Poe in Context*, ed. Kevin J. Hayes (Cambridge: Cambridge University Press, 2013), 179–87.

50. Argersinger identifies marketplace economics as a facet of global studies. See Argersinger, "From an Editor's Easy Chair," 45. In the examples presented here, the overlap between marketplace economics and book history/material culture is evident.

51. Marcy J. Dinius, "Poe's Moon Shot: 'Hans Phaall' and the Art and Science of Antebellum Print Culture," *Poe Studies* 37 (2004): 7.

52. Laura Langer Cohen, *The Fabrication of American Literature: Fraudulence and Antebellum Print Culture* (Philadelphia: University of Pennsylvania Press, 2012); Sandra Tomc, *Industry and the Creative Mind: The Eccentric Writer in American Literature and Entertainment, 1790–1860* (Ann Arbor: University of Michigan Press, 2012).

53. Argersinger deems Meredith McGill's *American Literature and the Culture of Reprinting, 1834–1853* (Philadelphia: University of Pennsylvania Press, 2007) an exemplar of marketplace economics, for McGill examines Poe's place within a global literary market. In the wake of that seminal publication, many women have further investigated this subject. See Argersinger, "From an Editor's Easy Chair," 46.

54. Joan D. Grossman, *Edgar Allan Poe in Russia: A Study in Legend and Literary Influence* (Würzburg: Jal-Verlag, 1973); J. Lasley Dameron and Tamara Miller, "Poe's Reception in Russia," review of *Edgar Allan Poe in Russia: A Study in Legend and Literary Influence*, by Joan D. Grossman, *Poe Studies* 8 (1975): 27–28.

55. See *The Edgar Allan Poe Review* 10, no. 2 (2009); *The Edgar Allan Poe Review* 11, no. 1 (2010); and *The Edgar Allan Poe Review* 11, no. 2 (2010).

56. See Ángel Galdón and María Isabel Jiménez, "The Influence of E. A. Poe in the Spanish Short Subject Industry," *The Edgar Allan Poe Review* 10, no. 2 (2009): 78–86; Margarita Rigal-Aragón, "Spanish 'Misreadings' of Poe's Life and Works at the Beginning of the Twenty-First Century," *The Edgar Allan Poe Review* 10, no. 2 (2009): 36–48; Ana Olos, "Premises for the Reception of Edgar Allan Poe's Work in Romania at the Bicentenary of His Birth," *The Edgar Allan Poe Review* 11, no. 2 (2010): 9–20.

57. Argersinger, "From an Editor's Easy Chair," 44; Lois Davis Vines, *Poe Abroad: Influence, Reputation, Affinities* (Iowa City: University of Iowa Press, 1999).

58. Virginia Jackson, "Poe, Longfellow, and the Institution of Poetry," *Poe Studies* 33 (2000): 27.

59. Monica Peláez, "The Sentimental Poe," *The Edgar Allan Poe Review* 8, no. 2 (2007): 75.

60. Ibid., 81.

61. Eve Célia Morisi, "The Female Figure of Poe's Poetry: A Rehabilitation," *Poe Studies* 38 (2005): 17.

62. Grace Farrell Lee, "The Quest of Arthur Gordon Pym," *Southern Literary Journal* 4, no. 2 (1972): 22–33; Kathleen Sands, "The Mythic Initiation of Arthur Gordon Pym," *Poe Studies* 7, no. 1 (1974): 14–16.

63. Lee, "The Quest of Arthur Gordon Pym," 22; Sands, "The Mythic Initiation," 14.

64. Rachel Boccio, "'The Things and Thoughts of Time': Spatiotemporal Forms of the Transcendent Sublime in 'The Fall of the House of Usher,'" *The Edgar Allan Poe Review* 18, no. 1 (2017): 54–72.

65. Barbara Cantalupo, "'Of or Pertaining to a Higher Power': Involution in *Eureka*," *ATQ* 4, no. 2 (1990): 82.

66. Maura Grace Harrington, "'My Narrative': The Story of the Non-Disinterested Narrator in Poe's 'Hop-Frog,'" *The Edgar Allan Poe Review* 5, no. 1 (2004): 98.

67. Joan Tyler Mead, "Poe's 'The Man That Was Used Up': Another Bugaboo Campaign," *Studies in Short Fiction* 23, no. 3 (1986): 281–86.

68. Alissa Burger, "'You Fancy Me Mad': The Unreliable Narrator's Defense in Poe, Lovecraft, and King," in *The Lovecraftian Poe*, ed. Sean Moreland (Bethlehem: Lehigh University Press, 2017), 179–94.

69. Bonita Rhoads, "Poe's Genre Crossing: From Domesticity to Detection," *Poe Studies* 42 (2009): 18. This article received the 2009 James W. Gargano Award.

70. Ibid., 39.

71. Susan Amper, "The Biographer as Assassin: The Hidden Murders in 'The Assignation,'" *Poe Studies* 35 (2002): 14–21.

72. Karen Roggenkamp, *Narrating the News: New Journalism and Literary Genre in Late Nineteenth-Century American Newspapers and Fiction* (Kent: Kent State University Press, 2005); Dorothea E. von Mücke, *The Seduction of the Occult and the Rise of the Fantastic Tale* (Stanford: Stanford University Press, 2003).

73. Carmen Trammell Skaggs, *Overtones of Opera in American Literature from Whitman to Wharton* (Baton Rouge: Louisiana State University Press, 2010).

74. Charity McAdams, "Music, Madness, and Disenchantment: Roderick Usher and the Ballad 'The Mad Trist,'" *The Edgar Allan Poe Review* 16, no. 1 (2015): 54–69. See also Charity McAdams, *Poe and the Idea of Music: Failure, Transcendence, and Dark Romanticism* (Bethlehem: Lehigh University Press, 2017).

75. Barbara Cantalupo, *Poe and the Visual Arts* (University Park: The Pennsylvania State University Press, 2014); Judith Saunders, "'If This I Saw': Optic Dilemmas in Poe's Writings," *ATQ* 62 (1986): 63–80; Laura Saltz, "'Eyes Which Behold': Poe's 'Domain of Arnheim' and the Science of Vision," *The Edgar Allan Poe Review* 7, no. 1 (2006): 4–30; Elvira Osipova, "Aesthetic Effects of 'King Pest' and 'The Masque of the Red Death,'" *The Edgar Allan Poe Review* 8, no. 2 (2008): 25–33. See also Barbara Cantalupo, "Poe's Responses to Nineteenth-Century American Painting," in *Edgar Allan Poe: Dosciento Años Después*, ed. Beatriz González-Moreno and Margarita Rigal-Aragón (Cuenca: Universidad de Castilla–La Mancha, 2010), 111–20; and Susan Elizabeth Sweeney, "The Magnifying Glass: Spectacular Distance in Poe's 'Man of the Crowd' and Beyond," *Poe Studies* 36 (2003): 3–17.

76. Cordelia Candelaria, "On the Whiteness at Tsalal: A Note on *Arthur Gordon Pym*," *Poe Studies* 6 (1973): 26; Gayle Denington Anderson, "Demonology in the 'Black Cat,'" *Poe Studies* 10 (1977): 43–44. See also Elizabeth G. Lord's translation of Gerhard Hoffman's article, "Space and Symbol in the Tales of Edgar Allan Poe," *Poe Studies* 12 (1979): 1–14.

77. Susan Elizabeth Sweeney, "The Horror of Taking a Picture in Poe's 'Tell-Tale Heart,'" *The Edgar Allan Poe Review* 18, no. 2 (2017): 142–62; Susan Williams, "Daguerreotyping Hawthorne and Poe," *Poe Studies* 37 (2004): 14–20; Lauren Curtright, "Moving Daguerreotypes and Myths of Reproduction: Poe's Body," in *Deciphering Poe: Subtexts, Contexts, Subversive Meanings*, ed. Alexandra Urakova (Bethlehem: Lehigh University Press, 2013): 121–37.

78. Barbara Cantalupo received the 2014 Patrick F. Quinn Award for an outstanding monograph on Poe. Laura Saltz received the James W. Gargano Award in 2006, and in 2017, Susan Elizabeth Sweeney won that award.

79. Yonce, "The Spiritual Descent," 29.

80. Amy C. Branam [Armiento], "Mother Goddess Manifestations in Poe's 'Morella' and 'Catholic Hymn,'" in *Deciphering Poe*, ed. Alexandra Urakova (Bethlehem: Lehigh University Press, 2013), 27–40.

81. Elizabeth Vincelette, "Beauty, Truth, and the Word: The Prophecy and Theology of Poe's *Eureka*," *The Edgar Allan Poe Review* 9, no. 2 (2008): 37.

82. Barbara Cantalupo, "Interview with Elvira Osipova," *The Edgar Allan Poe Review* 2, no. 1 (2001): 75.

83. Nancy Berkowitz Bate, "'I Think, but Am Not': The Nightmare of William Wilson," *Poe Studies* 30 (1997): 27.

84. Ibid., 29.

85. Christina Murphy, "The Philosophical Pattern of 'A Descent into the Maelstrom,'" *Poe Studies* 6 (1973): 25–26.

86. Ruth M. Harrison, "Poe's Möbius: An Exploration of Poe's Fractal Universe," *Poe Studies* 36 (2003): 32.

87. Harriet Holman, "Splitting Poe's 'Epicurean Atoms': Further Speculation on the Literary Satire of *Eureka*," *Poe Studies* 5 (1972): 37.

88. Sara Brio, "The Shocking Truth: Science, Religion, and Ancient Egypt in Early Nineteenth-Century Fiction," *Nineteenth-Century Contexts* 40, no. 4 (2018): 339.

89. Margaret Alterton, *Origins of Poe's Critical Theory* (Hamburg: Severus-Verlag, 1925), 18, 24.

90. Wendy Flory, "Usher's Fear and the Flaw in Poe's Theories of the Metamorphosis of the Senses," *Poe Studies* 7 (1974): 19. For Flory's interrogation of Poe's personal beliefs regarding death, see "Rehearsals for Dying in Poe and Emily Dickinson," *American Transcendental Quarterly* 18 (1973): 13–18.

91. Justine Murison, *Politics of Anxiety in Nineteenth-Century American Literature* (New York: Cambridge University Press, 2011), 48.

92. J. Alexandra McGhee, "Morbid Conditions: Poe and the Sublimity of Disease," *The Edgar Allan Poe Review* 14, no. 1 (2013): 55–70; Vicki Hester and Emily Segir, "Edgar Allan Poe: 'The Black Cat' and Current Forensic Psychology," *The Edgar Allan Poe Review* 15, no. 2 (2014): 175–93; Suzanne Ashworth, "Experimental Matter, Unclaimed Death, and Posthumous Futures in Poe's 'Valdemar,'" *Poe Studies* 49 (2016): 52–79; Ashworth, "Cadaverous Intimacies," 565–92. See also Hannah Murray, "'I Say to You That I Am Dead!': Medical Experiment and the Limits of Personhood in Edgar Allan Poe's 'The Facts in the Case of M. Valdemar' (1845)," *Irish Journal of Gothic and Horror Studies* 16 (2017): 22–40.

93. Dana Medoro, "Introduction: Edgar Allan Poe and Nineteenth-Century Medicine," *Poe Studies* 50 (2017): 2–11; Kristie Schlauraff's "Do You Hear What I Hear? Stethoscopic Listening in Poe's 'The Tell-Tale Heart,'" *Poe Studies* 50 (2017): 26–45; Sara Crosby, "A Weird Tonic for the Anthropocene: Poe's Use of Gardenesque Landscapes as Nature Cure," *Poe Studies* 50 (2017): 69–86; Susan Scheckel, "Home-Sickness, Nostalgia, and Therapeutic Narrative in Poe's 'The Fall of the

House of Usher,'" *Poe Studies* 50 (2017): 12–25. Elsewhere, Medoro has published on abortion in Poe. See her "So Very Self Evident: Adultery and Abortion in 'The Purloined Letter,'" *Literature and Medicine* 26, no. 2 (2007): 342–63.

94. Lynne Piper Shackelford, "'Infected by Superstitions': *Folie à Deux* in 'The Fall of the House of Usher,'" *The Edgar Allan Poe Review* 18, no. 2 (2017): 110.

95. Vanessa Warne, "'If You Should Ever Want an Arm': Disability and Dependency in Edgar Allan Poe's 'The Man That Was Used Up,'" *Atenea* 25, no. 1 (2005): 95–105. Laura Behling argues that "The Man That Was Used Up" anticipates medical advancements in the area of prosthetics, using Poe's tale as a springboard for studying this technology today. Therefore, her reading is not directly in line with other disability studies interpretations of this tale. See Behling's "Replacing the Patient: The Fiction of Prosthetics in Medical Practice," *Journal of Medical Humanities* 26, no. 1 (2005): 53–66.

96. Heidi Hanrahan, "'A Series of Mere Household Events': Poe's 'The Black Cat,' Domesticity, and Pet-Keeping in Nineteenth-Century America," *Poe Studies* 45 (2012): 40–56.

97. Colleen Glenney Boggs, *Animalia Americana: Animal Representations and Biopolitical Subjectivity* (New York: Columbia University Press, 2013), 109–31.

98. Rosemary Franklin, "The Cabin by the Lake: Pastoral Landscapes of Poe, Cooper, Hawthorne, and Thoreau," *ESQ* 22 (1976): 59–70; Linda Miller, "The Writer in the Crowd: Poe's Urban Vision," *American Transcendental Quarterly* 44 (1979): 325–39. Miller further explores Poe's relationship to urban spaces in a later article that identifies his precarious financial position as the motive for writing pieces for popular audiences. See her "Poe on the Beat: 'Doings of Gotham' as Urban, Penny Press Journalism," *Journal of the Early American Republic* 7, no. 2 (1987): 147–65.

99. Whitney May, "The Influence of Place on Identity in Poe's 'Morella' and 'William Wilson,'" *The Edgar Allan Poe Review* 18, no. 2 (2017): 218–33; Katherine Bowers, "Haunted Ice, Fearful Sounds, and the Arctic Sublime: Exploring Nineteenth-Century Polar Gothic Space," *Gothic Studies* 19, no. 2 (2017): 71–84.

100. Philip E. Phillips, ed., *Poe and Place* (New York: Palgrave Macmillan, 2018). See Katherine J. Kim, "Poe and Boston," 21–41; Amy C. Branam [Armiento], "Poe in Philadelphia," 123–43; Sonya Isaak, "Poe's German Soulscape: Influenced by Angst or Anxiety of Influence?," 215–40; Alexandra Urakova, "'Demon of Space': Poe in St. Petersburg," 243–63; and Emily James Hansen, "Poe, Egypt, and 'Egyptomania,'" 265–88.

101. See the following essays in *Approaches to Teaching Poe's Prose and Poetry*, ed. Jeffrey Andrew Weinstock and Tony Magistrale (New York: Modern Language Association of America, 2008): Alison Kelly, "Loving with a Love That Is More Than Love: Poe, the American Dream, and the Secondary School Classroom," 161–69; Desirée Henderson, "Understanding the Fear and Love of Death in Three Premature-Burial Stories: 'The Premature Burial,' 'Morella,' and 'The Fall of the House of Usher,'" 69–75; Rebecca Jaroff and Domenick Scudera, "From Page to Stage: An Interdisciplinary Approach to Teaching 'The Philosophy of Composition' through Performing 'The Raven,'" 204–9; and Lesley Ginsberg, "A New-Historicist Approach to Teaching 'The Black Cat,'" 97–103.

102. Pamela Bedore, "Exploring the Origins of American Detective Fiction: Teaching Poe and Dime Novels," in *Murder 101: Essays on the Teaching of Detective Fiction*, ed. Edward J. Reilly (Jefferson: McFarland, 2009); Diane Long Hoeveler, "Teaching 'The Purloined Letter' and Lacan's Seminar: Introducing Students to Psychoanalysis through Poe," in *Approaches to Teaching Poe's Prose and Poetry*, 109–14.

103. Marcy J. Dinius, "Teaching the Mechanics of Deception: 'Hans Pfaall,' Science Fiction, and Hoaxing in Antebellum Print Culture," in *Approaches to Teaching Poe's Prose and Poetry*, 55–60.

104. Eliza Richards, "Poe, Women Poets, and Print Circulation," in *Teaching Nineteenth-Century American Poetry*, ed. Paula Bennett, Karen Kilcup, and Philipp Schweighauser (New York: Modern Language Association of America, 2007); Lois Davis Vines, "Rediscovering Poe through the Eyes of World Authors: What Do They See in Him?," in *Approaches to Teaching Poe's Prose and Poetry*, 186–91. For an earlier pedagogical essay related to reader-response criticism, see Patricia Donahue, "Misreading Students' Texts," *Reader: Essays in Reader-Oriented Theory, Criticism, and Pedagogy* 17 (1987): 1–12.

105. See Adeline Tintner, "Fire of the Heart in 'Al Aaraaf': Beckford and Byron as Source," *Poe Studies* 22, no. 2 (1989): 47–48; Tintner, "A Possible Source in Dickens for Poe's 'Imp of the Perverse,'" *Poe Studies* 18, no. 2 (1985): 25; E. Kate Stewart, "An Early Imitative Ape: A Possible Source for 'The Murders in the Rue Morgue,'" *Poe Studies* 20, no. 1 (1987): 24; Stewart, "Another Source for 'The Black Cat,'" *Poe Studies* 18, no. 2 (1985): 25.

106. Dorothy Z. Baker, "'A wilderness of error': Edgar Allan Poe's Revision of Providential Tropes," in *America's Gothic Fiction: The Legacy of Magnalia Christi Americana* (Columbus: Ohio State University Press, 2007), 37–64.

107. Bonnie Shannon McMullen, "'A Desert of Ebony': Poe, Blackwood's, and Tales of the Sea," *The Edgar Allan Poe Review* 11, no. 1 (2010): 70–78.

108. Diane Long Hoeveler, "Reading Poe Reading Blackwood's: The Palimpsestic Subtext in 'The Fall of the House of Usher,'" in *Double Vision: Literary Palimpsests of the Eighteenth and Nineteenth Centuries*, ed. Darby Lewes (Lanham, MD: Lexington Books, 2012): 227–37.

109. Gina Claywell, "'A worn, weary, discontented look': The Influence of West Point and the Hudson River Valley on Poe," *The Edgar Allan Poe Review* 19, no. 2 (2018): 137–52; Ellen M. Bayer, "The Ecocritical Implications of Downing's Influence on Poe's Landscape Aesthetic," *The Edgar Allan Poe Review* 19, no. 2 (2018): 250–73.

110. Judy Osowski, "Fugitive Poe References," *Poe Studies* 8 (1975): 21–22; Osowski, "Fugitive Poe References: A Bibliography," *Poe Studies* 9 (1976): 49–51.

111. Linda T. Prior, "A Further Word on Richard Wright's Use of Poe in *Native Son*," *Poe Studies* 5, no. 2 (1972): 52–53; Adeline Tintner, "Poe's 'The Spectacles' and James' 'Glasses,'" *Poe Studies* 9 (1976): 53–54; J. Aretta Stevens, "Faulkner and 'Helen': A Further Note," *Poe Newsletter* 1 (1968): 31; Iola S. Haverstick, "A Note on Poe and *Pym* in Melville's *Omoo*," *Poe Newsletter* 2, no. 2 (1969): 37. See also Janette S. Johnson and Michael C. Hillman, "The Blind Owl, Nerval, Kafka, Poe

and the Surrealists: Affinities," in *Hedayat's The Blind Owl: Forty Years After*, ed. Michael Hillman (Austin: University of Texas, 1978), 125–41; Mildred K. Travis, "The Idea of Poe in *Pierre*," *ESQ* 50, supp. (1968): 59–62; Adeline Tintner, "James Corrects Poe: The Appropriation of *Pym* in *The Golden Bowl*," *American Transcendental Quarterly* 37 (1978): 87–91; Grace Farrell Lee, "*Pym* and *Moby-Dick*: Essential Connections," *American Transcendental Quarterly* 37 (1978): 73–86; Marilyn Gaddis Rose, "'Emmanuele'—'Morella': Gide's Poe Affinities," *Texas Studies in Literature and Language* 5 (1963): 127–37; Carole Shaffer-Koros, "Edgar Allan Poe and Edith Wharton: The Case of Mrs. Mowatt," *Edith Wharton Review* 17 (2001): 12–16.

112. Ana Hernández del Castillo, *Keats, Poe, and the Shaping of Cortázar's Mythopoesis* (Amsterdam: Benjamins, 1981); Erika Hulpke, "On First Translations of 'The Raven' into German," *Poe Studies* 15, no. 2 (1982): 41; Lois Davis Vines, *Valéry and Poe: A Literary Legacy* (New York: New York University Press, 1992); Barbara Cantalupo, ed., *Poe's Pervasive Influence* (Bethlehem: Lehigh University Press, 2012).

113. Mary E. Phillips, *Edgar Allan Poe the Man* (Philadelphia: John C. Winston Co., 1926); Marie Bonaparte, *Life and Works of Edgar Allan Poe*, trans. John Rodker (London: Imago Publishing, 1949); Frances Winwar, *The Haunted Palace: A Life of Edgar Allan Poe* (New York: Harper, 1959). For more information on nineteenth-century women biographers, see Sandra Tomc's chapter in this collection.

114. Agnes Bondurant, *Poe's Richmond* (Richmond: Poe Associates, 1978).

115. Barbara Moore, *The Fever Called Living* (New York: Doubleday, 1976).

116. Bettina Knapp, *Edgar Allan Poe* (New York: Ungar, 1984): 205.

117. Liliane Weissberg, *Edgar Allan Poe* (Stuttgart: J. B. Metzlersche, 1991).

118. Dawn B. Sova, *Critical Companion to Edgar Allan Poe: A Literary Reference to His Life and Work* (New York: Facts on File, 2007). This version is an update to her 2001 *Edgar Allan Poe, A to Z: The Essential Reference to His Life and Work*.

119. See "Poe, Decoded," *The New Yorker*, April 17, 2009; "A Poe Coda," *The New Yorker*, April 17, 2009; "The Humbug: Edgar Allan Poe and the Economy of Horror," *The New Yorker*, April 20, 2009; *Edgar Allan Poe: Buried Alive*, directed by Eric Stange (PBS, *American Masters*, 2016).

120. See *The Short Fiction of Edgar Allan Poe: An Annotated Edition* (Indianapolis: Bobbs-Merrill, 1976); *Edgar Allan Poe: Thirty-Two Stories* (Indianapolis: Hackett Publishing Co., 2000); *Edgar Allan Poe: Eureka* (Urbana: University of Illinois Press, 2004); *Edgar Allan Poe: Critical Theory, The Major Documents* (Urbana: University of Illinois Press, 2009). For more information on Maureen Cobb Mabbott's contributions, see Travis Montgomery's afterword to this collection.

121. Frederick Frank and Diane Long Hoeveler, eds., *The Narrative of Arthur Gordon Pym of Nantucket* (Peterborough: Broadview, 2010).

122. I would like to thank Scott Peeples, Richard Kopley, and John Edward Martin for helping me locate this information.

123. The masthead of the first issue of *The Edgar Allan Poe Review* lists four editorial board members. Joan Tyler Mead was the first woman to serve in this role for the journal.

124. Although *Poe Studies* and *The Edgar Allan Poe Review* have had a good record of including women contributors, multiple issues in both runs include neither literary criticism nor reviews by women, even in recent years.

125. See Patricia Merivale and Susan Elizabeth Sweeney, eds., *Detecting Texts: The Metaphysical Detective Story from Poe to Postmodernism* (Philadelphia: University of Pennsylvania Press, 1999); Jeffrey Andrew Weinstock and Tony Magistrale, eds., *Approaches to Teaching Poe's Prose and Poetry* (New York: Modern Language Association of America, 2008); James Hutchisson, ed., *Edgar Allan Poe: Beyond Gothicism* (Newark: University of Delaware Press, 2011); Dennis Perry and Carl Sederholm, eds., *Adapting Poe: Re-Imaginings in Popular Culture* (New York: Palgrave, 2012); Barbara Cantalupo, ed., *Poe's Pervasive Influence* (Bethlehem: Lehigh University Press, 2012); J. Gerald Kennedy and Jerome McGann, eds., *Poe and the Remapping of Antebellum Print Culture* (Baton Rouge: Louisiana State University Press, 2012); Kevin Hayes, ed., *Edgar Allan Poe in Context* (Cambridge: Cambridge University Press, 2013); Richard Kopley and Jana Argersinger, eds., *Poe Writing/ Writing Poe* (New York: AMS, 2013); Alexandra Urakova, ed., *Deciphering Poe: Subtexts, Context, Subversive Meanings* (Bethlehem: Lehigh University Press, 2013); Philip E. Phillips, ed., *Poe and Place* (New York: Palgrave Macmillan, 2018).

126. Argersinger, "From an Editor's Easy Chair," 42.

Chapter Four

Transnational Poe and Women Scholars Abroad

Clara Petino

According to George Bernard Shaw, Poe "wrote always as if his native Boston was Athens, his Charlottesville University Plato's Academy, and his cottage the crown of the heights of Fiesole," so it comes as little surprise that his work resonates with writers all over the world.[1] Women scholars abroad number among those writers intrigued by Poe. To illustrate, Sybille Haage, Katrina Bachinger, and Stephanie Sommerfeld—Europeans all—have published, in English, critical analyses of Poe's writings.[2] Other important contributions to the field have been made by their successors. This chapter offers an overview of their work, the following paragraphs indicating many ways that female critics from such diverse places as Brazil, Russia, and Japan have brought the transnational qualities of Poe to the fore, but the limited scope of this essay allows only for the discussion of a few scholars who have been particularly prominent in Poe studies in recent decades. Although many of those women have also published on Poe in their native language, this chapter will address only studies in English with an emphasis on comparative work, much of which appears in the collected editions *Poe Abroad* (1999) and *Translated Poe* (2014).

The Japanese poet and scholar Noriko Mizuta Lippit has made significant contributions to Poe studies. She entered the field with her dissertation *Crime and Dream: A Study on Edgar Allan Poe* and established a critical reputation with her in-depth study of Poe's use of the terms *grotesque* and *arabesque*.[3] Most of Lippit's work is, however, comparative. She is the first scholar to study the Japanese novelist Natsume Sōseki's early-twentieth-century essays on Poe. Lippit looks at the connection between Sōseki, one of "the first Japanese writers to be drawn to Poe," and the Japanese aesthetic school that Poe greatly influenced.[4] In *Reality and Fiction in Modern Japanese Literature*, she focuses on the relation between Western Dark Romanticism and Japanese aesthetic literature. For Lippit, the attraction of modern Japanese writers such as Tanizaki Junichiro, Akutagawa Ryūnosuke, Hagiwara Sakutaro, and Mishima Yukio to Western writers of Dark Romanticism, particularly Poe, derives from shared themes and concerns: "the question of evil, the role of the grotesque and the ugly in art, and the relation of art to life."[5] Through her analysis of *fin-de-siècle* Japanese literature, Lippit traces the development of Japanese cultural identity under the influence of the Dark Romantics, explaining that their "romantic quest for a vision of destructive transcendence" is in line with Japanese writers' "skepticism toward and criticism of progress, Western civilization, and capitalist economic development."[6] Drawing upon her studies of the grotesque, Lippit compares Poe and Sakutaro, and she points out similarities in their notions of transcendence. She concludes the chapter with a detailed analysis of Tanizaki's work, a subject she had addressed in a 1977 publication, wherein she discussed Poe's influence on Tanizaki.[7] Lippit took up the topic again in one of her two contributions to *Poe Abroad*. In that piece, she shows how the Japanese author "developed his early Poesque world of Romanticism in the Japanese literary tradition," indicating similarities between the (female) characters of Tanizaki and those of Poe, fictional figures that Lippit describes as "unattainable" while identifying differences in the ways the two authors portray women.[8] She also observes convergences and divergences in the writers' treatments of four themes: "fear of death, the sadomasochistic pursuit of feminine beauty, the discovery of perversity or cruelty in human nature, and the relation of art to these themes."[9] Her comparative analysis of "The Domain of Arnheim" and "Konjiki no shi" ("The Golden Death") is notably comprehensive. Lippit finds that Tanizaki managed to transfer Poe's Gothic themes into Japanese natural settings.[10]

Other links between Poe and Japanese culture have received her critical scrutiny. In the second contribution to *Poe Abroad*, Lippit traces Poe's literary significance in Japan since the nineteenth century as well as his importance in Japanese pop culture, where his influence is evident in everything from manga books to science fiction and from horror movies to computer games. Aware that Poe was "one of the earliest foreign writers to be introduced in Japan," she considers the history of Poe translations (starting with Aeba Koson's first translations in 1888) and analyzes Poe's influence on different literary genres in Japan.[11] According to Lippit, not only did the American writer inspire independence "from the tradition of the regulated short poems of tanka and haiku," but he also piqued interest in short fiction as well as "Japanese literature of the city."[12] Furthermore, Lippit recognizes Poe's female readership in

Japan, and although Poe's writing apparently had "little to offer to promote feminism itself," its publication in the first Japanese feminist journal, *Seito*, confirms, Lippit argues, Poe's transnational appeal to women:

> *Seito* initially was mainly a literary journal, a forum for literary and artistic expression for women, and in that context the publication of Poe's tales did not appear unnatural. Poe continued to be translated even after the journal moved on to become a forum for political issues concerning women's rights and other ideological issues of feminism. . . . It is clear, however, that Poe was read and appreciated by the feminists of *Seito* enough to be repeatedly published, often translated by Raicho [Hiratsuka]. Although Raicho was a committed feminist, her interest in and connection with Poe opened among women writers and artists new areas of sensitivity for the mysterious and fantastic, for the grotesque and arabesque in Modernism.[13]

Lippit's work on Poe's reception in Japan from the nineteenth century to the present, particularly in the context of aestheticism, is a valuable contribution to bringing seemingly different cultures together. The Poe Society of Japan (established in 2008) as well as its journal and website demonstrate Japan's unabated interest in Poe. Another testament to that fascination is a major event: the 2018 International Hawthorne and Poe Conference hosted in Kyoto by the Poe Society of Japan and other scholarly organizations. Significantly, the conference program complements this chapter's theme. To illustrate by referencing only one of the papers presented in Kyoto, Maki Sadahiro's "The Birth of American Poe and the Transatlantic Triangular Literary Exchanges" demonstrates international women scholars' interest in a transatlantic Poe.

Popular in Japan, Poe is also a major figure in Russia, where he "appears to be the most translated U.S. author," and the writer has attracted the critical attention of Russian women.[14] For example, Elvira Osipova, a former editorial board member of *The Edgar Allan Poe Review*, has studied the history of Russian Poe translations. Osipova notes that, although Poe's "psychological tales" appeared in Dostoyevsky's magazine *Vremya* in 1861, textual parallels between "The Black Cat" and "The Double" suggest that the Russian writer's tale actually influenced the Poe translation. According to Osipova, it was above all the Russian Symbolists' fascination with Poe's tales at the turn of the twentieth century that fueled the Poe cult in Russia. French being more widely spoken than English in nineteenth-century Russia, Poe was introduced there through Baudelaire, and Konstantin Bal'mont, who translated from the French into Russian and became the "Russian Baudelaire," helped create "'the Russian face' of Edgar Poe."[15] In 2004, Osipova addressed the specific case of Bal'mont's faulty but influential translation of *Eureka*. She states, "The reception of *Eureka* in Russia has always been conditioned by what a scholar relies on—translation or original text."[16] The inseparability of Russian Poe scholarship and translations is an important theme in Osipova's contribution to *Translated Poe*, in which she shows how translators' often incomplete understanding of Poe's work led scholars to dwell on Gothic material in his work.[17] Discussing Poe's influence on Russian Symbolism, Osipova emphasizes the vital role of translations as opinion-forming texts of their own, especially in the case of one of Poe's most controversial works: *Eureka*.[18]

Another scholar prominent in Russian Poe scholarship is Alexandra Urakova who, like Osipova, complicates the Poe presented to the (Russian) reader. Of special importance is her editing of the 2013 collection *Deciphering Poe: Subtexts, Contexts, Subversive Meanings*, in which contributors examine Poe's "heritage in its complex interrelation with contemporary notions of race, sexuality, and gender"—among other topics.[19] Her work on Poe also includes studies on publication history as well as innovative readings of Poe's works. She interprets "The Purloined Letter" as hidden criticism of the Gift Book tradition within which the tale was first printed, and she shows how the pieces Poe published in *Godey's Lady's Book* fit the "carnivalesque and interactive spirit of the magazine."[20] She also makes a compelling case that Poe ridicules the "antebellum rhetoric of youth" and the radical rejection of old forms and ideas within the Young America movement.[21] Urakova has penned an article about Poe adaptations for the Russian stage, and her comparative work includes an essay (written with Timothy Farrant) about Poe's influence on Baudelaire and the two writers' prominent use of uncanny, emblematic bird figures.[22]

Urakova's work on Poe and Gogol is particularly important. Many readers consider Nikolai Gogol the Russian counterpart of Poe, and taking seriously the writers' imaginative kinship, Urakova offers a comparative analysis of Poe's "The Man of the Crowd" and Gogol's "The Portrait," tales with some important similarities despite their seemingly dissimilar content.[23] Focusing on the figure of the old wanderer in the vicious modern city, she finds that both writers "combine the cursed restlessness of the Wandering Jew with overtly demonic features."[24] Yet while Gogol's protagonist follows a classic Faustian plot, Poe's wanderer remains a mystery.[25] The stories end differently, too. According to Urakova, "Replacing the soul-for-money exchange by the endless circuit of desire, Poe surpasses Romantic dualism of the demonic and the divine, and of the material and the spiritual."[26] For this reason, she concludes that Poe's story "became one of the emblems of literary modernity due to the fluidity of its meaning" as well as its reliance on "a new set of binary oppositions to describe the modern urbanity: privacy and publicity, transparency and obscurity, consumption and waste."[27]

In addition, Urakova has shed light on the Russian publication history of "The Gold-Bug" and its unique reception. Whereas Poe's Gothic tales are popular among U.S. students, Poe's famous tale of ratiocination and buried treasure—the first Poe story translated into Russian—remains a favorite among young Russian readers.[28] Urakova explains this popularity by recounting the first appearance of "The Gold-Bug" in a Russian juvenile journal and identifying the "educative purpose" of solving mysteries.[29] Poe's tale contains many puns that are difficult to render into Russian, and Urakova asserts that the translated text in itself "was turned into a 'mental quiz' for a schoolchild to solve," for "the reader has to master a complicated text that is a translation of the translation of the translation."[30] The tale had little appeal for the Russian Symbolists, who preferred other stories by Poe, but with the rise of Communism, "The Gold-Bug" took on new significance. Urakova explains that change: "his detective and logical tales were in every respect 'safer' for a Soviet reader, and particularly for a young reader, than his renowned mysticism. Soviet criticism refused to acknowledge any mysteries that could not be explained positively and rationally."[31] Urakova's sophisticated interpretations as well as her demonstration of the inseparability of Poe's Russian reception from the region's political realities remain impressive.

In Portugal, Poe has also attracted the attention of female critics. Scholar, translator, and poet Margarida Vale de Gato wrote her dissertation on "Poe's rewrites by late-19th century Portuguese poets," and with Emron Esplin, she edited the collection *Translated Poe*, showing that "[f]ew, if any, U.S. writers are as important to the history of world literature as Poe, and few, if any, U.S. authors owe so much of their current reputations to translation."[32] Fittingly, the first chapter, which Vale de Gato wrote herself, demonstrates how "translations of Poe were used in Portugal to challenge installed systems, support literary revolutions, and uphold or complement authorial agendas."[33] She discusses the curious situation that the first Portuguese translation of a Poe story was a version of "Hans Pfaall" published in 1857, the year that saw the first balloon journey of a Portuguese citizen. Thereafter, "Poe was . . . tentatively framed as a herald of technology and modernity instead of as the dark Romantic . . . ," and Vale de Gato observes how the themes of the Poe tales translated during the 1870s—mostly from Baudelaire's French texts—deal with "topics of social critique, realism, and deductive analysis devoted to the exploration of the human psyche" relevant to "the attack on the formality of morals in the Portuguese Catholic society."[34] Vale de Gato also addresses other political issues such as Portuguese nationalism during the nineteenth century as well as the relationship between the Geração de 70 and Poe.[35]

In addition, she has studied the Portuguese modernist and Poe translator Fernando Pessoa, noting his debts to the American writer, particularly the notion that "obscurity was at the core of modernity."[36] Vale de Gato discusses Pessoa's English poetry under the pseudonym Alexander Search, the name of the "Poesque persona of Pessoa."[37] She presents a new in-depth analysis of Poe's "The Bells" as "genetic subtext" to Pessoa's/Search's "Ode to the Sea" and "Insomnia," attending to the ways that the two writers use sounds to suggest changing moods.[38] She then illustrates Pessoa's departure from Symbolism and *saudosismo*, a dominant poetic trend "advocating recollection through landscape contemplation and evoking the pan-psychic nature of the Portuguese soul."[39] For Vale de Gato, Pessoa found "both tendencies to be lacking in complexity and bordering on vagueness, and ascribed to Poe the sobering cautionary remark against 'obscurity of expression' when striving for the 'expression of obscurity.'"[40] Stressing the interrelations between music and poetry in both writers' verse once more, Vale de Gato identifies Poe's influence on Pessoa's "modernist hallmark—the forgery of emotion and commitment to intellectual composition," suggesting that Poe's influence may have played a key role in shaping early Portuguese modernism.[41] Pessoa's translations of "The Raven," "Ulalume," and "Annabel Lee" do not escape Vale de Gato's critical attention, for she and Maria Antónia Lima interpret that translation work as not only an expression of the Portuguese author's "Poesque fascination for young ethereal women" but also a "commitment to an intellectual rationale for prosody and his interest in the romance of a lost kingdom of spirituality, foreshadowing Portuguese claims at the outset of the 20th century for the foundation of a '5th Empire,'" an ideology made particularly famous through the writings of Pessoa.[42]

Vale de Gato has highlighted the Poe/Portugal connection in other ways. A special issue of *The Edgar Allan Poe Review* that she coedited with Lima showcases scholarly work from the 2009 "Poe and Gothic Creativity" international symposium at the University of Lisbon, and that publication strikingly demonstrates the persistence of Portugal's interest in Poe. Vale de Gato also observes that interest in "Poe's 'Nevermore,' Lisbon's Ravens, and the Portuguese Ideology of *Saudade*." Here, she explains how the "sweet yet painful sensation created by the contemplation of a beloved object from which we are separated" and the emotion at the heart of the *saudosismo* trend correspond to melancholia in "The Raven."[43] Through analyses of three nineteenth-century Portuguese re-inscriptions of Poe's poem, Vale de Gato reveals how these texts, with their references to dead women, employ Poe's sentimentality to express "national bereavement" and to participate in "the ideological attempt to restore Portugal's wounded national identity" after the country's "perceived descent into decadence."[44] For example, in his rewriting of "The Raven," Alberto d'Oliveira "combines Poe's refrain 'Nevermore' with the raven motif of the arms of Lisbon," emphasizing the "deployment of Poe in nationalist nostalgia" associated with Portugal's capital city.[45] Vale de Gato's work illuminates Poe's influence on Portuguese national identity, and her scholarship remains invaluable to the study of Poe's worldwide significance.

Poe criticism has also flourished in Brazil, where Renata Philippov has been active. Philippov begins her contribution to *Translated Poe* by recognizing the hegemony of French literary and intellectual culture in Brazilian life during the years following independence from Portugal. As she observes, Poe came to Brazil through French translations, but in 1883, Joaquim Maria Machado de Assis became the first to translate "The Raven" into Portuguese. Philippov devotes special attention to a particular Brazilian translation of a famous Poe tale. Invoking Haroldo de Campos's idea of "translation as transcreation," Philippov examines Oscar Mendes's 1944 translation of "The Fall of the House of Usher" ("A Queda do Solar de Usher"), investigating the extent to which Mendes's language, specifically "solar" ("mansion") instead of "house" ("casa") "keeps and/or distorts the allegorical meaning conceived by Poe"—especially in light of the "polysemantic richness the original title carries . . . and which, at least partially, got lost in translation."[46]

Known best for her work on Poe's influence on Machado de Assis, Philippov emphasizes both writers' reputations as critics, their stylistic affinities for humorous elements, their passion for short fiction, and their use of similar motifs and themes such as "the fantastic, insanity, death, [and] the doppelgänger."[47] She does, however, point out important ways in which Poe differed from his Brazilian counterpart. For example, she notes that whereas Machado enjoyed financial success, Poe languished in poverty throughout his career. Philippov also identifies artistic distinctions between the two writers, insisting that Machado moved beyond Poe by transforming the latter's themes and forms for new aesthetic ends:

> If Poe sought in his writings a way of denouncing alienation and humanity's inexorable destruction, Machado seems to have had another mission: to openly criticize his times without isolating himself and his characters from reality. . . . His later characters and more mature stories are set in an open-air space: the streets of Rio de Janeiro during Brazil's Second Empire. As opposed to the indeterminable gothic ambience of Poe's stories, Machado places his narrators in the easily recognizable petty situations and the well-known places of ordinary citizens in Rio de Janeiro.[48]

To Machado, Philippov concludes, Poe was "a source rather than an influence to be used uncritically."[49]

She continues this line of inquiry in a study of Baudelaire's influence on Machado's transformations of Poe themes, paying special attention to the French writer's aesthetics.[50] According to Philippov, this artistic "transatlantic voyage" shows "how Machado de Assis may have actually incorporated and, paradoxically, subverted Poe's and Baudelaire's imagery, topoi and aesthetics into his own literary project."[51] In particular, Philippov looks at the 1885 short story "Só!" in relation to "The Man of the Crowd" and Baudelaire's poem "À une passante." As a representative for Poe studies in South America, Philippov—like Elvira Osipova in Russia—impressively demonstrates the significance of "translation as transcreation" as well as Poe's global influence.

Another hub for Poe scholarship is Spain, where Margarita Rigal-Aragón has noted the discrepancy between a long tradition of Spanish translations of Poe's writings and a lack of scholarly work devoted to Poe before the 1980s, her own dissertation being one of the first in the field. Commenting on the anonymous 1857 version of "Three Sundays in a Week," she argues that the Poe story was adapted to a Spanish environment and thus "perfectly suited the spirit of the epoch in Spain: a likeness to introduce local customs in literary works."[52] Rigal-Aragón also traces Baudelaire's influence on *Historias extraordinarias,* the first Spanish collection of Poe's tales, and she discusses Lasso de la Vega's twentieth-century translations as products of the "Spanish avant-garde movement called 'Ultraísmo[,]' a reaction against the dominating *Modernismo.*"[53] In addition, she comments upon the first Spanish biographies of Poe, most of which offer one-sided depictions of Poe as a melancholic drug-addict.[54] Another research interest of Rigal-Aragón is Argentine Julio Cortázar, whose Poe translations were commissioned by UNESCO in 1956 and "continue to attract Spanish readers because of his ability to place Poe's fiction within the context, both national and personal, in which Poe wrote it."[55] She concludes her overview with an account of translations from the 1990s and the early twenty-first century. Among them are her own efforts, on which she reflects critically.

Rigal-Aragón's contributions to Poe studies include conference planning and public education. She co-organized the 2009 "Edgar Allan Poe: Two Hundred Years Later" conference at the University of Castilla–La Mancha. A particularly interesting read in light of that event is her paper titled "Spanish 'Misreadings' of Poe's Life and Works at the Beginning of the Twenty-First Century." After she and Beatriz González-Moreno received an invitation to participate in a radio program celebrating the bicentennial of his birth, Rigal-Aragón accepted, and the questions during the interview inspired her to explain why the persistent image of Poe as a drunken lunatic is so hard to erase in Spain and South America. She singled out Baudelaire as the source of that misperception, for it has been "tradition in Spain to accept Baudelaire's opinion regarding the life and works of Poe, and thus, to inherit the Frenchman's mistaken assumptions."[56] A second major influence was, she insisted, Ramón Gómez's 1953 biographical study, which lacks references, takes drastic liberties with Poe's real biography, and perpetuates Baudelaire's portrayal.[57] There was perhaps another reason, Rigal-Aragón suggested, why Spanish and South American readers associated Poe the man with gloom and terror. Cortázar's aforementioned translations promoted the notion that Poe was essentially a horror author, for the Argentine writer put the Poe works that he considered the best—the terror stories—in the first volume of *Cuentos*, leaving the tales that he considered inferior—the satirical pieces—to fill the second book.[58]

Rigal-Aragón also points out the disturbing fact that academic works are largely ignored in Spanish appreciations of Poe and his writings while long outdated references (such as Gómez's) are still in use. Throughout Spain, Baudelaire's account of Poe remains a frequently cited biographical source.[59] The public, Rigal-Aragón writes, seems to prefer "personal appreciations" over academic work, an inclination most dramatically displayed in the case of writer Fernando Iwasaki, who prepared the 2008 edition of Poe's *Cuentos Completos* financed by the Spanish Ministry of Culture. In that publication, the translator not only "belittles Spanish scholarship on Poe" but also "perpetuates misinformation that Poe was a drug abuser, a sex fiend, who wrote only about terror, phantoms, dreams, nightmares, dying ladies, illnesses, and devastating love."[60] Rigal-Aragón bemoans how editorial apathy and politics play a role in "helping to perpetuate mistakes about Poe's life and his artistic achievements."[61]

A desire to clear the air inspired Rigal-Aragón and Beatriz González-Moreno, whose coedited volume, *A Descent into Edgar Allan Poe and His Works: The Bicentennial*, offers a corrective view of the American writer. Departing from an interpretative approach that features Poe's personal life, the editors draw "together a group of scholars who are Poe-conscious, who are aware of the many Poe-related mysteries which are still to be unveiled," and who "aim to 'redeem' Poe on the occasion of the second centenary of his birth, validating, through scientific investigation, that he was no erratic star but a BRILLIANT one."[62] The work thus marks an essential contribution not only to the study of the Spanish reception and translation of Poe but also to correcting a one-sided image of Poe's life and work in Rigal-Aragón's native country and beyond.

In her own contribution to that collection, Rigal-Aragón argues that the ratiocination traditionally associated with Poe's detective stories pervades the Poe oeuvre. In fact, that theme surfaces in early tales such as "MS. Found in a Bottle" and "Berenice," stories in which the narrators are "masters of solving puzzles."[63] Even the narrator of the "Tell-Tale Heart" and Poe's other murderers "plan crimes with mathematical precision, and have acute and awake brains, like Dupin's."[64] Highly interesting in this interpretative vein is Rigal-Aragón's description of Kate in "Three Sundays in a Week" as "the first woman detective-like character, and the two of them [Kate and Bobby], the first detective-like couple, since they both work together in order to deceive their uncle in a prodigious way."[65] Rigal-Aragón not only illuminates Poe's role as the father of detective fiction, significantly highlighting Kate's mental acuity, but she also sheds new light on one of Poe's most important literary achievements.

Other contributions by Rigal-Aragón merit attention here. Among her recent publications is an essay (written with José Manuel Correoso-Rodenas) about "Poe's Spaces" in the TV series *The Following*.[66] In another piece, Rigal-Aragón conducts (with Fernando González-Moreno) an analysis of the "pictorial dimensions of Poe's tales," his textual references to works of art, and the ways that Poe's unique verbal images have inspired illustrators.[67] The authors study how the largely forgotten illustrator Fernando Xumetra interpreted Poe's prose visually in the first illustrated Spanish edition in 1887, highlighting the "originality" of those interpretations.[68] Building relationships with scholars around the world remains important to Rigal-Aragón, and as president of the Edgar Allan Poe Spanish Association, she helped the organization launch its first international conference ("Poe in the Age of Populism") in 2018.

The remainder of this chapter accounts for the scholarship of Lois Davis Vines, a U.S.-based professor. In 1993, a year after the publication of her *Poe and Valéry: A Literary Legacy*, Vines received the *Chevalier dans l'ordre des Palmes Academiques*, one of the highest French scholarly awards, and she has published so extensively on Poe's French legacy that she is indispensable for this collection. In *Poe and Valery*, Vines notes that "Paul Valéry's death in 1945 marks the end of the century-long Poe cult in France."[69] Beginning with Baudelaire's legendary discovery of Poe, this cult "was carried out with missionary-like fervor by his successors Mallarmé and Valéry."[70] According to Vines, Poe's influence on Valéry has rarely been studied, and redressing this oversight, she highlights how Poe helped Valéry understand his own mind during the creative act, a major theme of Valéry's own poetry.[71] This subject dominates Vines's study. She points out Valéry's distinction between creative influence that elicits imitation and influence that produces what he considered "extreme originality."[72] With that distinction in mind, Vines asserts that "Poe's influence on Valéry is unique and goes far beyond the effect of the American writer on his predecessors. It had the effect of turning Valéry against literature and orienting him toward the quest of pure intellectual power."[73]

Although Vines shows how Valéry's "On Literary Technique" is, indeed, an imitation of Poe's "The Philosophy of Composition," she demonstrates how Valéry transforms Poe's detective type. Valéry's detective Teste, a character based upon Poe's Dupin, is preoccupied with comprehending his own mind. As a "silent, uncelebrated genius," he differs from Poe's character, who focuses on solving cases and getting praise.[74] In addition, Vines addresses Valéry's—as well as Baudelaire's and Mallarmé's—indebtedness to Poe's idea of "pure poetry," which is perfect in sound, verse, and imagery but free from politics, history, and morality, and she shows how Poe stimulated Valery's interest in science.[75]

Paul Valéry, Charles Baudelaire, and Stéphane Mallarmé figure prominently in Vines's contribution to *Poe Abroad: Influence, Reputation, and Affinities*, a 1999 collection of essays that she edited. Vines identifies sources for Baudelaire's 1852 article "Edgar Allan Poe: sa vie et ses ouvrages" in Poe's writings, particularly Baudelaire's fascination with Poe's "psychological condition of a poem."[76] She also discusses the high quality of Baudelaire's Poe translations, works that profoundly shaped Poe's transnational reputation. In the chapter "Poe in France," she surveys the history of French translations and academic studies of Poe, documenting the American writer's influence on French prose writers from Guy de Maupassant to Jules Verne as well as on French dramatists, philosophers, and psychoanalysts such as Marie Bonaparte, whose Freudian study of Poe's life and work remains influential.[77] She concludes: "From the precursors of Symbolism to the New Novel, Poe has had an influence on the major literary movements in France for a century and a half."[78] Topically similar to her work in *Poe Abroad* is her contribution to *Translated Poe,* in which she identifies recent academic developments and translation projects that evince a thriving French Poe cult.[79] Vines demonstrates that Poe's stories have lost nothing of their influential power in the twenty-first century.

Vines has also discussed how Poe was influenced by the French authors François Rabelais and Alain-René Lesage, who "exert a crucial, but so far largely neglected influence on the development of American literature in general and especially on the writings of Edgar Allan Poe."[80] Poe mentions Rabelais repeatedly in his writings, and Vines subjects "Hop-Frog" and "Lionizing" to thorough analysis, drawing on studies of Rabelais by Mikhail Bakhtin. "Hop-Frog," she claims, "is a tale of laughter and merrymaking reminiscent of Rabelais's carnival scenes, except that Poe's story ends in horror."[81] Characterization in "Lionizing" mirrors the satiric depiction of society in *Gargantua*, and Vines asserts, "[t]hrough their use of negative laughter, Poe and Rabelais place themselves above the objects of their mockery."[82] According to Vines, "The Cask of Amontillado" is a text in which Poe diverges from Rabelais: "Whereas the Rabelaisian carnivalesque integrates life and death in triumphant celebration, Poe's carnival creates an oppressive contrast to emphasize the omnipresence of death."[83] In addition to examining connections between Poe and Rabelais, Vines identifies some of Poe's debts to Lesage, particularly the devil motif from *The Devil on Two Sticks (Le Diable boiteux)*. Citing stories such as "The Man That Was Used Up," "The Spectacles," and "Never Bet the Devil Your Head," Vines claims, "For both Poe and Lesage the devil is a metaphor for the absurd, the elements in life that escape reason and logic."[84] Her in-depth analysis of Poe's influence on French writers as well as her research about the French impact on Poe's reputation is unrivaled in Poe scholarship.

The collection *Poe Abroad*, which Vines edited, was "in no way an exhaustive study" of Poe's international prestige, but the book was a model for *Translated Poe* and other critical works.[85] To be sure, *Poe Abroad* inspired this overview, which confirms that Poe is not only one of the most important American writers but also an author of world literature. Women scholars have long recognized that fact, for their work has shown that Poe's themes and styles sparked and shaped literary movements abroad, from Japanese aestheticism to Russian Symbolism, proving that he truly has a global reach. These women have changed Poe studies, and although the overview offered here is not all-inclusive, it emphasizes that female scholars who study Poe— like the writer's literary women, including German Ligeia, English Rowena, and French Marie Rogêt—come from all over the world.

NOTES

1. George Bernard Shaw, "Edgar Allan Poe," in *The Recognition of Edgar Allan Poe. Selected Criticism since 1829*, ed. Eric W. Carlson (Ann Arbor: Michigan University Press, 1970), 98.

2. In *Edgar Allan Poe's "Tales of the folio club": Versuch der Rekonstruktion einer zyklischen Rahmenerzählung* (Frankfurt am Main: Peter Lang, 1978), Sybille Haage analyzes Poe's earliest prose tales in their largely unknown first editions, interpreting them as embedded narratives in a cyclical frame. Austrian scholar Katrina Bachinger is known for her monograph *Edgar Allan Poe's Biographies of Byron: Byrons Differed/Byrons Deferred in the Tales of the Folio Club* (Lewiston: Mellen, 1994). Here, she not only corrects the widely held belief that Byron ceased to be an influence on Poe in the second half of his life, but she also shows that many of Poe's stories, from "Metzengerstein" to "Morella," can be read as responses to Byron's life and work. She has also contributed repeatedly to *Salzburger Studien zur Anglistik und Amerikanistik/Salzburg Studies in English Literature*, often refuting other scholars' criticism of Poe's works. See "A Fit Horror': Edgar Allan Poe's 'The Raven'" (1979: 48–60); "The Poetic Distance of the House of Usher" (1979: 61–74); and "Tit for Tat: The Political Poe's Ripostes to Nineteenth Century American Culture and Society" (1981: 46–90). Stephanie Sommerfeld has published at length on Poe and sublimity. See "The Sublime's Invasion of Ellisonland" in *Edgar Allan Poe: Doscientos años después,* ed. Beatriz González-Moreno and Margarita Rigal-Aragón (Cuenca: Ediciones de la Universidad de Castilla–La Mancha, 2010), 141–54; "Post-Kantian Sublimity and Mediacy in Poe's *Blackwood Tales*," *The Edgar Allan Poe Review* 13, no. 2 (2012): 33–49; and "From the Romantic to the Textual Sublime: Poesque Sublimities, Romantic Irony, and Deconstruction" in *Deciphering Poe*, ed. Alexandra Urakova (Bethlehem: Lehigh University Press, 2013), 75–85.

3. Noriko Mizuta Lippit, "The Grotesque and Arabesque in Poe," *Josai Jinbun Kenkyu/Studies in the Humanities* 1 (1973): 132–72.

4. Noriko Mizuta Lippit, "Natsume Sōseki on Poe," *Comparative Literature Studies* 14, no. 1 (1977): 32.

5. Noriko Mizuta Lippit, *Reality and Fiction in Modern Japanese Literature* (New York: M. E. Sharpe, 1980), 70.

6. Ibid., 71, 74.

7. Noriko Mizuta Lippit, "Tanizaki and Poe: The Grotesque and the Quest for Supernatural Beauty," *Comparative Literature* 29, no. 3 (1977): 221–40.

8. Noriko Mizuta Lippit, "Tanizaki Junichiro," in *Poe Abroad: Influence, Reputation, Affinities*, ed. Lois Davis Vines (Iowa City: Iowa University Press, 1999), 244, 247.

9. Ibid., 245.

10. Ibid., 248.

11. Noriko Mizuta Lippit, "Poe in Japan," in *Poe Abroad: Influence, Reputation, Affinities*, ed. Lois Davis Vines (Iowa City: Iowa University Press, 1999), 135.

12. Ibid., 137.

13. Ibid., 142, 143.

14. Elvira Osipova, "The History of Poe Translations in Russia," in *Translated Poe*, ed. Emron Esplin and Margarida Vale de Gato (Bethlehem: Lehigh University Press, 2014), 65. The Russia/Poe connection has also intrigued U.S. scholars. See, for example, Joan Delaney Grossman's *Edgar Allan Poe in Russia* (Würzburg: Jal-Verlag, 1973) and the chapters that Eloise M. Boyle contributed to *Poe Abroad*: "Poe in Russia" (19–25) and "Valery Brjustov and Konstantin Bal'mont" (177–82).

15. Osipova, "History of Poe Translations," 68, 72.

16. Elvira Osipova, "The Reception of 'Eureka' in Russia," *The Edgar Allan Poe Review* 5, no. 1 (2004): 17.

17. Osipova, "History of Poe Translations," 70.

18. Osipova, "Reception of 'Eureka,'" 16–28.

19. Alexandra Urakova, ed., *Deciphering Poe: Subtexts, Contexts, Subversive Meanings* (Bethlehem: Lehigh University Press, 2013), xii.

20. Alexandra Urakova, "Poe, Fashion, and *Godey's Lady's Book*," *The Edgar Allan Poe Review* 15, no. 1 (2014): 37; Alexandra Urakova, "'The Purloined Letter' in the Gift Book: Reading Poe in a Contemporary Context," *Nineteenth-Century Literature* 64, no. 3 (2009): 323–46.

21. Alexandra Urakova, "Why Old? Edgar Allan Poe and the Antebellum Rhetorical Constructions of Youth," in *"Forever Young"?: The Changing Images of America*, ed. Philip Coleman and Stephen Matterson (Heidelberg: Universitätsverlag, 2012), 161.

22. Alexandra Urakova, "Edgar Poe on the Russian 'Stage': Between 'Depths' and 'Surfaces,'" in *Cultural Exchanges Between Central/Eastern Europe and America*, *ZENAF Conference Proceedings*, vol. 3 (Frankfurt: J. W. Goethe-Universität, 2003), 24–39; Timothy Farrant and Alexandra Urakova, "From 'The Raven' to 'Le Cygne': Birds, Transcendence, and the Uncanny in Poe and Baudelaire," *The Edgar Allan Poe Review* 15, no. 2 (2014), 156–74.

23. Alexandra Urakova, "'Breaking the Law of Silence': Poe's 'Man of the Crowd' and Gogol's 'The Portrait,' in *Poe's Pervasive Influence*, ed. Barbara Cantalupo (Bethlehem: Lehigh University Press, 2012), 63–73.

24. Ibid., 65.

25. Ibid., 68.

26. Ibid., 69.

27. Ibid., 70–71.

28. Alexandra Urakova, "Code for Kids: The Story of 'The Gold-Bug's' First Translation in Russia," in *Translated Poe*, ed. Emron Esplin and Margarida Vale de Gato (Bethlehem: Lehigh University Press, 2014), 221–29.

29. Ibid., 224.

30. Ibid., 227.

31. Ibid., 228.

32. Margarida Vale de Gato, "Poetics and Ideology in Fernando Pessoa's Translations of Edgar Allan Poe," *The Edgar Allan Poe Review* 11, no. 1 (2010): 127; Emron Esplin and Margarida Vale De Gato, eds., *Translated Poe* (Bethlehem: Lehigh University Press, 2014), xi.

33. Margarida Vale de Gato, "Poe Translations in Portugal: A Standing Challenge for Changing Literary Systems," in *Translated Poe*, ed. Emron Esplin and Margarida Vale de Gato (Bethlehem: Lehigh University Press, 2014), 4.

34. Ibid., 5.

35. Ibid., 5–6.

36. Ibid., 9.

37. Margarida Vale de Gato, "'Around Reason Feeling': Poe's Impact on Fernando Pessoa's Modernist Proposal," in *Poe's Pervasive Influence*, ed. Barbara Cantalupo (Bethlehem: Lehigh University Press, 2012), 92.

38. Ibid.

39. Ibid., 99.

40. Ibid.

41. Ibid., 100, 106.

42. Margarida Vale de Gato and Maria Antónia Lima, "From the Guest Editors," *The Edgar Allan Poe Review* 11, no. 1 (2010): 6, 7; see Vale de Gato, "Poetics and Ideology," 121–30.

43. Margarida Vale de Gato, "Poe's 'Nevermore,' Lisbon's Ravens, and the Portuguese Ideology of *Saudade*," in *Trans/American, Trans/Oceanic, Trans/lation: Issues in International American Studies*, ed. Susana Araújo, João Ferreira Duarte, and Marta Pacheco Pinto (Cambridge: Cambridge Scholars Publishing, 2010), 219.

44. Ibid., 228, 219.

45. Ibid., 229.

46. Renata Philippov, "Poe in Brazil: The Case of 'The Fall of the House of Usher,'" in *Translated Poe*, ed. Emron Esplin and Margarida Vale de Gato (Bethlehem: Lehigh University Press, 2014), 243–44, 249.

47. Renata Philippov, "Edgar Allan Poe and Machado de Assis—How Did Machado Read Poe?" *The Comparatist* 35 (2011): 222–23.

48. Ibid., 225.

49. Ibid.

50. Renata Philippov, "Blurring Borders: The Self, the Wanderer and the Observer in Edgar Allan Poe, Charles Baudelaire and Machado de Assis," *AmeriQuests* 12, no. 1 (2015): 1.

51. Ibid., 1.

52. Margarita Rigal-Aragón, "A Historical Approach to the Translations of Poe's Narrative Works in Spain," in *Translated Poe*, ed. Emron Esplin and Margarida Vale de Gato (Bethlehem: Lehigh University Press, 2014), 13.

53. Ibid., 19.

54. Ibid., 20.

55. Ibid., 23.

56. Margarita Rigal-Aragón, "Spanish 'Misreadings' of Poe's Life and Works at the Beginning of the Twenty-first Century," *The Edgar Allan Poe Review* 10, no. 2 (2009): 37.

57. Ibid., 38.

58. Ibid., 40.

59. Ibid., 41.

60. Ibid., 42–43.

61. Ibid., 43.

62. Beatriz González-Moreno and Margarita Rigal-Aragón, eds., *A Descent into Edgar Allan Poe and His Works: The Bicentennial* (Bern: Peter Lang, 2010), xvi–xvii.

63. Margarita Rigal-Aragón, "The *Thousand-and-Second* Dupin of Edgar A. Poe," in *A Descent into Edgar Allan Poe and His Works: The Bicentennial*, ed. Margarita Rigal-Aragón and Beatriz González-Moreno (Bern: Peter Lang, 2010), 51. For her earlier work on this subject, see "Dupin and Quinn 'Deconstructing' the North American Detective Character," in *Popular Texts in English*, ed. Lucía Mora and Antonio Ballesteros (Cuenca: Servicio de Publicaciones de la Universidad de Castilla-La Mancha, 2001): 203–13; and Margarita Rigal-Aragón and Beatriz González-Moreno, "The Detective Narration: Another of Poe's Legacies," *Nexus/Aedean* 1 (2009): 91–96.

64. Ibid., 55.

65. Ibid., 54.

66. José Manuel Correoso-Rodenas and Margarita Rigal-Aragón, "Poe's Spaces and *The Following*," *Studia Neophilologica* 89 (2017): 14–33.

67. Margarita Rigal-Aragón and Fernando González-Moreno, "Poe and the Art of Painting: Tales to Be Seen—The First Spanish Illustrated Edition," *The Edgar Allan Poe Review* 19, no. 1 (2018), 7.

68. Ibid., 22.

69. Lois Davis Vines, *Poe and Valéry: A Literary Legacy* (New York: New York University Press, 1992), 1.

70. Ibid., 1.

71. Ibid., 3.

72. Ibid., 3.

73. Ibid., 76.

74. Ibid., 82.

75. Ibid., 8.

76. Lois Davis Vines, "Charles Baudelaire," in *Poe Abroad: Influence, Reputation, Affinities*, ed. Lois Davis Vines (Iowa City: Iowa University Press, 1999), 168.

77. Lois Davis Vines, "Poe in France," in *Poe Abroad: Influence, Reputation, Affinities*, ed. Lois Davis Vines (Iowa City: Iowa University Press, 1999), 14.

78. Ibid., 16.

79. Lois Davis Vines, "Poe Translations in France," in *Translated Poe*, ed. Emron Esplin and Margarida Vale de Gato (Bethlehem: Lehigh University Press, 2014), 47–54.

80. Lois Davis Vines, "Rabelais and Lesage," in *Edgar Allan Poe in Context*, ed. Kevin J. Hayes (Cambridge: Cambridge University Press, 2013), 232.

81. Ibid., 234.

82. Ibid., 236.

83. Ibid., 236.

84. Ibid., 237.

85. Lois Davis Vines, Introduction to *Poe Abroad: Influence, Reputation, Affinities*, ed. Lois Davis Vines (Iowa City: Iowa University Press, 1999), 4.

Chapter Five

"Can You See Me?"

Poe's Female Characters and the Struggle for Self-Definition on Film

Alexandra Reuber

Many of Edgar Allan Poe's tales exemplify the narrator's encounter with the Other, which represents opposition to what is known, identifiable, and accepted. Its existence puts conventions into question, demands a reevaluation of established social roles, and exemplifies that identity is not fixed but a fluid concept that is formed through engagement with difference. In "Morella" (1835), "Berenice" (1835), and "The Black Cat" (1843), the Other finds representation in the female character who is often initially voiceless, passive, and inferior to the male counterpart. Signaling submission, her silence suggests her dependent role in "the masculine universe," sets her apart from a speaking man, and reduces her to an objective status within the text.[1] This situation gives the impression that the male narrator "is the true central character" of the text, which his domineering voice controls.[2] Yet, in each of these stories, the narrator suffers from a nervous agitation that takes hold of him like "a forbidden spirit" and leads him to question his understanding of himself and of his surroundings.[3] His mind is seemingly rattled by the existence of the female figure, who revolts against a nineteenth-century androcentric society and (silently) questions its societal norms and gender roles. By doing so, she opposes the "historical situation" and perception of womanhood as well as the respective cultural construction of identity and agency.[4] Initially presented "as an *object* rather than the subject of constitutive acts," she actually establishes her own voice from within the text and slowly outgrows her previously imposed inferior position.[5] This "episodic autonomy" leaves behind a deeply disturbed narrator, who no longer is able to control his nervousness.[6] "As a strategy of survival," he either attempts to "compel the [female] body to conform to an historical idea of 'woman'" or exhibits uncontrollable aggression toward her.[7]

This struggle of self-direction and definition has intrigued filmmakers for decades but has never been better expressed than in three recent cinematographic adaptations of Poe's stories: Jeff Ferrell's *Edgar Allan Poe's "Morella"* (2008), Vlad Latosh's *Berenice* (2015), and Stuart Gordon's *The Black Cat* (2007).[8] While keeping "the story [as] the common denominator," these adaptations feature female characters who challenge social conventions, gender roles, and the notion that identity and agency are "constrained by available historical conventions."[9] In each case, the male narrator misperceives the female body as Other, a symbolic reminder of a patriarchal society in which men wield power and treat females as objects. Nevertheless, the presence of the woman points toward the weakness and insufficiency the man senses within himself when exposed to her. Filled with anxiety, he not only objectifies but also introjects the female body to enrich himself without recognizing the risk this introjection-identification entails. Illustrating a woman's intellectual superiority to a man and the feminine personification of his personality disorders or fear of death, each film "bring[s] female specificity into visibility" and shows how the female character challenges the male subject while elevating her own social position.[10]

FERRELL'S *EDGAR ALLAN POE'S "MORELLA"* (2009)

Like many of Poe's tales, "Morella" features a male narrator who tells the reader about his personal life. However, he has experienced a family tragedy that makes him unique. His wife, Morella, died while giving birth to a daughter who took her mother's name. Grieving for his late beloved, the husband tells the tale of their marriage, and as narrator, he automatically occupies a position superior to the one held by his wife, leaving the reader with the impression that the account is *his* story. Morella speaks only once—a short time before her death. At that moment, she warns her husband that "the hours of thy happiness are over, and joy is not gathered twice in life," indicating that her passing will generate *his* endless "days of sorrow."[11] The narrator, who once defined himself through her, who allowed her interests to become his own in process of time, abandoned himself "implicitly to the guidance of [his] wife."[12] Following her death, he lost any sense of self-sufficiency and happiness. Although the narrator unconsciously alludes to *his* inferiority to Morella, Poe's text reduces *her* "to a single dimension," namely the intellect.[13] She appears lifeless and essentially voiceless, and she enjoys an intellectual existence only within the narrator's tale. In this respect, "Morella" dramatizes "the repressiveness of androcentric culture" of the nineteenth century, during which "upper- and middle-class women's choices were limited to marriage and motherhood, or spinsterhood."[14]

Succeeding where former adaptations of the tale like Roger Corman's and Jim Wynorski's failed, Jeff Ferrell's version gives the female character a powerful presence that is true to life. Corman's "Morella" and Wynorski's *The Haunting of Morella* showcase beautiful but evil-minded women who physically or spiritually feed on younger women. In Wynorski's adaptation, Morella engages in occult practices and human sacrifice with the sole goal of obtaining eternal youth, and in Corman's film, she seeks to gain power and strength by accessing her daughter's and her husband's thoughts. Consequently, both films turn Morella into a grim supernatural being resembling a witch or vampire more than an actual woman of the nineteenth century. As a result, Corman and Wynorski misrepresent the female to the extent that she becomes a harbinger of evil who, according to folklore, can be destroyed only by fire. Her domineering and forceful presence, which supersedes her husband's mundane existence, provides the viewer with a better understanding neither of his mental state nor of gender roles within nineteenth-century society.

Ferrell's cinematographic interpretation of Poe's story does, however, illuminate those subjects. In that film, Morella is depicted as beautiful, "delicate[,] and weak."[15] Moreover, she exhibits "great self-control" and fulfills her social duty of motherhood, honoring obligations that many antebellum Americans "valued as the most fulfilling and essential of all women's duties."[16] That said, Ferrell's Morella also revolts against social conventions of Poe's time. She opposes male dominance and refuses to be described solely by a man and reduced to the status of a character in *his* story, the role that she plays in Poe's tale. In Ferrell's film, Morella leaves her subordinate role behind, appearing the equal—and in some cases, the superior—of her husband. For example, she sits next to him on a garden bench, holds hands with him while walking in the garden, reads to him in front of the fireplace, points out illustrations to him while gently pushing his hand aside, stands behind him while he plays the piano, and after her death, places a spectral hand on his shoulder while he sits at her dressing table. These actions illustrate that, despite being confined by the cultural and historical norms of womanhood, Morella exhibits "episodic autonomy" in "isolated situations."[17] Her husband, however, does not.

Throughout the 09:33 minutes of the film, Morella appears on screen a total of 05:55 minutes, roughly 58 percent of the total run time. This prominence reflects the husband's fascination with Morella's beauty, elegance, and curiosity, which grows until he realizes that she surpasses him in intelligence. Furthermore, her presence and intellectual superiority illustrate her influence over his underdeveloped self, which derives "from the integration of multiple self-images" and "an integrated view of the other."[18] As her pupil, he blindly abandons himself to her guidance, adopting her views, decisions, and tastes as his own.[19] Her dying words—"I will never leave you"—underline this psychic attachment.[20]

Yet, despite Ferrell's devotion of screen time to Morella and his corresponding emphasis on the husband's subjective dependence, Morella often appears as "prone to fainting and illness" and exhibits the frailty that many nineteenth-century Americans associated with womanhood.[21] However, Morella's physical weakness in the film suggests the husband's subjectivity crisis, which results from the merging of "the self and other" or from a definition of the self through the Other.[22] It is this "despairing loss of self" that actually draws the viewer's attention to Morella's power, not her weakness.[23]

Ferrell visualizes the husband's increasing loss of selfhood and autonomy by placing him in a subordinate position to his wife, thus stressing the woman's increasing agency. Only in the first one and a half minutes does the narrator seem the equal of his spouse. Here, he sits next to Morella on a stone bench, and he reads and walks through the gardens alongside her. Nonetheless, this seemingly equal relationship between husband and wife soon changes, and the viewer realizes that *he* follows *her*. She is the agent, who seeks out "pockets of autonomy" that allow for "partial access to and expression of the self" in an androcentric society.[24] At 01:38 minutes, he sits on the ground and looks up to *her* while she reads to him. Some minutes later, Ferrell shows *her* removing her husband's hand from the book. In both instances, Morella wields intellectual power over the man even though "the mind [was] associated with the masculine" during the nineteenth century.[25] By doing so, Morella assumes the role of lead character in the story and sets herself apart from her husband as well as from her own sex because, in the antebellum world, "intellectual women . . . were condemned as 'unfeminine.'"[26] Consequently, she is the one who engages in othering, rhetorically and socially. Moreover, her empowerment leads to the castration of her husband, a symbol of his inferiority to her. Her dominance over the man is evident in two additional moments. In one of these, Morella makes the patronizing gesture of standing behind him and placing her hand on his shoulder while he plays the piano. The second occurs amidst her death throes when she pulls herself up above her husband and whispers "I will never leave you" into his ear.[27]

Promise or threat, these words find fulfillment in the birth of her daughter, who not only carries her mother's name but also looks, behaves, and dresses exactly like her maternal forebear. The mirror image of her mother, young Morella functions as her mother's double, and as such, she reasserts the domineering presence of the female in her father's life. On the one hand, young

Morella's existence reminds the narrator of his sorrow and unhappiness after his wife's passing. Thus, the daughter prolongs the father's mourning. On the other hand, her presence further symbolizes his fragmented state of self and consequential lack of identity, an insufficiency he once sought to resolve through introjection-identification of the child's mother. No matter the reading, the father transfers his inner conflict onto the child, who loses her own status as independent subject and steadily becomes the shadow figure of her dead mother until the child herself dies. Like her mother, young Morella exerts power over her father, who attempts to define himself through her. Young Morella, then, is the embodiment of her mother's exclamation—"I will never leave you!"—*and* of her father's projective identification causing self-fragmentation.[28] In addition, her presence emphasizes the man's grief and is a constant reminder of a passage in Poe's original text, in which Morella claims: "the hours of thy happiness are over."[29]

The last two minutes of the film convey the emotional and psychological implications of these words. Here, Ferrell shows the widower sitting at his wife's dressing table. Entranced, the man stares into the mirror for ten seconds, looks down, and sees objects dear to his wife: a small mirror, a hairbrush, and a ring. While he touches her comb, the body of his deceased wife materializes. Standing behind him and placing her left hand on his shoulder, she seemingly encourages him to look into the mirror, which consists of three individual glass panels representing the past, the present, and the future. This scene serves as a visual confirmation of Morella's assertion, "I will never leave you," and of her power to suppress her husband's voice, to undermine his identity, and to force him to tell *her* story.[30] It is the story of the wife and mother "that has previously gone untold."[31] To this narrative usurpation the husband consents, leaning back against her body, closing his eyes, and reminiscing. For the first time in the film, the man smiles. He is at peace with himself. When the camera turns and the screen darkens, a medium shot reveals him sitting alone in front of the mirror with his eyes closed. The message of Ferrell's adaptation is clear: even though the widower has lost his autonomy as well as the fight to assert his patriarchal power over the female, he seems content to have found "enhanced self-acceptance and a greater ability to tolerate [his previously] ambivalent emotional states."[32]

VLAD LATOSH'S *BERENICE* (2015)

Poe's short story "Berenice," in which the male narrator Egaeus unconsciously introjects and negates the female body, opens with a woman's oppression and ends with her agency. Throughout Poe's text, Berenice is utterly silent. She apparently has a tenuous existence, a body that first is "agile, graceful, and overflowing with energy" but that later suffers from a transformation of "her mind, her habits, and her character . . . disturbing even the identity of her person!"[33] Escaping any characteristic denominator that could inform the reader about her personality, she becomes the "perfect figure of negative identity," taking on the role of a shadow character in a patriarchal narrative featuring a deathbed mutilation, an indignity that underlines Berenice's subjective insignificance in a man's world.[34]

Nevertheless, it does not take the reader long to discover that her transformation reflects Egaeus's changing psychological condition and relates to his disease, which is, he acknowledges, a form of monomania. This disorder manifests itself in his obsessions with the fantasies outlined in books, Berenice's ethereal presence, and her teeth. His "pathological obsession with one idea or subject" distorts his perception to the extent that "the realities of the world affected [him] as visions, and as visions only, while the wild ideas of the land of dreams became, in turn . . . that existence utterly and solely in itself."[35] In other words, infatuation with fantasy renders the narrator incapable of distinguishing between "real and illusion, dream and reality, conscious and unconscious, natural and supernatural, masculine and feminine," and that failure keeps him from seeing Berenice as a real person.[36] Described as a being of a dream, of a memory, just "like a shadow—vague, variable, indefinite, unsteady," she is there but not there, and she appears to live only within the parameters of the narrator's mind.[37] Representing something that stems from within "the disordered chamber of [his] brain," she apparently personifies a repressed fear the narrator is either unable to pronounce or unwilling to admit.[38] It is a fear expressed through his words, which suggest darkness, sorrow, and death.

That fear finds its ultimate representation in Berenice and in the tale's dominant images: her teeth. These objects penetrate the narrator's well-being, becoming first "the essence of [his] mental life" and later the harbinger of his mental degradation.[39] Appearing "here, and there, and everywhere," her teeth soon become the narrator's sole identifiers as well as omnipresent threats to his physical and mental existence.[40] The teeth thus symbolize change or the fear of that change, a transformation signaled by the narrator's utterance: "I had died."[41] Thus, Berenice is Other, not only because she is a woman but also because she functions as the narrator's double, whose "unhappy malady" and physical deterioration mirror his psychological decline.[42] Seemingly belonging to the imaginary realm that lies beyond verbal expression, she embodies the narrator's all-consuming fear of death represented powerfully by "[t]he teeth!—the teeth!"[43]

Although Poe's narrator names Berenice sixteen times and alludes to her seven times through references to her teeth, it is Vlad Latosh's short film *Berenice,* narrated by Vincent Price that stresses the titular character's destabilizing effect on her male counterpart. In this film, which lasts 17:34 minutes, Berenice is on screen for a total of 05:01 minutes. She appears in various places—outside Egaeus's dilapidated house, inside one of its labyrinthine hallways, and in the middle of the library—and in various forms (i.e., a body at the end of a couloir, a figure within a painting, a face in the mirror, a corpse in a coffin, and the reduced form of extracted teeth placed on a spoon or kept in a box).[44] The visualization of place, in combination with shots of the female character inside and outside of Egaeus's house, is indicative of his physical and mental condition. Berenice inhabits everything that once was known and familiar to him and "disturbs any straightforward sense of what is inside and outside."[45] She ushers him into the shadows of his mind, where reality, dream, and illusion—as well as self and Other—collide, and by doing so, she triggers his fear of death. It is a fear that the text insinuates but that the film explores.

On screen, Egaeus reacts to his fearful thoughts expressed in his books and nourished in the confined world of his library, the architectural manifestation of his highly imaginative and disturbed mind. It is here, in the turret of his dilapidated house, that Latosh introduces Berenice, whom Egaeus desires, objectifies, introjects, and eventually fears. She haunts his psyche, prompting the reevaluation of ideas, perceptions, and actions. For instance, Latosh repeatedly projects Berenice's face, then her white teeth, through close-ups against the backdrop of the library. He combines them with black-and-white art sketches of floating skeletons, teeth, and skulls that transform into drawings of monsters latching onto each other, creatures conveying the narrator's "dread and horror."[46] These close-ups constitute the female body as a composite dream figure personifying Egaeus's occupied mind, which is filled with imagery from books and thoughts of death. Because Berenice was "born" and "framed" in the library, it is no surprise that this room is the location she seeks out the most. A place that can be reached only by a long, narrow, dark hallway, the library represents the unconscious. Due to its general inaccessibility, Latosh portrays the room as a dimly lit or even dark place that triggers Egaeus's "wild ideas" and nourishes his "most intense and abnormal meditation": his fear of death, which Berenice represents.[47] As such, Berenice is nontangible yet there. Like his books, her mere presence causes Egaeus to question being and becoming; thus, he simultaneously desires and fears her. Berenice then is an internal *and* external being who silently but visually informs the viewer of Egaeus's "morbid irritability of those properties of the mind . . . termed the *attentive*," his fear of death.[48] Consequently, the library represents the birth chamber of his latent fears, which promote bodily disease and bewilderment.

To represent Egaeus's growing confusion, Latosh juxtaposes low-angle and eye-level medium shots with high-angle dolly shots, capturing the library, the books, and the female body before zooming in and out on the narrator's face or focusing on the framed picture of a woman in the library. Later, he captures Berenice moving around freely, inside and outside of the house. Allowing her to leave the confined space of the picture, Latosh not only frees Berenice from her subordinate and restricted position but also permits her to constitute "a reality that in some sense is new" to her and to the narrator, a reality where *she* dominates *his* house and library as well as *his* "disordered chamber," which symbolizes his mind.[49] Thus, Latosh instills in Berenice a novel agency and allows her to take charge of the story.[50]

Latosh's film conveys Berenice's unsettling, dominating presence in a long scene in the library. Something at the door startles Egaeus, who looks up from the pages of a book with a devil on its cover. Before disclosing what has captured his attention, the camera cuts to a portrait of Berenice in which she poses with a close-lipped smile. As Egaeus's eyes adjust to the darkness created by shadows, Berenice comes into his view as well as the audience's. The camera zooms in on her face. At first, all of its features are visible, and the lips conceal her teeth. Next, the camera cuts to a close-up of Egaeus, who seems puzzled. When the camera cuts back to Berenice, thick tresses of hair cover her eyes and frame her mouth, the lips of which form a grin revealing her teeth. Egaeus immediately has a flashback to the moment he proposed to Berenice, and the viewer sees tears running down his cheek. Then the camera returns a final time to the grinning Berenice. This shot sequence recalls two passages from Poe's text: "[I]n an evil moment, I spoke to her of marriage" and "The shutting of a door disturbed me, and, looking up, I found my cousin had departed from the chamber. But from the disordered chamber of my brain, had not, alas! departed, and would not be driven away, the white and ghastly spectrum of the teeth."[51] This connection between Berenice, her teeth, and death is beautifully underscored in the film's editing. The director ends the scene in the library and follows it with Egaeus encountering "a servant maiden" who informs him "that Berenice [is]—no more."[52]

As Egaeus's own death approaches, Latosh symbolically references the end of life through a series of long shots in soft focus. The audience sees the lake in the evening hours, low lighting in the house, and a camera, tilted and shaking, zooms in on Egaeus's face when he descends the steep staircase prior to proceeding through the subterranean vaults to a tomb. The camera focuses on funerary objects, including candles, a casket, and a mirror covered by a black shawl. This covered mirror is the first object the narrator encounters upon reaching the underground room. The black shawl blocks any reflection, even his own, suggesting that Egaeus's death is near. This reality finds symbolic representation in his position as well as in the open casket holding Berenice's dead body. Egaeus first gazes down at Berenice's corpse, but seconds later, she looks up into the eyes of her beholder, symbolically rising from her position of inferiority to usurp his personality, his voice, and ultimately his sanity. The following alternation between long-lasting close-ups of the narrator's face and of freshly extracted teeth—objects that stand for consummation, annihilation, and transcendence—lying on the narrator's spoon further suggest Berenice's increasing dominance of the narrator's thoughts as well as "the theoretical death of an old, fixed subject, and the birth of a new, constructed one characterized by subversive possibility and agency."[53]

Latosh underlines this transcendence and the power transfer when presenting Egaeus's as well as Berenice's images within a framed mirror reflecting the narrator in the foreground and a woman looking over his shoulder in the background. The director's message is clear: not only has Egaeus entered the realm where all objects such as books, paintings, and teeth represent Berenice, but he has also succumbed to the command and control of the Other, whose place of origin is that realm of the imagination closely connected to his perceptions.[54] His loss of selfhood is evident when he blows out the only candle illuminating his room. Surrounded by darkness, Berenice's face emerges first in soft then in deep focus before disappearing completely in the dark library while Vincent Price's eerie voice repeats the phrases "des sentiments" and "des idées."[55]

Latosh's subsequent juxtaposition of close-ups (e.g., Egaeus's face and Berenice's, Berenice's body and open books, as well as Berenice's face and the small box holding her teeth) further visualizes her psychological power over Egaeus. In addition, Latosh uses shots to emphasize the effect her agency and dominance have on him. A close-up of a drawing showing a monster consuming bodies—a visual allegory for the narrator's all-consuming fear of death—precedes the final scene, in which he runs through the dark, tortuous passageways of his house. It is Egaeus's final attempt to escape from his fear of death represented by Berenice, her teeth, and the artwork in his home.

Like Ferrell's short film "Morella," Latosh's adaptation of Poe's "Berenice" rattles the author's original tale and challenges the notion "of woman as a selfless, passive object."[56] Despite the fact that in both films Morella and Berenice are "portrayed as delicate and weak, prone to fainting and illness," they are strong-willed and refuse to be obedient.[57] In addition, instead of being silenced by their husbands, both women take on "the roles of teachers," enlightening their male counterparts about themselves.[58] By doing so, these women step out of the shadows and assume roles of empowerment. While "exercising self-direction," they express their agency and reduce the once-domineering male narrators "to conditions of passivity" previously associated with femininity.[59] As a consequence, the male narrators lose their ability to communicate, relating their losses to insanity.[60]

GORDON'S *THE BLACK CAT* (2007)

This loss is nowhere else better outlined than in Poe's short story "The Black Cat," a story that Stuart Gordon reimagines as an account of a man suffering from writer's block and the fear of professional extinction. In the original tale, Poe strips the narrator's anonymous and "uncomplaining wife" of any personal identifiers, not even granting her an opportunity to speak.[61] She is mentioned only when needed before being killed and walled up. Even the story's title underlines her subordinate position within the tale. Whereas the titles "Morella" and "Berenice" carry the names of the female characters, "The Black Cat" does not. Furthermore, the unnamed woman's relationship with her insane husband remains undeveloped in Poe's tale. In a similar vein, the film adaptations of "The Black Cat" by Roger Corman, Dario Argento, and Rob Green also leave unexplored the effect of the wife on the male narrator.

Gordon's fifty-minute film *The Black Cat* is, however, different. This adaptation presents an alcohol-dependent narrator whose mental and emotional instability leads to violent outbursts directed at animals and at people close to him. To underline the man's irritability, Gordon juxtaposes the narrator's mood swings with the kindness and good heartedness as well as the mental and emotional strength of his wife, Sissy (Poe's affectionate name for his wife, Virginia). Unlike Poe but like Argento, Gordon gives the woman a name, assigning her a major role in the story. Both women—Annabel in Argento's film and Sissy in Gordon's—differ significantly from their partners. These women are emotionally present, understanding, truthful, and artistic, but their partners—Rod Usher in Argento's film and Eddy (i.e., Edgar Allan Poe) in Gordon's—are absent-minded and emotionally unavailable alcoholics who are professionally unsuccessful. Beyond these similarities, Gordon's film differs from Argento's. Whereas Argento concentrates on Rod's substance-fueled rage, Gordon elaborates on the origins of Eddy's addiction and its effects on his private and professional lives. In this respect, Gordon's work resembles Roger Corman's adaptation of "The Black Cat" (from his film *Tales of Terror*), which dramatizes the psychologically destructive effects of alcohol. Significantly, the reason for the man's addiction is missing in Corman's film. Thus, Corman does not offer the viewer any insight into the alcoholic's troubled psyche.

Gordon's film corrects this oversight, providing the viewer with a profound understanding of Eddy's inner conflicts—turmoil that he tries to escape by drinking. While intoxicated, Eddy loses touch with reality. In addition, he exemplifies a "subjective distress and presence of social malfunctioning" that expresses itself in his uncontrollable spending and continuous lying about his whereabouts.[62] His "consistent irresponsibility" about working and fulfilling financial obligations illustrates his "reckless disregard" for social norms and etiquette.[63] This behavior contributes to his "affective instability" characterized by "intense episodic dysphoria," a condition that manifests itself in depression as well as frequent "displays of temper" directed at the black cat Pluto and his wife.[64] Looking at these character traits closely, one realizes that this man suffers from antisocial and borderline personality disorder (PD): "a pervasive pattern of instability across multiple domains, including affect, interpersonal relationships, and self-image."[65] The viewer also detects a strong correlation between the writer's psychic distress and his wife's declining health. Like Ferrell and Latosh, Gordon exposes degradation in Eddy's mental constitution that reflects his wife's physical decline, a link that is missing from previous adaptations of "The Black Cat."

At the very beginning of the film, Gordon establishes this correlation between physical and mental health. The film opens with Sissy lying in bed and listening attentively to her husband's poetry recital with Pluto beside her. Her facial expression is encouraging when she says, "Oh Eddy, that's beautiful."[66] This moment of intense admiration and encouraging support is, however, short-lived. Two minutes later, Sissy coughs up blood, and this first sign of her declining health parallels Eddy's growing emotional and mental instability. Gordon stresses this correlation via a series of alternating close-ups of Sissy's and Eddy's faces before homing in on her bloodstained white cushion, an image that foreshadows Eddy's loss of selfhood. As a symbolic manifestation of Eddy's self, Sissy personifies her husband's goodness and "tenderness of heart," softer traits of character that get pushed aside as his emotional instability worsens.[67]

For Gordon, the relationship between Sissy and Pluto is also significant. In his film, he introduces Sissy and Pluto simultaneously, but in Poe's text, the cat appears before the wife. Moreover, in the original tale, the narrator defines the cat as *his* "favorite pet and playmate," but in Gordon's film, Pluto is *Sissy's* companion, not Eddy's.[68] Throughout the film, the cat continually seeks her presence. He lies next to her in bed, sits on her chest during her death throes, and licks her expectorated blood from the floor, yet Pluto hisses at the narrator upon his approach, scratches and bites him, or runs away from him whenever the man is intoxicated. Argento's film features a similar relationship between the cat and his mistress, for the creature is peaceful in Annabel's arms but attacks or flees from Rod whenever he gets too close.

In Gordon's adaptation, cat and wife serve as one antagonistic force challenging Eddy's definition of self, a situation with no parallel in Argento's, Corman's, and Green's cinematic treatments of Poe's story. Argento leaves the viewer wondering about Annabel's overall role within the film as well as the reason for the sudden appearance of the black cat at the couple's door. At no point does the director explore the correlation between the couple's relationship troubles, Rod's increased alcohol consumption, his violent mood swings, and his sadistic treatment of Annabel and Pluto. Instead of examining the effect of the Other on Rod, Argento's film suggests that the man's anger and aggression directed at his spouse as well as the cat are merely the results of excessive drinking. A similar critique applies to Corman's and Green's adaptations of "The Black Cat." Neither one of these films elaborates on the functionality of the woman, on her power over the male character, or on her effect on his weak self-image. In addition, Green's and Corman's films even fail to establish a link between the cat and the wife.

Gordon's film is unique in that it represents woman and cat as what Emmanuel Levinas once called "the face of the other," and in the film, that entity "faces [the narrator] and puts [him] in question and obliges [him]" to confront his weaknesses and flaws.[69] Sissy's demands that Eddy not destroy his genius by drinking and Pluto's staring eyes compel the writer to question himself, to recognize his PD, and to acknowledge his shortcomings as a writer, husband, and gentleman. His reaction to this challenge is in line with the psychological properties of his antisocial and borderline PD. He exemplifies a "failure to conform to social norms" as well as "intense mood shifts" when engaging with his fellowmen at the bar or when being asked to pay his dues.[70] In addition, he shows "inappropriate, intense anger" at his editor's office and at home.[71]

Sissy's prefatory request, "Eddy write for me, please," then no longer has a comforting effect on him.[72] It rather reminds him of his personal failures and only accentuates his already highly conflicted self. Instead of being a provider to his wife and a respected author within the literary community, Eddy is a failed and abusive alcoholic writer. Moreover, instead of being a submissive and obedient wife exhibiting nineteenth-century social values, Sissy dares to speak up, exemplifying a new liberation and bodily agency that challenges not only the male narrator but also "the category of woman itself."[73] She addresses "situation-specific [problems] that occasion introspective reflection," trigger his self-doubt, and undermine his authority.[74] That authority destabilized, Eddy attacks Sissy, and in a dissociative state, he imagines taking an axe to her piano. This patriarchal fantasy represents Eddy's attempt to separate himself from the one who "awakens, accuses, and judges" him.[75] Anticipating his self-destruction and self-dissolution, that imagined act serves two purposes. First, it is an effort to suppress personal failures in his private life. As such, it is an attempt to regain control. Second, it provides relief from his profound anger at his wife and at everything she represents: softness, artistic talent, morality, and change.

Although Sissy maintains her social standing while opposing and disapproving of her husband's behavior at home, Eddy no longer follows the social etiquette associated with a "public man."[76] His behavior "deviates markedly from the expectations of the individual's culture."[77] As a nineteenth-century husband, he must provide for his wife, who finds herself in a "dependent situation."[78] As a famous writer, the narrator has the obligation to offer his readership a constant flow of "fantastic tales."[79] As a law-abiding citizen, he should respect and "honor financial obligations" to fellow citizens instead of exploiting them.[80] Nevertheless, he is a man whose writer's block and alcohol abuse fuel his PD and mark *him* as "Other." Socially, professionally, and emotionally marginalized, he finds himself in a position inferior to his wife's. To regain any sense of control, Gordon's Eddy needs to liberate himself from Sissy's judgment and the obligation to take responsibility for his actions and shortcomings. Perceiving wife and cat as one and the same, Eddy decides to cut out one of Pluto's eyes in order to eliminate Sissy's admonitory gaze, which challenges his being and becoming.[81] By doing so, Eddy extinguishes his moral conscience and suppresses the unpleasant feelings associated with his inferiority complex and unstable self-image.

Without considering the consequence "that repression of the softer tendencies will reinforce the aggressive ones, making them all the more compulsive," Eddy takes another step toward self-annihilation.[82] Convincing himself that only the death of Pluto will end his shame, he follows the cat into the dark cellar of the house, the symbol of Eddy's psyche. Once again, he takes up the axe in the attempt to separate himself from the burden of moral responsibility that Pluto personifies. He swings the axe at the black cat only to bury it in Sissy's skull, which splits in half. That splitting symbolizes Eddy's agonizing struggle between good and evil, between former and current self—a psychological struggle missing from the cinematic adaptations of "The Black Cat" mentioned above.

To ease his pain after the axe episode, he takes again a big sip out of a bottle before discovering both Sissy and Pluto unharmed in the room. When he realizes that he had only imagined the bloody deed, Eddy's previous anger and anxiety give way to joy and creativity. This dramatic shift in mood illustrates once more the emotional and mental instability characteristic of antisocial and borderline PD, yet Eddy seems to have realized that, despite social rules and values that privilege masculinity, it is *he* who finds himself in a "dependent situation," and that it is *he* who relies on his wife's moral guidance and supervision.[83] In short, he recognizes that he is inferior to his wife.

Like the narrator of "Morella," who finds inner peace after accepting a position inferior to that of his female counterpart, Eddy does so, too. He smiles and looks content when sitting at his desk with Sissy bending over him and Pluto lying next to his papers. Guided by his wife and cat, Eddy writes down the title of his next fantastic tale, "The Black Cat": a tale that expresses the man's family and professional situation and whose title refers to both cat and wife, *one* superior force that shifts from threatening the narrator to nurturing him.

By portraying the narrators as men whose identity crises derive from unhealthy relationships to their female counterparts, Ferrell's, Latosh's, and Gordon's adaptations subvert the gender hierarchies established in Poe's original tales. In each of these films, the seemingly unimportant female character of the text refuses to adhere any longer to "the tacit conventions that structure the way the body [of the woman] is culturally perceived," the tendency to see that body as naturally silent, submissive, subjectified.[84] By opposing feminine norms "circumscribed by historical convention," Morella, Berenice, and Sissy challenge male autonomy and superiority.[85] Changing places with men, these women assume voices and agency while forcing the male narrators to reassess their identities. Consequently, Morella, Berenice, and Sissy invade their male counterparts' egocentric monism and intensify their mental instability. In each film, the troubled male character, desperate to preserve an assumed sense of self, tries to free himself from the female presence and its influence. However, the attempt fails, for the woman returns "from a dimension that surpasses" the male beholder.[86] Having found her voice, she claims her superior status.

NOTES

1. Simone de Beauvoir, *The Second Sex*, trans. Constance Borde and Shelia Malovany-Chevallier (New York: Vintage, 2011), 725, 734.

2. Craig Howes, "The Fall of the House of Usher" and Elegiac Romance," *The Southern Literary Journal* 19, no. 1 (1986): 71.

3. Edgar Allan Poe, "Morella," in *The Complete Works of Edgar Allan Poe,* ed. James A. Harrison, vol. 2 (New York: AMS Press, 1965), 28.

4. Judith Butler, "Performative Acts and Gender Constitution: An Essay in Phenomenology and Feminist Theory," *Theatre Journal* 40, no. 4 (1988): 521.

5. Ibid., 519.

6. Kathryn Abrams, "From Autonomy to Agency: Feminist Perspectives on Self-Direction," *William & Mary Law Review: Institute of Bill of Rights Symposium. Reconstructing Liberalism* 40, no. 3 (1999): 814.

7. Butler, 522.

8. Examples are Roger Corman's *courts-métrages* "Morella" and "The Black Cat" in his film anthology *Tales of Terror* (1962), Dario Argento's film segment "The Black Cat" included in his portmanteau film *Two Evil Eyes* (1990), Jim Wynorski's movie *The Haunting of Morella* (1990), Rob Green's short film *The Black Cat* (2012), and James McTeigue's feature film *The Raven* (2012). Some of these more faithful to the original texts than others, the adaptations share common features: they depict the irritability of men who cannot control a woman's resistance to historical conventions

of womanhood, their agitation leading to severe depression, to heightened imagination, and to isolation from society—*or* to irrational verbal outbursts and aggressive behavior, even, in one case, to serial killing. Nevertheless, these films neither explore the psychological impact of an autonomous female character on her male counterpart nor challenge *his* false notions of selfhood and identity.

9. Linda Hutcheon, *A Theory of Adaptation* (New York: Routledge, 2006), 10; Butler, 521.

10. Ibid., 523.

11. Poe, "Morella," 30.

12. Ibid., 28.

13. Allan G. Johnson, *Privilege, Oppression, and Difference* (New York: McGraw Hill, 2006), 19.

14. Yonjae Jung, "The Return of the Real: A Lacanian Reading of Poe's Dying Women Stories," *American Studies in Scandinavia* 37, no. 1 (2005): 59; Susan M. Cruea, "Changing Ideals of Womanhood during the Nineteenth-Century Woman Movement," *General Studies Writing Faculty Publications* 1 (2005): 187.

15. Cruea, 189.

16. Ibid., 188.

17. Abrams, 814; Diana T. Meyers, "Personal Autonomy and the Paradox of Feminine Socialization," *The Journal of Philosophy* 84, no. 11 (1987): 624.

18. Althea Horner, *Psychoanalytic Object Relations Therapy* (Lanham, MD: Jason Aronson, 1991), 9, 27.

19. See Poe, "Morella," 28.

20. *Edgar Allan Poe's "Morella,"* YouTube video, directed by Jeff Ferrell (Seattle Film Institute: July 23, 2008), accessed December 3, 2018, https://www.youtube.com /watch?v=LguIwF48VGc.

21. Cruea, 189.

22. Mardi J. Horowitz, "Self-Identity Theory and Research Methods," *Journal of Research Practices* 8, no. 2 (2012): 5.

23. David E. Scharff, *Refinding the Object and Reclaiming the Self* (Lanham, MD: Jason Aronson, 1992), 27.

24. Meyers, 624–26.

25. Cruea, 189.

26. Ibid., 189.

27. Ferrell, *Edgar Allan Poe's "Morella."*

28. Ibid.

29. Poe, "Morella," 31.

30. Ferrell, *Edgar Allan Poe's "Morella."*

31. Cynthia S. Jordan, *Second Stories: The Politics of Language, Form, and Gender in Early American Fictions* (Chapel Hill: University of North Carolina Press, 1989), 135.

32. Horowitz, 4.

33. Edgar Allan Poe, "Berenice," in *The Complete Works of Edgar Allan Poe,* ed. James A. Harrison, vol. 2 (New York: AMS Press, 1965), 18.

34. Judith Halberstam, *Skin Shows: Gothic Horror and the Technology of Monsters* (Durham: Duke University Press, 2000), 73.

35. Ibid.; Poe, "Berenice," 17.

36. Jung, "Return of the Real," 58.

37. Poe, "Berenice," 17.

38. Ibid., 23.

39. Ibid., 24.

40. Ibid., 23.

41. Ibid., 23.

42. Ibid., 21.

43. Ibid., 23.

44. If one counts the images of death paraphernalia and books, objects that are closely tied to the female Other, Berenice's onscreen time is 07:48 minutes.

45. Nicholas Royle, *The Uncanny* (New York: Routledge, 2003), 2.

46. Sigmund Freud, "Papers on Applied Psychoanalysis. The Uncanny," in *Collected Papers*, vol. 4, trans. Joan Rivière (London: Hogarth Press, 1949), 368.

47. Poe, "Berenice," 21.

48. Ibid., 19.

49. Butler, 527; Poe, "Berenice," 23.

50. Similar observations can be made of McTeigue's 2012 film *The Raven*, in which the main female character, Emily Hamilton, dominates the male mind, especially after being kidnapped at her father's masquerade ball. First silenced and dominated by her father, then objectified and sexualized by her lover Edgar, Emily is a woman whose physical absence torments both men. Their effort to find her—the object of their affection—is the narrative core of the film. Although the fear of her death immobilizes Emily's father and lover, Emily's own fear of death drives her to fight for her life. Her attempt to free herself from the small wooden box, in which her captor places her, symbolizes her desire to escape the social constraints of nineteenth-century womanhood. Whereas Berenice rises from her position of inferiority and supersedes male autonomy, Emily does not. Her inability to free herself represents her bondage to social expectations that involve female subordination to patriarchal power. Nevertheless, Emily's fear suggests that those expectations are problematic. The men's fear, however, signals their anxiety about the potential loss of autonomy as well as their dependence on the female body, the external object through which they seek identification. Present or absent, Emily and Berenice dominate the narratives in which they appear and the minds of men whom they haunt.

51. Poe, "Berenice," 22–23.

52. "Edgar Allan Poe's 'Berenice,'" YouTube video, directed by Vlad Latosh (Latosh, 2015), accessed December 3, 2018, https://www.youtube.com/watch?v=BTm0i9k12Ig&t=10s.

53. Sara Salih, "On Judith Butler and Performativity," in *Judith Butler* (New York: Routledge, 2002): 59, http://www2.kobe-u.ac.jp/~alexroni/IPD2020/IPD2020%20No.2/Salih-Butler-Performativity-Chapter_3.pdf

54. Poe, "Berenice," 24.

55. Ibid., 24.

56. Jung, "The Return of the Real," 59.

57. Cruea, 189.

58. Ibid., 191.

59. Abrams, 823; Leland S. Person, *Aesthetic Headaches: Women and a Masculine Poetics in Poe, Melville, and Hawthorne* (Athens: University of Georgia Press, 1988), 175.

60. See Christopher Benfey, "Poe and the Unreadable: 'The Black Cat' and 'The Tell-Tale Heart,'" in *New Essays on Poe's Major Tales*, ed. Kenneth Silverman (Cambridge: Cambridge University Press, 1993), 30.

61. Edgar Allan Poe, "The Black Cat," in *The Complete Works of Edgar Allan Poe*, ed. James A. Harrison, vol. 5 (New York: AMS Press, 1965), 152.

62. Paul Emmelkamp and Jan Henk Camphuis, *Personality Disorders* (New York: Psychology Press, 2007), 4.

63. Ibid., 10.

64. Ibid., 11.

65. Ibid., 11.

66. *Masters of Horror*, "The Black Cat," directed by Stuart Gordon (Starz Media, January 19, 2007), 3:47, accessed, December 3, 2018, https://www.amazon .com/Family/dp/B0016BN9NM/ref=sr_1_2?ie=UTF8&qid=1545272857&sr=8–2 &keywords=masters+of+horror+season+2. In this scene, Sissy bears some resemblance to Emily Hamilton, an important character in the aforementioned film *The Raven*. Like Hamilton and the female audience attending a poetry recitation by Poe, Sissy is an attentive and admiring listener to the poet, a man with a fragile ego who is highly dependent on audience approval.

67. Poe, "The Black Cat," 143.

68. Ibid., 144.

69. Emmanuel Levinas, *Totality and Infinity: An Essay on Exteriority*, trans. Alphonso Lingis (Dordrecht: Kluwer Academic Publishers, 1991), 207.

70. Emmelkamp and Camphuis, 11.

71. *National Institute of Mental Health*, s.v. "Borderline Personality Disorder," last modified 2017, accessed December 20, 2018, https://www.nimh.nih.gov/health/topics /borderline-personality-disorder/index.shtml.

72. *Masters of Horror*, "The Black Cat."

73. Butler, 523.

74. Meyers, "Personal Autonomy and the Paradox of Feminine Socialization," 625.

75. Adriaan Peperzak, *To the Other: An Introduction to the Philosophy of Emmanuel Levinas* (West Lafayette: Purdue University Press, 1993), 25.

76. Glenna Matthews, *The Rise of Public Women: Woman's Power and Woman's Place in the United States, 1630–1970* (New York: Oxford University Press, 1992), 4.

77. Emmelkamp and Camphuis, 2.

78. Cruea, 187.

79. *Masters of Horror*, "The Black Cat."

80. Emmelkamp and Camphuis, 10.

81. Although the removal of one of Pluto's eyes is a key moment in Poe's text, it is missing from Corman's adaptation. Without this scene, the man's abusive and

aggressive tendencies toward the Other are not evident before the murder of his wife. Consequently, the husband's slowly intensifying madness—so pronounced in the tale—is not sufficiently illustrated in Corman's adaptation. For that reason, his film denies viewers a deeper understanding of the relationship between the disturbed male self and the female Other.

82. Karen Horney, *Our Inner Conflicts: A Constructive Theory of Neurosis* (New York: Norton, 1966), 71.

83. Cruea, 187.

84. Butler, 524.

85. Ibid., 521.

86. Peperzak, 20.

Chapter Six

"And She Grew Strangely"

Poe, Women, and Comics

John Edward Martin

The wide variety of comic book and graphic novel adaptations of Poe's work over the past near-century offers fertile ground for a range of interpretations and re-imaginings that both pay homage to the originals and expand their artistic, philosophical, and cultural horizons, particularly in regard to the roles of women as characters in and creators of these texts. Just as scholars have re-examined how women are figured as influences, inspirations, audiences, critics, and interpreters of Poe's work, comics creators have performed a similar revisioning of Poe through the forms and tropes of a popular culture medium. The survey of recent comics and graphic novel adaptations below reveals not only how these artists tackle the challenges of adaptation on a formal and contextual level, but also how they depict Poe's women characters in new, sometimes subversive, ways. Beginning with the particular challenges of adapting Poe's literary work into comics form and proceeding to the ways that various creators, particularly women, have used that form to reimagine Poe's tales, this chapter suggests that comics adaptations provide a rich vein of inquiry for understanding the relationship between gender and form in Poe. The process of adaptation into the visual, spatial, and linguistic registers of the comics medium necessarily involves a transformation of the original texts that mirrors, in many ways, the transformations of Poe's women into haunting, disruptive, and revelatory presences for both Poe's narrators and for audiences. Of particular interest in this essay is how women creators have adapted Poe's tales to their own personal and cultural contexts in order to address some of Poe's appropriations, or misappropriations, of women's experience that Eliza Richards and others have noted, including his depictions of female bodies, agency, and relationships.[1]

*****

"Gosh, when you mess up an introduction, there's no telling *what* trouble you're causing."[2] It is a fair warning delivered by Mag the Hag, a horror host in the tradition of The Crypt-Keeper or Cousin Eerie, who serves as spectator, narrator, and occasional participating character in *Spirits of the Dead* (2014), a graphic anthology of Poe's stories adapted and illustrated by Richard Corben. Mag's comment offers an ironic postscript to Corben's adaptation of "Morella," Poe's tale of transposed identities and the potential power of a woman to transgress the boundary between life and death. The "introduction" Mag refers to is the pivotal moment when Morella's daughter (named "Orella" here) is introduced by the narrator as "Morella." Upon hearing the name, the young woman—who has assumed the appearance of her dead mother and become the narrator's forbidden lover—grips her throat in agony and falls to the ground a decaying corpse, screeching, "You fool! You've killed me!"

It is not the introduction, of course, but the revelation of Morella's reincarnation in her daughter's body that breaks the spell and plunges the narrator into his own fit of madness and regret. By acknowledging both her arcane power and his own transgressive sin (i.e., treating the daughter *as if* she were the mother), he suddenly realizes the grim irony of Morella's revenge: he has killed the daughter with his desire, just as he killed the mother by withholding it. As penance, he hurls himself from a cliff and plunges into the churning waters below—all the while clinging to Orella's rotting corpse. A messy introduction, indeed!

Many details of this adaptation differ from material in the tale familiar to Poe fans. In the original story, Poe writes:

> Yet, as she had foretold, her child—to which in dying she had given birth, and which breathed not until the mother breathed no more—her child, a daughter, lived. And she grew strangely in stature and intellect, and was the perfect resemblance of her who had departed, and I loved her with a love more fervent than I had believed it possible to feel for any denizen of the earth.[3]

Although the narrator's love for the as-yet-unnamed daughter might be read here as an overabundance of paternal affection, Corben clearly reads "a love more fervent" as incestuous desire. Likewise, Corben takes liberties with the relationship between the narrator and Morella herself. In the first scene of his comic, he depicts the narrator standing on a cliff and shouting, "Bitch! She's ruined my life!" In contrast, Poe's original narrator expresses "a feeling of deep yet most singular affection" for his friend and cousin Morella, though he also says of their marriage, "I never spoke of passion, nor thought of love."[4] This admission adds mystery to the later birth of a daughter and suggests the child's unnatural origin. The heightening of marital tensions between the narrator and Morella and the overtly sexual relationship between the narrator and Morella's "daughter" (a *step-daughter* in Corben's retelling) are but two of the not-so-subtle changes that Corben makes in adapting Poe's tale to the comics medium. Other modifications include the additions of Mag the Hag, who assists Morella in her occult studies; a pair of lavender-colored glasses that becomes a visual symbol of Morella's as well as her daughter's spiritual vision; and the narrator's ultimate suicide at the end—a fate perhaps implied by Poe's tale but made explicit by Corben.

Such changes emphasize the tension between fidelity and originality that mark any attempt at artistic adaptation, especially one that moves between media, rhetorical conventions, and cultural contexts, as do all modern comic book and graphic novel adaptations of Poe's work. Corben, himself one of the most prolific adapters of Poe's work into the comics medium, has suggested three reasons why these alterations are inevitable. First, his adaptations are "contrived imitations" of the deep *feelings* elicited by his readings of the original tales—feelings that by their subjective and changeable nature tend to drive the narrative in new directions. Second, there is a willingness on his part to pursue narrative threads that are consistent with his own sense of playfulness and curiosity about alternate situations, reactions, endings, or cultural contexts. Third, there is the influence of earlier adaptations of Poe's work, particularly those by filmmakers like Roger Corman, whose work overlays that of Poe in Corben's memory and experience. The resulting mash-up of stories, characters, and situations on display in *Spirits of the Dead* constitutes a hybrid of Corben's, Poe's, and other adapters' visions.[5] Like "Morella" itself, the act of adaptation is necessarily one that involves *transposition* and *transgression*—a blurring of identities that results in uncanny new forms that have the potential to "grow strangely" in relation to the originals.

Significantly, Poe's story "Morella" is itself an adaptation of both the biography of a real woman, Sor Juliana Morell, a seventeenth-century nun and philosopher, and an earlier tale, Henry Glassford Bell's "The Dead Daughter" (1831), which features a dead child apparently reincarnated in her sibling.[6] From the life of the learned nun, Poe borrows the name of his title character, who is, like her religious forebear, precocious and spiritually gifted, and from the horror tale, he gleans Gothic themes of death, interment, and uncanny rebirth or reincarnation. What Poe invents are *motive* (Morella's conscious desire to return), *conflict* (the narrator's contradictory feelings of admiration, desire, and horror), and *moral questioning* (the narrator's and the readers' doubts about the benevolence of Morella's unnatural power). The tale takes on new significance when read in relation to Poe's other stories about powerful, lost, and supernaturally or psychologically revenant women such as Lenore, Ligeia, Berenice, Madeline Usher, and Annabel Lee. That context raises critical questions about the place of women in Poe's writings, aesthetics, philosophy, and politics. One could argue that "Morella," like many of Poe's tales and poems, is *haunted* by women, just as his text is haunted by the palimpsestuous presence of earlier texts.[7] As Eliza Richards says, "Women are everywhere and nowhere in Poe studies. . . . [S]he is never fully forgotten, and she threatens or promises to rise again."[8]

Whether one considers comics adaptations of Poe's writings as mash-ups, hybrids, or palimpsests, a consistent theme in many of these works—as in Poe's original texts—is the need to grapple with the ghostly yet potent presence of women. Although Poe neither fully explains his troubling representations of women nor adequately acknowledges his debts to women writers, patrons, caretakers, and audiences, the modern artists who have adapted his work, especially in the comics form, have found ample opportunity to explore these issues.

Poe's pervasive presence in comics and his influence on their creators is significant enough to provide plenty of material for this study. M. Thomas Inge, who has prepared the most comprehensive survey of comic book adaptations of Poe to date, suggests that there were well over three hundred such adaptations as of 2008.[9] According to Inge's count, at least twenty more collections or individual adaptations appeared between 2008 and 2011.[10] Since that time, the present author has identified at least a dozen more, including works that feature Poe himself as a character.[11] Impressive as the full list is, Inge omits the innumerable stories and characters "inspired" by Poe or drawing upon conventions of Gothic, mystery, or detective stories employed by him. The number of Poe-inspired comics is, in any case, substantial, and Inge feels comfortable asserting that Poe's works have likely been adapted into comics more frequently than have the writings of any other American author.[12]

Furthermore, Inge suggests that one reason why Poe's tales and poems are so popular with adapters is that those works suit the comic book writer's need for short-form narratives that may be resolved within a few pages.[13] The same might, however, be said of the short fiction of other writers whose works have been in the public domain during the modern comics era. To be sure, Poe's use of popular genres does appeal to comics audiences, but those types of writing are not unique to Poe. Nevertheless, there is clearly something more compelling to comics creators about Poe's works than those of his contemporaries such as Hawthorne and Irving, or the literary efforts of later authors (e.g., Ambrose Bierce, Jules Verne, and H. P. Lovecraft) who wrote in forms and genres similar to those used by Poe. Perhaps Poe's popularity with comics audiences derives from the writer's stylistic peculiarities: his emphasis on dramatic *effects* that engage and titillate readers; his rich, descriptive prose; his attentiveness to colors, shadows, and textures; and his vivid, symbolic imagery. These characteristics lend themselves to a visual medium like comics. Likewise, the historical, geographical, and cultural ambiguities of many of his tales allow for the kinds of transpositions and recontextualizations—the key mechanisms of adaptation—that comics creators like Corben might use to facilitate their own "contrived imitations." One cannot, of course, ignore Poe's iconic status. Although other authors have worked in similar forms and genres, few have attained the cultural currency or instant recognizability of Poe. That familiarity is evident in the number of comics adaptations that present Poe himself as a central character: over thirty, not counting those that offer just a cameo or an image of the writer.[14] Poe's *image*, literal and metaphorical, provides the kind of aesthetic and thematic reference point that allows comics creators to capture their audiences' interest.

In addition to these practical considerations, comics artists seem to have a particular fascination with Poe's *characters*—especially his women characters, who are among the most memorable figures in American fiction. Given that many of his male protagonists are nameless, faceless, and unreliable first-person narrators, it is no wonder that comics creators often choose to portray these generic "heroes" as Poe himself. At the same time, many artists indulge their creative impulses by visually reimagining those powerful women—or, in some cases, supernatural creatures—who are objects of fascination and fear for Poe's hapless narrators as well as for his audiences. More than his nameless narrators, or even named characters like C. Auguste Dupin or Arthur Gordon Pym, Poe's women seem to provide the most compelling opportunities for comics creators to explore new visions, themes, plots, and interpretations of Poe's classic tales. In their attempts to depict these characters, adapters face both formal and cultural challenges. How does one simultaneously capture the complexities and powerful presences of these women in a new medium *and* address changing social attitudes toward gender?

*****

The formal challenges of adaptation may seem tangential to the topic of women in Poe's works, but without considering those matters, one cannot fully understand the possibilities for innovative or transgressive revisioning of Poe. *How* such revisioning occurs, and in what forms, may be as important as *why* it occurs in these texts. For example, women comics creators have often been limited in the genres and formats in which they are paid to work—and yet, by taking advantage of the popularity and creative potential of literary adaptations, they have found ways to expand readers' understanding of Poe through comics. There is, however, no single format or formal structure that can easily be defined as "comics," and there are various methods of adaptation. Derek Parker Royal notes that recent graphic adaptations of Poe include individual tales adapted as graphic novels, multiple stories adapted by a single artist or creative team collected in a volume, stories by various creators in an anthology, and original fictional narratives using Poe and/or his characters as central figures.[15]

But while there is value in delineating the formats of graphic adaptations for the purposes of comparison, such distinctions are less important to this study than some key concepts in adaptation identified by Linda Hutcheon, Siobhan O'Flynn, and other theorists—namely, "transcoding" from one medium to another, notions of "fidelity" versus "originality," modes of engagement (e.g., "showing" and "telling"), and modes of reception.[16] Examples of all of these concepts in the comics will be examined later. Diverse adaptive practices have allowed comics artists and writers to "transpose and transgress" the boundaries of Poe's original texts in startlingly original ways. For example, re-telling the story of one of Poe's narrators from the perspective of a woman—an approach employed in some of the following examples—offers comics writers the opportunity to explore both the universality and the specificity of these characters' experiences in new ways. Similarly, by working in a visual format, comics artists confront the challenge of rendering the mysterious scenes in Poe's writing (e.g., the destruction of the House of Usher and the grotesque decay of M. Valdemar) in more concrete and specific forms.

Moving from text to graphic form involves a shift of medium and rhetoric that can be jarring to those unfamiliar with the comics form. Michelle Kay Hansen suggests that comics may involve a third mode of engagement beyond showing and telling: "interacting" via the dynamics of "closure," the mental process of filling in the gaps that occur between panels and pages of a comic book or graphic novel.[17] Making this leap between forms requires textual and visual literacy, knowledge of literary and cultural context, and the ability to synthesize these things. Such competencies help readers interpret even a relatively straightforward illustrated work like Gareth Hinds's *Poe: Stories and Poems: A Graphic Novel Adaptation*, a Candlewick Press edition aimed at younger readers. Hinds's adaptation of "Annabel Lee," for example, features a colorful backdrop showing a beach scene, a sky filled with white angelic figures ("the winged seraphs of heaven"), and red and green mermen riding huge sea serpents ("demons down under the sea"). Six suited men bear a coffin toward a white mausoleum, and, in the top left corner is the profile of a young, fair-haired woman with two smaller figures—a woman and a dark-skinned man—running happily down the slope of her hair (Fig. 6.1).[18]

In the bottom left corner of that page, the same man kneels in the sand, covering his face in grief. It takes a moment to realize that these figures represent the speaker and Annabel Lee herself, and another moment to understand that what is forbidden about their "love that was more than love" is not just their youth. Posing additional obstacles are racial, and perhaps cultural, differences. Those differences are reinforced by the direction of their faces—hers turned upward toward the white angels, his downward toward the dark

Fig. 6.1. "Annabel Lee," from *Poe: Stories and Poems.*

"demons" in the sea. These racial implications are, of course, an addition to Poe's poem made by the artist, but they add a layer of meaning that evokes not only the classic themes of forbidden love and lost youth but also cultural taboos about interracial relationships that may challenge conventional interpretations of the poem and speak to contemporary readers. Moving away from a traditional reading of the text, Hinds uses the visual tools of the comics artist to expand the poem's interpretive possibilities. To read this adaptation properly, one must understand how Hinds's visual rhetoric works with and against Poe's text to produce a new understanding of a classic work.

Being familiar with Poe's more famous works, as many readers are, presents its own challenges for comics adapters. Such familiarity amplifies what Hutcheon and O'Flynn call the "palimpsestuous intertextuality" that exists within all adaptations, for audiences come to these tales with layers of predetermined expectations based on earlier encounters with the stories.[19] Among these are varying expectations of fidelity to the originals, which may clash with an adapter's desire for originality. How comics creators negotiate these challenges can reveal their own cultural, critical, or ideological stances toward Poe and his work. Inge notes that many of the early comic book adaptations of Poe's work, such as the *Classics Illustrated* series that ran from 1944–1962, tend to remain as faithful to the original stories as possible—in terms of plots, themes, settings, and characterizations—due to the necessarily abbreviated format.[20] For Royal, however, such fidelity suggests that these adaptations lack the "romantically ironic spirit of Poe's aesthetics" encouraging the playfulness that might allow an adapter to experiment freely. More recent adaptations, like those of Corben and others, partake of a postmodern spirit of irony and free play that Royal believes is more consistent with Poe's own aesthetics.[21]

Two notable examples of such postmodern takes on Poe are Jason Asala's *Poe* series, which ran from 1996–2000, and Dwight MacPherson and Thomas Boatwright's two-part comic *The Surreal Adventures of Edgar Allan Poo*.[22] Both texts showcase Poe himself as the fictional hero. In Asala's *Poe,* the poet mourns the death of his lost love, "Lenoir." But, unlike most of Poe's tales, this bereaved lover gets an opportunity to be reunited with his beloved if he can defeat thirteen demons who have escaped into the physical world. Thus begins an Orpheus-like quest that leads Poe through a series of adventures, many of them based on Poe's own tales, including "The Black Cat," "The System of Doctor Tarr and Professor Fether," and "The Fall of the House of Usher." What is notable about Asala's versions of these tales is that they are segments of a longer journey enacted by the author/hero in pursuit of a larger truth or personal goal rather than distinct literary artifacts. These adaptations offer a way of reading Poe's oeuvre as the record of a continuous spiritual and psychological pilgrimage instead of a series of discrete aesthetic moments. The convoluted, mysterious, sometimes nonsensical journey that Poe takes through various alternate realities is reminiscent of works by other twentieth-century authors such as Thomas Pynchon and Jorge Luis Borges—writers who owe an artistic debt to Poe, a literary forefather of surrealism and postmodernism.

MacPherson and Boatwright's *Edgar Allan Poo* takes this notion of surreal journey in a more absurd and perhaps challenging direction. Poo is, as his name implies, an abject product of the bowels of the original Edgar Allan Poe. Although he resembles—fortunately, for readers—a miniature version of the original, Poo actually represents the creative soul of the poet, his "Dream Child" who has somehow been cast out as a result of Poe's own suffering and desire not to dream. The loss of this crucial part of himself comes at an inopportune moment, as the demonic forces of the Nightmare King, a psychic manifestation of Poe's own despair, have set out to destroy the poet by urging him toward self-destruction. Poo's mission, which he only comes to discover through the help of various dream-figures who aid him along the way, is both to discover his own true nature and to rescue his "father" by confronting the Nightmare King and releasing Poe from his influence. Poo's adventures are humorous, exciting, heart-rending, and, at times, genuinely frightening. Designed to engage and titillate readers, this sensational material obscures the absurd premise of the tale, which is grounded in precisely that ironic and self-mocking "distance" that Royal deems central to the best contemporary adaptations of Poe. Both Asala's *Poe* and MacPherson and Boatwright's *Poo* demonstrate the liberating and playful power of the comics medium for artists eager to explore Poe's ideas and themes in ways that are at once transgressive and true to the spirit of Poe's own aesthetics. Taking these various aspects of adaptation—translation between media, various degrees of fidelity and originality, and the ironic playfulness suggested by Poe's aesthetics—together, one begins to see the great potential for powerfully re-envisioning Poe's works in the comics medium.

None of the examples in the section above presents, however, any real re-evaluation of the role of women, as characters or creators, in the works of Poe. Produced by male writers and artists, these works tend to reiterate the roles that women have typically played in Poe's writing as objects of longing, desire, loss, aesthetic pleasure, or, at times, revulsion and terror for the male protagonist. It seems fair to say that the comics medium as a whole has long been dominated by such stereotypes and conventions, even though adaptations of Poe's work often reflect or even amplify the writer's own ambivalent attitudes toward women. Rarely do Poe's women appear as complex characters with inner lives, agents of their own fates, or first-person narrators with identifiably female perspectives. Such revisioning goes beyond the formal challenges and opportunities of adaptation and requires a consideration of the cultural, economic, and gendered dynamics that have shaped comics and their creators.

Whether the limited and stereotyped roles of women in comics derive from source material, the conventions of popular genres like horror and science fiction, or cultural attitudes, one factor that has certainly shaped the creation of comics is the relative lack of diversity in the comics industry and in the audiences of comics and graphic novels.[23] Women are employed in that industry, but they generally earn substantially less than men. Furthermore, they often lack creative control over their work because publisher needs, opportunities, reader demand, and/or financial incentives—rather than personal artistic considerations—typically dictate selection of material.[24] Opportunities for independent or creator-owned production are also rarer for women than for men.[25] Another problem is the infrequency with which comics present female characters. According to one study, only about 30 percent of all the characters in Marvel and DC publications are women.[26]

Although gender disparities limit opportunities for women creators in the industry, the comics audience has changed significantly in recent decades, with encouraging results. In 1944, a Market Research Company of America report showed that, although comics readership among children aged six to seventeen was nearly identical for boys and girls, by age eighteen that rate had changed significantly, with only 28 percent of women and 41 percent of men indicating that they read comics. By 2011, both numbers had increased, with 38 percent of adult women and 59 percent of adult men indicating on a social media survey that they read comics, perhaps a result of the increased production of adult-targeted comics in the modern era.[27] More recent surveys of comics retailers and attendance at comics conventions indicate that comics readership may be up to 45–47 percent female and 52–54 percent male, with percentages nearer equivalence for female and male fans under age eighteen.[28] Certain genres of comics, including manga, webcomics, graphic novels, and comic strips actually show consistently higher readership among women than men. Significantly, these are also the genres in which women creators are more frequently employed.[29]

Such industry realities have several consequences for comics production. For one thing, these demographic studies indicate that most comics adaptations of Poe are the work of white males and that for a good portion of the twentieth century those adaptations were tailored to a largely male readership. That is not to say that all these earlier adaptations failed to include female characters or to address potential female audiences in interesting ways. For example, Richard Corben creates a uniquely subversive vision of "Morella," and he offers similarly critical takes on stories like "Berenice," "The Fall of the House of Usher," and "Ligeia." However, Corben is an unusual artist, both in terms of the depth and breadth of his engagement with Poe and in terms of his willingness to depart from Poe's original stories in significant, transformative ways. Although other male artists such as Asala and MacPherson have certainly taken writings by Poe in interesting new directions, those artists have not often challenged his stereotypical depictions of women as victims, idealizations, or monsters. Perhaps not surprisingly, creative teams that *do* challenge those depictions have often included women of various backgrounds and orientations.

Many women in the comics industry have found the greatest creative freedom outside the series produced by mainstream publishers, and this situation has largely been true of those who have adapted Poe's work. A notable exception is the writer Caitlin R. Kiernan, who worked for several years on DC/Vertigo's *Sandman* spinoff series *The Dreaming*. One of Kiernan's most popular stories during that run was "The First Adventure of Miss Catterina Poe."[30] The tale features one of the less-heralded companions in Poe's life: Catterina, the tortoise-shell cat that lived with Poe and his wife, Virginia, during their years in Philadelphia. In this story, Catterina must rescue Poe from the Conqueror Worm lurking beneath Virginia's grave, which Poe visits all too frequently in his grief. Warned by emissaries of the Lord of Dreams (the Sandman himself), who feels that Poe has many tales yet to tell, Catterina ventures underground, battling rats, dangerous mazes, and finally, the Worm itself, to save Poe from an early grave.

That Catterina, Poe's protector as well as his companion, is the heroine of the tale hints at the central role that women—including Virginia, his aunt Maria Clemm, and numerous female benefactors and friends—played in Poe's survival and success. In the final scenes, readers learn that Catterina's "real name" is Kate, the name given by her mistress, Virginia Poe, whom the cat feels proud to have served by saving Poe from himself. This protective behavior resembles the rescue in *Edgar Allan Poo*, but Kiernan gives the salvation in her text a distinctly feminine spin. More important than protecting Poe is Catterina's service in protecting *the stories* that Poe has yet to write. As an agent of the Lord of Dreams, she distinguishes herself as a heroine of the imagination by preserving Poe's legacy.

Kiernan's tale is an original one and less an "adaptation" than a commentary on Poe's life and work from the perspective of an important female figure connected to him. Other comics adaptations address his stories directly. Some, like Denise Despeyroux and Miquel Serratosa's *Dark Graphic Tales by Edgar Allan Poe*, offer a fairly faithful re-telling of Poe's tales "The Gold-Bug," "The System of Doctor Tarr and Professor Fether," and "The Fall of the House of Usher." Although "Usher" has long been popular with adapters working in the comics mode, the other two tales are rarer choices for imaginative reworking. It may be that Despeyroux, a playwright, and Serratosa, a painter, illustrator, and graphic design artist, selected stories that they found both character-driven and dramatically or visually "stageworthy." For example, "The System of Doctor Tarr and Professor Fether" provides an ensemble cast of idiosyncratic characters who have the opportunity to enact a humorous yet chilling performance of "madness" during a lavish dinner party. In this extended scene (Fig. 6.2), Serratosa's lush, grotesque watercolor illustrations and carefully delineated characters suggest a staged production complete with wild costumes and rehearsed lines—a performance that mirrors what the inmates of Poe's asylum produce for the unwitting narrator.[31]

But beyond the humor and the visual staging, the story also provides Despeyroux with an opportunity for social commentary on the place of women in this institutionalized setting. After a particularly risqué scene in which Mademoiselle Salsafette (one of the inmates of the hospital masquerading as a member of the staff) nearly performs a striptease in front of the entire company, the party is interrupted by the screams of the guards locked in the patients' cells. The narrator, oddly clueless throughout the tale, asks how many patients there are, and an exchange follows:

Monsieur Maillard: Right now, we have ten.

Narrator: I assume they are mostly women.

Maillard: Actually, they are all men, strong men at that.

Fig. 6.2. Denise Despeyroux and Miquel Serratosa, "The System of Doctor Tarr and Professor Fether," from *Dark Graphic Tales by Edgar Allan Poe* [Relatos de Poe], 2013, page 60. © Denise Despeyroux, 2013.

Narrator: It was my understanding that a majority of the mentally ill are female.

Maillard: There was a time when we had twenty-six patients, of which fifteen were women. But things have really changed.

Dinner guests [together]: Things have really changed! Have really changed . . . Yes, they've really changed![32]

In the preceding scene with Mademoiselle Salsafette, there are fifteen women at the table—former patients now liberated and free to express themselves in increasingly eccentric and, by the narrator's standards, socially inappropriate ways. That the narrator can at once believe that women are particularly prone to mental illness and yet fail to see that the women masquerading as well-dressed and cultured dinner guests are, in fact, patients of the hospital reveals his gender and class assumptions, which are viciously satirized. This situation adds a touch of irony in the closing scene when the guards, covered in black tar and feathers, burst into the room to subdue the company of patients. The narrator notes, "They did not seem too fond of the system of soothing, but rather they embraced more conventional methods."[33] These "conventional methods" exhibit violence and sadism, for the guards choke, tackle, and brutalize the dinner guests, bringing an end to their masquerade. In this scene, who are the real threats to civility and society? Like Poe, Despeyroux and Serratosa do not explicitly answer that question, but they leave readers with a powerful visual image of two contrasting forms of distinctly gendered "madness." For the women in this hospital, madness is a form of creative resistance to social norms and propriety; for the men, those deemed mad are subject to violent domination and control. That this adaptation appears in an edition for younger readers suggests the importance of the story's subversive message for Despeyroux and Serratosa.

Other adaptations by women creators offer even more radical re-imaginings of Poe's work. One recent anthology, *Nevermore: A Graphic Adaptation of Poe's Short Stories* (2008), offers several tales rewritten or drawn by women artists. In Leah Moore and John Reppion's "The Black Cat," readers encounter familiar elements of the original tale (e.g., a drunken, abusive husband, an animal-loving wife, and, of course, a black cat), but in this case, they are all members of a struggling traveling circus. The cat in question is an exotic female black panther upon whom the husband (the ringmaster) projects all of his own failures and frustrations. Similar to the narrator in Poe's tale, the husband tries to get rid of the offending creature by luring it into the woods and shooting it, but visions, dreams, and obsessive thoughts plague him wherever he goes. Tormented by guilt, he sees images of cats in everyday objects (Fig. 6.3).[34]

In a final attempt to destroy the beast, he instead shoots his wife on the spot where circus performers later discover the reanimated cat hunched protectively over the woman's corpse. Confronted by the image of his wife's body and the uncanny cat, the narrator blurts out, "But I killed her!" With this exclamation, the narrator refers to the cat, but the outburst is, in fact, an

Fig. 6.3. Leah Moore and John Reppion, "The Black Cat," from *Nevermore: A Graphic Adaptation of Poe's Short Stories*, 2008, page 73. © SelfMadeHero, 2008. Reproduced with kind permission.

unintentional confession of *two* crimes. As in Poe's original tale, the narrator's association of the cat with his wife and his hostility toward both result in violence and self-incrimination.

Some differences between tale and adaptation are quite significant, though. Poe's original black cat is a male named Pluto after the Roman god of the underworld, but Moore and Reppion dub their female panther "Galenthias"—a name derived from "Galanthis" or "Galinthias," monikers for a figure from Greek mythology transformed by the goddess Hera into a weasel or a polecat.[35] Commonly used to ward off rats and snakes, such feline creatures were believed to have magical powers allowing them to cause or abort births, to disrupt harmonious relationships, or even to stave off death.[36] After her metamorphosis, Galanthis becomes a servant of Hecate, a goddess sometimes associated with ghosts, magic, witchcraft, necromancy, and, through her association with Demeter, the protection of domestic spaces.[37] Renaming the creature and changing its gender, Moore and Reppion reconceptualize the animal as a figure of feminine power and revenge that acts not as a manifestation of the husband's conscience but as an avenger of his wronged wife, a victim of patriarchal violence. In poisoning his own domestic space with alcohol, resentment, and violence—toward the cat and his wife—the husband summons the wrath of a goddess, who resembles some of Poe's other vengeful women, including Ligeia and Madeline Usher. Rather than viewing the cat through the paranoid, obsessive lens of Poe's narrator, readers see Galenthias exercise an independent will that thwarts the husband's efforts to control others.

The same anthology includes Jeremy Slater and Alice Duke's "The Tell-Tale Heart," in which the narrator of the original tale is reimagined as a blind woman caring for an elderly man in a rehabilitation center. This interpretative approach was first suggested by Gita Rajan, who argues that the old man's eye is "a metaphor of patriarchal scrutiny and social control" and that the nongendered narrator assumes the "female situation" in a patriarchal culture.[38] Adopting a feminist psychoanalytic perspective, Mary J. Couzelis follows Rajan's lead while analyzing the Slater/Duke adaptation.[39] Couzelis points out that the artist, Alice Duke, emphasizes the patriarchal gaze, first by showing the audience the blind female protagonist from the perspective of the old man, whom she suspects of faking his blindness, and then by showing his disembodied eyes following her even outside the room where he is confined, thus "changing the role of the narrator from hunter to haunted."[40] The narrator's final act of violence might then be read as an act of desperate self-defense against not just one creepy old man but also an entire cultural apparatus that sees her as an object of both pity and desire. In the climactic scene (Fig. 6.4), the narrator expresses fear even as she approaches the old

Fig. 6.4. Jeremy Slater and Alice Duke, "The Tell-Tale Heart," from *Nevermore: A Graphic Adaptation of Poe's Short Stories*, 2008, page 97. © SelfMadeHero, 2008. Reproduced with kind permission.

man with the intention of trying to "sort things out."[41] However, her claim that she "never had a choice" belies that design. Her choice is negated not by any particular actions of the old man but by her belief that "his kind never slept." Here, the old man is not an individual but a "kind," a representative of a larger threat that she perceives as surveilling her at all times and that she must eliminate.

Two other recent titles, entirely written and drawn by women artists, present re-imaginings of Poe's work that are even more original than the adaptations in *Nevermore*. Dawn Brown's 2005 graphic novel *Ravenous* offers a contemporary murder mystery inspired by several Poe works, including "The Tell-Tale Heart," "The Pit and the Pendulum," "The Masque of the Red Death," "William Wilson," and "The Raven"—each of which appears in its entirety at the end of the volume with illustrations by Brown.[42] Her original murder tale *Ravenous* explores "the perverse," a psychic faculty that prompts people to act against their moral and philosophical convictions—a recurring subject in Poe's work. Brown's story features a young detective named Mason on the trail of a serial killer in the isolated town of Good Fortune. Mason displays many of the familiar qualities of Poe's male narrators: he is plagued by anxiety; paranoia; heroic and romantic fantasies that derive from childhood dreams; egomania; barely repressed desires for recognition and revenge; and obsessive longing for a fellow detective, Catherine (or "Cat"), who fails to return his affections. He also has an unusual tendency to lapse into verse while narrating his tale, sometimes echoing Poe directly. All of these traits serve to undermine his credibility as the "hero" of the tale, which suggests a darkly satirical critique of Poe's narrators while maintaining Poe's own ironic stance toward those figures.

Although Poe's tales often focus on the self-destructive nature of the perverse, Brown emphasizes the *communal* effects of such acts. A conceptual artist and filmmaker who has primarily worked in film design, she has created visual worlds that directors and writers use to tell their stories.[43] In *Ravenous*, Brown utilizes her cinematic eye to create a physical and social space that puts each of the crime scenes in her serial killer's rampage into a broader perspective. Readers see how the lives of the police officers, families, children, and members of the larger community may be changed by one man's perverse violence. Whether this perspective is particularly feminist is debatable, but Brown clearly approaches Poe with the intention of seeing beyond his obsessive narrators' limited (always male) perspectives, something that Poe rarely does.

Wendy Pini's webcomic *The Masque of the Red Death* addresses another topic often muted or absent in Poe's work: sexuality. Pini presents a futuristic world dominated by the wealthy, pansexual Anton Prosper, a man seeking the secret to eternal life. He is aided by a young scientific prodigy, Steffan Kabbala, who longs to be Anton's lover.[44] The unapologetically homoerotic elements of the comic as well as its exploration of themes of desire, power, and privilege transform Poe's original tale. Described by Pini as "part Byron, part Frankenstein," Prosper is a figure who not only hoards wealth in the face of a biotechnical plague (unleashed by the conflicting passions of Prosper and Steffan) but also attempts to defy the "illimitable dominion" of Death.[45] The colored rooms of his "Rainbow Suite" represent things that he hopes to master through his scientific discoveries—Truth, Spirit, Words, Feelings, Power, Passion, and Choice (in this case, the choice of Life or Death). Gender and sexuality become one of many "choices" in this world that Pini's characters are free to explore, experiment with, and even transcend—assuming they can survive their own selfish desires and jealousies, which the figure of the Red

Death ultimately forces them to confront. Drawing upon the aesthetics of Erté, Hollywood film, 1980s fashion, and Japanese manga, Pini has suggested that she particularly targets a female-identifying audience attracted to the artwork, the eroticism, and the free play of gender roles in her work.[46] Whether her assumptions about her audience's tastes are accurate, Pini's revisioning of Poe's tale expands the social and sexual awareness of its audience by presenting a world in which identities are fluid, manipulable, and individualized while still bound by ethical consequences.

The examples presented above suggest just a few of the ways women artists have approached Poe's work in the comics medium—sometimes directly, sometimes obliquely, with varying degrees of "fidelity" or "irony," just as male artists have done. But what these particular artists seem to bring, in addition to the creative choices inherent in adaptation, is a desire to expand Poe's work through methods that address the concerns, interests, and aesthetic preferences of diverse audiences. The cartoonist Gale Galligan has suggested that such approaches reflect two strains of fandom: "curative" fans, who "prioritize canonical knowledge," and "transformative fans," who "use the canon for launching new ideas and discovering subtext."[47] From her own experience, Galligan suggests that curative fans are disproportionately male while transformative fans are disproportionately female. Whether that distinction actually holds or has been consistent over time is debatable, and such a model does not adequately account for queer, nonbinary, or trans experiences. Fan labeling of that sort does, however, suggest that artists like Galligan consider the needs of their audiences in making choices about how to adapt canonical works. If they perceive female audiences as especially receptive to transformation or subversion of the canon and create works for those audiences, these artists are more likely to produce the kinds of adaptations represented in this chapter.

Of course, transformative adaptation, irony, postmodern "distance," and subversion are unique neither to male nor to female artists, and Poe seems to invite such treatments by virtue of his canonical status. A recent parody series from Ahoy Comics titled *Edgar Allan Poe's Snifter of Terror* offers a salient example of the extent to which contemporary comics artists feel inclined to transform and subvert Poe's work and his place in the canon. Built on the kind of absurdist humor that one might find in *MAD* magazine or *Cracked*, *Snifter of Terror* offers not only humorous takes on classic Poe stories but also frequent appearances by Poe himself, who acts as the "horror host" of his own series. At times a gross caricature of the worst assumptions about Poe, whom many people envision as a drunken, angry, vision-obsessed madman, the Poe from *Snifter of Terror* is nevertheless a perceptive observer of readers and an effective anticipator of their expectations. In Rachel Pollack and Rick

Geary's adaptation of "Ligeia," for example, Poe confronts the audience on the opening page:

> Oh . . . it's you again. No doubt this is how you view me: a pathetic drunk in a dingy fetid tavern. This . . . this image of me is the doing of those who would pull me down from the Parnassian heights. . . . Down to their own wretched level. Cleanse your eyes that you might see beyond the lies of my enemies, those jealous scribblers.[48]

Invoking his own tarnished reputation at the hands of "enemies" (no doubt a reference to Rufus Wilmot Griswold and his heirs) and his desire to be seen with new eyes, Poe then proceeds to show readers a "magic lantern" that will allow them to perceive things never before imagined, including, perhaps, forbidden longings and desires. Comic scenes of homoerotic love, bondage, and sexual roleplay featuring other famous writers such as Oscar Wilde, Virginia Woolf, and James Joyce unfold, only to be dismissed by Poe as "obvious." Then begins his own tale of a longing that is less obvious—the longing for death and return featured in "Ligeia." Throughout the tale, Poe frequently interrupts with his own observations about everything from tense changes, to the sudden need for an "exquisite poem" that reflects the "exquisite death" of the beautiful woman, to readers' assumptions about the narrator's marriage to Rowena: "Yes, yes, I know what you're thinking. How the terrible Poe married his own cousin and underage to boot. I assure you, in my native Baltimore there is nothing unseemly about such a match. My wife and I are devoted to each other."[49]

Thus he continues until, at one point, he pauses to get feedback from the audience through the "magic lantern," which is, in fact, a computer screen with a message board and notes from such fans as "@Nevermore," "@M. Valdemar," and "@MME Dupine." Those fans regale him with comments, suggestions, insults, and, worst of all, attempts to "intrude their own . . . extensions" into his work.[50] His outrage goes beyond frustration with their misperceptions of his life, his work, and his marriage to his hatred for a modern world in which everyone is literally a critic—or worse, an adapter of his work! In the closing scenes, just as Ligeia makes her climactic return from the grave, Poe enjoys a climax of his own—a perverse, drug-induced, masturbatory moment in which he seems to ridicule everyone for taking him, his story, and his outrage seriously.

At once humorous, irreverent, absurdist, and critically insightful, Pollack's "Ligeia" engages in the kind of ironic play that Derek Royal feels is crucial to modern adaptations of Poe's work. It also makes audience members aware of their roles—as readers, spectators, critics, and creators—in determining how such adaptations or "hybrids" evolve to fit various cultural contexts.

Refusing to submit to reader expectations or to abandon them altogether, Pollack's Poe seems an appropriate spokesperson for an artistic form—the comics adaptation—that can exist only within that tension between transposition and transgression of the original texts, of Poe's own assumptions about his women characters, and of the audience's expectations. As recent comics adaptations go, "Ligeia" is one of the most unapologetically transformative and subversive of the genre, for Pollack treats both Poe and his work as material for contemporary cultural criticism and artistic play, not as unquestionable genius and inviolable canon. Her adaptation also demonstrates how the comics form can contribute something unique and vital to our understanding of Poe by providing a visual, popular, and constantly evolving medium for presenting Poe's tales.

Interestingly, Pollack is also one of the first "out" trans creators in the mainstream comics industry, and she is perhaps as well known for her award-winning science fiction novels and books on occultism, women's spirituality, and tarot.[51] Common to much of her work is the theme of "transformation" on physical, spiritual, and cultural levels, and this topical emphasis affords her a unique perspective on the process of artistic adaptation. To adapting "Ligeia" Pollack brings a sensibility that is indicative of both her lived experience and cultural moment and in tune with Poe's own imaginative explorations of gender, identity, artistic vision, and adaptation. The original Ligeia is, of course, a woman of profound spiritual and occult learning who, through the power of her own will and imagination, transcends both death and her own body, much to the horror of her former husband. However, in re-telling "Ligeia," Pollack chooses to focus not on the character who would seem to be most reflective of her own perspective and interests but on the intrusive, absurd, and ultimately repulsive figure of Poe the host, who seems to steal the scene from Ligeia at every perverse turn. In doing so, Pollack draws attention to the tendency of Poe, as well as many of his readers, to focus obsessively on the male narrator—or on Poe himself—rather than on the woman who is nominally at the center of the story. By rendering Poe as an obscene, hostile, and self-pleasing author getting in the way of his own story, Pollack turns the satirical tables on Poe while allowing him to excoriate his faithless readers and critics.

The work of Pollack and others proves that comics provide fertile ground for further adaptations and revisionings of Poe's work. That many of the most subversive comics are created by women—cis, queer, and trans—is perhaps not an accident, given the growing number of women among both the creators and audiences of these works. Poe's popularity with these diverse comics creators suggests that these artists still have a lot to say about Poe, his stories, and his treatment of women as characters and inspirations. There are still unexplored avenues of imagination, social and cultural critique, and formal

experimentation that the comics medium, particularly in the hands of women
and queer artists, can open up for readers and critics.

NOTES

1. See Eliza Richards, "Women's Place in Poe Studies," *Poe Studies/Dark Roman-
ticism: History, Theory, Interpretation* 33, nos. 1–2 (2000): 1–12; Colin Dayan,
"Poe's Women: A Feminist Poe?," *Poe Studies/Dark Romanticism: History, Theory,
Interpretation* 26, nos. 1–2 (1993): 1–12; and Cynthia S. Jordan, *Second Stories: The
Politics of Language, Form, and Gender in Early American Fictions* (Chapel Hill:
University of North Carolina Press, 1989). Dayan and Jordan offer a more generous
reading of Poe's use of women's voices and works than Richards does, but Dayan and
Jordan still recognize the exploitative dimension of such appropriations.

2. Richard Corben, *Edgar Allan Poe's Spirits of the Dead* (Milwaukie: Dark Horse
Comics, 2014), 60.

3. Edgar Allan Poe, "Morella," in *Collected Works of Edgar Allan Poe*, ed. Thomas
Ollive Mabbott, vol. 2 (Cambridge: Harvard University Press, 1978), 233, The Edgar
Allan Poe Society of Baltimore, https://www.eapoe.org/works/mabbott/tom2t025
.htm.

4. Poe, "Morella," 229.

5. Richard Corben, "An Interview with Richard Corben," interview by Derek
Royal, *Comics Alternative*, 2014, https://web.archive.org/web/20140914110040/http:
//comicsalternative.com:80/interview-richard-corben/.

6. Thomas Ollive Mabbott, introductory note on "Morella," in *Collected Works of
Edgar Allan Poe*, ed. Thomas Ollive Mabbott, vol. 2 (Cambridge: Harvard University
Press, 1978), 222, The Edgar Allan Poe Society of Baltimore, https://www.eapoe.org
/works/mabbott/tom2t025.htm.

7. Linda Hutcheon and Siobhan O'Flynn, *Theory of Adaptation*, 2nd ed. (London:
Taylor and Francis, 2013). Hutcheon and O'Flynn suggest that adaptations are "inherently 'palimpsestuous' works, haunted at all times by their adapted texts" (6).

8. Richards, "Women's Place," 10. Richards identifies women not only as an
important symbolic presence and theme in Poe's writing but also among his most
formative aesthetic sources and audiences. She writes that "Early Poe biography and
criticism . . . is, to an unexamined degree, a product of women's memories, fantasies, and desires" (11). Richards sees Poe's appropriation of the feminine voice and
perspective as inherently exploitative and consistent with other patriarchal appropriations of female power, but she suggests that critics should look seriously at what he
finds valuable and inspiring in their work.

9. M. Thomas Inge, "Poe in the Comics," in *Approaches to Teaching Poe's Prose
and Poetry*, ed. Jeffrey Andrew Weinstock and Tony Magistrale (New York: Modern
Language Association of America, 2008), 198–203.

10. M. Thomas Inge, "Comic Book and Graphic Novel Adaptations of the Works
of Edgar Allan Poe: A Chronology," in *Adapting Poe: Re-Imaginings in Popular*

Culture, ed. Dennis R. Perry and Carl H. Sederholm (New York: Palgrave Macmillan, 2012), 245–47.

11. A few notable examples include the following texts: Kate Beaton, *Hark! A Vagrant* (Montreal: Drawn & Quarterly, 2011); Richard Corben, *Edgar Allan Poe's Spirits of the Dead* (Milwaukee: Dark Horse Comics, Inc., 2014); Denise Despeyroux (w) and Miquel Serratosa (a), *Dark Graphic Tales by Edgar Allan Poe* [Relatos de Poe], English ed. (Berkeley Heights: Enslow Publishers, 2013); Gareth Hinds, *Poe Stories and Poems: A Graphic Novel Adaptation* (Sommerville: Candlewick Press, 2017); Pete Katz, *Edgar Allan Poe's The Raven & Other Tales: A Graphic Novel* (New York: Metro Books, 2016); and *Edgar Allan Poe's Snifter of Terror* (Syracuse: Ahoy Comics, 2018)—the last being an ongoing anthology series.

12. M. Thomas Inge, *The Incredible Mr. Poe: Comic Book Adaptations of the Works of Edgar Allan Poe, 1943–2007* (Richmond: The Edgar Allan Poe Museum, 2008), 14.

13. Inge, "Poe in the Comics," 198.

14. "Edgar Allan Poe in popular culture," Wikipedia, The Free Encyclopedia, accessed December 10, 2018, https://en.wikipedia.org/wiki/Edgar_Allan_Poe_in _popular_culture. This is the only known list of Poe's appearances as a character in comic books, to which the current author has contributed.

15. Derek Parker Royal, "Illustrating the Uncertainty Within: Recent Comics Adaptations of Edgar Allan Poe," in *Drawn from the Classics: Essays on Graphic Adaptations of Literary Works*, ed. Stephen E. Tabachnick and Esther Bendit Saltzman (Jefferson: McFarland, 2015), 60–81. Royal considers neither illustrated editions of Poe's tales nor original stories only loosely inspired by Poe, though such works have been produced by notable comics artists and writers, including a number of women. Due to their brevity and formal simplicity, traditional comic strips or panel cartoons are not analyzed by Royal. Thus, he ignores artists like Kate Beaton.

16. Hutcheon and O'Flynn, *Theory of Adaption*, 17–21.

17. Michelle Kay Hansen, "Picturing Poe: Contemporary Cultural Implications of Nevermore," in *Adapting Poe: Re-Imaginings in Popular Culture*, ed. Dennis R. Perry and Carl H. Sederholm (New York: Palgrave Macmillan, 2012), 209. For a general introduction to "closure" and the visual rhetoric of comics, see Scott McCloud, *Understanding Comics: The Invisible Art* (New York: Harper Perennial, 1994).

18. Hinds, *Poe Stories and Poems*, 38–39.

19. Hutcheon and O'Flynn, *Theory of Adaptation*, 21. For Hutcheon and O'Flynn, "palimpsestuous intertextuality" is a dialogical process "in which we compare the works we know with the one we are experiencing" (21); this experience is complicated by the order in which readers encounter these texts, making the "original" text different for every reader.

20. Inge, "Poe in the Comics," 199.

21. Derek Parker Royal, "Sequential Poe-Try: Recent Graphic Narrative Adaptations of Poe," *Poe Studies/Dark Romanticism: History, Theory, Interpretation*, 39–40 (2006): 55–67. Royal references G. R. Thompson's understanding of romantic irony as a central aspect of Poe's writing. See: G. R. Thompson, *Poe's Fiction: Romantic Irony in the Gothic Tales* (Madison: University of Wisconsin Press, 1973).

22. Jason Asala, *Poe* (1996–1997) Cheese Comics; Jason Asala, *Poe* (1997–2000) Sirius Entertainment; Dwight L. Macpherson and Thomas Boatwright, *The Surreal Adventures of Edgar Allan Poe*, 2 vols. (Berkeley: Image Comics, 2007).

23. See David Harper, "SKTCHD Survey: What's the Life of a Comic Artist Like?" SKTCHD, June 16, 2015, http://sktchd.com/longform/whats-the-life-of-a-comic-artist-like/; and Walt Hickey, "Comic Books Are Still Made by Men, for Men and about Men," FiveThirtyEight, October 13, 2014, https://fivethirtyeight.com/features/women-in-comic-books/.

24. Jennifer Guzman, "Where's the Money in Comics? Breaking It Down by Gender," ComicsAlliance, last modified June 23, 2015, http://comicsalliance.com/money-in-comics-survey-by-gender/.

25. Jill S. Katz, "Women and Mainstream Comic Books," *International Journal of Comic Art* 10, no. 2 (2008): 108–09.

26. See Hickey, "Comic Books," 2014, and Amanda Shendruk, "Analyzing the Gender Representation of 34,476 Comic Book Characters," The Pudding, accessed May 18, 2018, https://pudding.cool/2017/07/comics/.

27. Noah Berlatsky, "The Female Thor and the Female Comic-Book Reader," *The Atlantic*, July 21, 2014, https://www.theatlantic.com/entertainment/archive/2014/07/just-how-many-women-read-comic-books/374736/.

28. Jason Rhode, "The Comic Industry's Struggle for Gender Diversity Will Always Be a Maze," *Paste Magazine*, August 11, 2018, https://www.pastemagazine.com/articles/2017/08/the-comic-industrys-struggle-for-gender-diversity.html.

29. Berlatsky, "Female Thor"; Guzman, "Where's the Money."

30. Caitlin R. Kiernan (w), Steve Leialoha (p), and Daniel Vozzao (i), "The First Adventure of Miss Catterina Poe," in *The Dreaming* 1, no. 56 (Burbank: DC Comics, 2001).

31. Despeyroux (w) and Serratosa (a), *Dark Graphic Tales*, 60.

32. Ibid., 62–63.

33. Ibid., 66.

34. Dan Whitehead, ed., *Nevermore: A Graphic Adaptation of Edgar Allan Poe's Short Stories* (New York: Sterling Publishing Co., 2008), 73.

35. Francis Celoria, *The Metamorphoses of Antoninus Liberalis: A Translation with a Commentary* (London: Routledge, 1992), 88.

36. Ibid., 191–92.

37. For more on Hecate, see Aaron J. Atsma, "Hekate," Theoi Project, https://www.theoi.com/Khthonios/Hekate.html; Walter Burkert, *Greek Religion: Archaic and Classical* (Hoboken: John Wiley & Sons, 1991), 171 and 200; and Sorita d'Este, *Circle for Hekate Vol. 1: History & Mythology* (London: Avalonia, 2017).

38. Gita Rajan, "A Feminist Rereading of Poe's 'The Tell-Tale Heart,'" *Papers on Language and Literature: A Journal for Scholars and Critics of Language and Literature* 24, no. 3 (1988): 292.

39. Mary J. Couzelis, "What Can 'The Tell-Tale Heart' Tell about Gender?" in *Adapting Poe: Re-Imaginings in Popular Culture*, ed. Dennis R. Perry and Carl H. Sederholm (New York: Palgrave Macmillan, 2012), 217–29.

40. Ibid., 219.

41. Jeremy Slater and Alice Duke, "The Tell-Tale Heart," Dan Whitehead, ed., *Nevermore: A Graphic Adaptation of Edgar Allan Poe's Short Stories* (New York: Sterling Publishing Co., 2008), 97.

42. Dawn Brown, *Ravenous: A Graphic Novel Inspired by the Works of Edgar Allan Poe* (Toronto: Speakeasy Comics, 2005).

43. Dawn Brown, "Dawn Brown: Concept Artist and Indie Filmmaker," http://www.dawnbrown.net/index.html.

44. Wendy Pini, *Wendy Pini's Masque of the Red Death, Volume One* (Agoura Hills: Go! Comi, 2008).

45. Wendy Pini, *Wendy Pini's Masque of the Red Death*, "The Players," http://masquemusical.com/characters; Edgar Allan Poe, "The Masque of the Red Death" (1842), in *Collected Works of Edgar Allan Poe*, ed. Thomas Ollive Mabbott, vol. 2 (Cambridge: Harvard University Press, 1978), 677, The Edgar Allan Poe Society of Baltimore, https://www.eapoe.org/works/mabbott/tom2t051.htm.

46. Elfen Moondaughter, "Looking Behind the Mask: Wendy Pini." Interview. *Sequential Tart*. August 13, 2007, http://www.sequentialtart.com/article.php?id=605.

47. Harper, "SKTCHD Survey."

48. Rachel Pollack (w), Rick Geary (p), and Michael Garland (i), "Ligeia," *Edgar Allan Poe's Snifter of Terror* 1, no. 2 (Syracuse, New York: Ahoy Comics, 2018).

49. Ibid., 7.

50. Ibid., 10.

51. Rachel Pollack, The Shining Tribe: The Website for Rachel Pollack, https://www.rachelpollack.com/bio/; Monika, "Interview with Rachel Pollack," The Heroines of My Life (Blog), http://theheroines.blogspot.com/2013/12/interview-with-rachel-pollack.html; Jeff Spry, "Rachel Pollack Returns to Comics in Our Exclusive Peek at Ahoy's 'Edgar Allan Poe's Snifter of Terror' #2," *SYFY Wire* https://www.syfy.com/syfywire/rachel-pollack-edgar-allan-poes-snifter-of-terror-2.

Chapter Seven

"Sort of E. A. Poeish"

Edgar Allan Poe and Female Pulp Writers

Kevin Knott

The history of the early pulp magazine has been well documented, yet the contributions of female pulp writers inspired by Poe constitute a rich archive for critical exploration and discussion.[1] This is the case even though the inter-war period (1920–1940) in the United States saw successful runs of several major pulp magazines dedicated to the Weird and Gothic that featured women authors whose work would eclipse even the lauded H. P. Lovecraft.[2] Scholars know that Jacob Clark Henneberger founded the U.S. pulp magazine *Weird Tales* not only to fill the commercial void of a horror-oriented pulp magazine but also to declare himself an ardent admirer of Edgar Allan Poe's Gothic fiction.[3] Traditional Victorian ghost stories could be found in other pulps, but the magazine Henneberger envisioned would, he thought, appeal to writers like Poe, as a February 1927 subscription insert indicated. "If Poe Were Alive! There is no doubt whatever that Edgar Allan Poe would be a contributor to WEIRD TALES if he were alive today," the unnamed author exclaims, crowing that "[t]he brilliant success of WEIRD TALES has been built upon tales of the grotesque and terrible, such as that great American fictionist used to write. . . . "[4] The advertisement continues to suggest that the editors tried to recover the spirit of Poe's Weird fiction, a body of work featuring "tales that send eery [*sic*] shivers up the spine; tales of the spaces between the worlds; weird-scientific stories that peer into the marvels of the future; gooseflesh tales, and tales of the supernatural; stories that are utterly strange, artfully written tales, that take the reader into a deathless world of the imagination."[5] Contributors and their editors would adopt the adjective *weird* to describe the overall speculative nature and uncanny mood of their work, borrowing the adjective from Poe himself.[6] In this way male *and* female authors helped to restore Poe's reputation and pushed subgenres of Gothic literature in new and interesting directions, further developing the Weird tradition inherited from Poe.

For female pulp authors looking to establish commercial and artistic reputations, it was critically important to experiment, to rewrite the Weird model derived from Poe, in order to claim space for themselves in the "shudder pulps," a catch-all term frequently used for those pulp magazines of horror or the grotesque.[7] The artistic goal for many female writers was not only to imitate but also to innovate by capitalizing on the literary style and subject matter of Poe's short stories and by being "Poe-like" without imitating the antebellum master so nearly as their male counterparts did. Pastiches of Poe's works were commonplace in the pulps, but for female authors, rewriting his stories into surprising homages or even completely new genres legitimized their work for skeptical, and mostly male, readers who identified female authorship with the dwindling vogue for Victorian-inspired ghost fiction.

Eric Leif Davin observes in *Partners in Wonder: Women and the Birth of Science Fiction, 1926–1925* (2006) that the first issue of *Weird Tales*, which appeared in March 1923, included a story by Meredith Davis.[8] Citing her work as an example of the significant contributions of women writers, Davin highlights what is clearly a *Poesque* story with some elements appropriated from Victorian ghost tales. In "The Accusing Voice," the manic narrator is a juror named Allen Defoe (a perhaps too on-the-nose reference to Poe himself), a man haunted by the murder conviction of Richard Bland, whose case he heard some time before as a jurist. Aware of Bland's innocence, Defoe is pursued by a strange "accusing voice," which could be either an apparition returning for retributive justice or Defoe's conscience driving him insane. In the story's most interesting twist, Defoe goes to considerable lengths, just short of killing himself, to avoid hearing this mysterious voice and confronting the specter,[9] yet his efforts are futile. During a sea voyage, the Voice returns to convince Defoe of the accused killer Richard Bland's innocence. Bizarrely, Defoe threatens to become a drunkard or dope fiend rather than be moved to suicide by the Voice's incessant cackle, and eventually, the strange Voice offers to stop tormenting Defoe if he confesses the identity of the real murderer.[10] Like Poe's manic narrators tormented by the psychological manifestation of their guilt, Defoe is not certain whether the Voice is supernatural or natural; however, when he eventually admits to having committed the murder himself, he realizes that the Voice is Bland, the man whom Defoe helped a jury convict.[11] Neither purely a Victorian-style ghost story nor a psychological thriller à la Poe, Davis's tale still features Defoe's expected death, but with an ironic twist: Bland had already been pardoned by the time of Defoe's needless confession.[12]

Such narrative reconfiguration is the subject investigated throughout this chapter, in which Poe's influence will be charted from the early days of *Weird Tales* in the 1920s and 1930s to the later disengagement with Poe in *Unknown* during the early years of the 1940s, when female authors had become ubiquitous in the shudder pulps. At stake is the recognition not only that female authors were proponents of Weird fiction in the heyday of the pulp magazines but also that these women were innovators in the development of horror literature in the United States. They were certainly, like male authors, devoted to Poe's peculiarly *Weird* fiction, yet they also invited a modernist irony into their stories, playing with the audience's expectations of a singular emotional effect, which Poe had championed and Lovecraft would laud and enshrine as essential in horror literature.

Veneration for Poe was evident on the editorial pages of *Weird Tales'* first anniversary issue (May 1924). There, the editor Edwin Baird recounted the successes of the magazine's initial year and laid out his plans.[13] Though sometimes considered a disengaged editor, Baird shared cofounder Henneberger's desire to promote Poe's Weird fiction.[14] In a piece titled "Why Weird Tales?" Baird announced:

> Up to the day the first issue of WEIRD TALES was placed on the stands, stories of the sort you read between these covers each month were taboo in the publishing world. Each magazine had its fixed policy. Some catered to mixed classes or readers, most specialized in certain types of stories, but all agreed in excluding the genuinely weird stories. The greatest weird story and one of the greatest short stories ever written, "The Murders of [*sic*] the Rue Morgue," would not have stood the ghost of a show in any modern editorial office previous to the launching of WEIRD TALES. Had Edgar Allan Poe produced that masterpiece in this generation he would have searched in vain for a publisher before the advent of this magazine.[15]

Baird's boast is the stuff of marketing embellishment, but he accurately describes the increasingly specialized foci of the major pulp publications in the 1920s. Unlike the "Big Four" pulp magazines that dominated the lowbrow literary landscape (namely *Adventure, Argosy, Blue Book,* and *Short Stories*), *Weird Tales* enjoyed a success that Baird attributed to the repetition of familiar tropes and plots from Poe's "masterpieces."[16] Even the "Big Four" would evolve to become synonymous with particular styles or subjects, so to create a steady audience, pulp editors like Baird narrowly defined their publications as air adventures, westerns, tales of romance, and science fiction stories.[17] *Weird Tales* had achieved the same goal by organizing itself around the style and conventions of a single author—and, in time, by aligning itself with Poe's most significant imitator in the interwar period, H. P. Lovecraft. Baird's assertion that Poe would not have been published anywhere other than the pages of *Weird Tales* is, of course, questionable. Weird fiction did appear regularly in other magazines, as Ambrose Bierce's career indicates.[18]

At any rate, Baird's readers were drawn to "the weird, the bizarre, the unusual," and those words signified more than just the subject matter of the magazine's stories.[19] Baird's editorial ends with a fascinating rhetorical flourish significant for a few reasons. He writes, "But enough of Poe. His works are immortal and stand today as the most widely read of any American author. The publishers of WEIRD TALES hope they will be instrumental in discovering or uncovering some American writer who will leave to posterity what Poe and Hawthorne have bequeathed to the present generation."[20] With the phrase "bequeathed to the present generation," Baird suggests that contemporary pulp readers have a responsibility to elevate and to sustain the reputations of the U.S. authors, perhaps even justifying the close imitations of Poe as culturally significant attempts to elevate him into the ranks of the great writers. Thus, Baird gestures to a literary nationalism that begins with a recognition of U.S. achievements in Gothic fiction and develops into the promotion of new Gothic and Weird writers for necessarily political reasons as well as literary ones. Baird had already placed Poe alongside Homer, Shakespeare, Dante, and Dickens as artists who delved into the Weird to explore universal fears at the heart of human existence, and Poe's rehabilitation as the first and perhaps the best of the Weird writers meant *Weird Tales* had a U.S. literary patron saint, an author whose influence might legitimize the magazine's efforts and in turn legitimize Poe himself.[21]

The magazine's initial commercial failures did not dampen Baird's faith in the periodical and its mission:

> Perhaps in the last year we have been instrumental in furnishing an outlet to writers whose works would not find a ready market in the usual channels. The reception accorded us has been cordial and we feel that we will survive. We dislike to predict the future of the horror story. We believe its powers are not yet exhausted. The advance of science proves this. It will lead us into unexplored labyrinths of terror and the human desire to experience new emotions will always be with us.[22]

Suggesting that the horror story finds justification in future critical acclaim rather than immediate commercial success, Baird's editorial leaves the readers aware of their participation in shaping the magazine and its reputation. This relationship between the magazine and its audience paid dividends in the initial thirty-one-year run of the magazine as well as in the cementing of Weird fiction as an important subgenre of speculative fiction. Regardless, Baird and other editors of *Weird Tales* were able to achieve this longevity, in part, by publishing the pioneering work of female pulp authors. As Davin pointedly reminds us, *Weird Tales* was a "magazine which published women from the very beginning of its existence, in which all editors published women writers during their tenures, a magazine with a long-time female editor [Dorothy McIlwraith 1940–1954], with a female artist [Margaret Brundage 1933–1938] sometimes called 'The First Lady of pulp magazine illustration' as the most famous of its cover artists, [and] with a readership which may have been a quarter female. . . ."[23] Like their male counterparts, most of these writers would have cited Poe's fiction as a significant influence, but they have not received the full recognition that Baird had predicted for all the contributors to *Weird Tales*.

Nearly twenty years after that magazine's founding, famed editor John W. Campbell, who had already proven his skill with *Astounding Science Fiction* (1930–1971), introduced *Unknown* in 1939.[24] Billed as "fantasy fiction," the magazine had a title placing it in direct competition with the more established *Weird Tales*, yet *Unknown* would not veer far from the Poe/Weird model already popular in the shudder pulps. Readers were assured that *Unknown* intended to offer something heretofore unseen. One key development was increased publication of works by female pulp writers. *Unknown* helped launch the careers of authors like Jane Rice, a phenomenal talent whose name is unfamiliar to contemporary audiences, and the magazine featured the work of pulp veterans such as Mona Farnsworth (pseudonym of beloved western writer Muriel Newhall), Marian O'Hearn (prolific writer for *Rangeland Romances* and noir publications), and Dorothy Quick (*Weird Tales* contributor and friend of Mark Twain), alongside fiction by other women writers whose work appeared in *Weird Tales* and whose names were recognizable among pulp readers. *Unknown* also showcased famed male writers like L. Ron Hubbard, L. Sprague de Camp, Theodore Sturgeon, and some members of the "Lovecraft Circle." Partially for that reason, Campbell struggled at first to make a distinction between his own magazine and its competitors; however, he would eventually find the storytelling mode that would distinguish *Unknown* in Jane Rice's modernist revision of Poe's central motifs and style.

In her unpublished short story "The Cats" (1943), Rice reimagines Poe's "The Black Cat."[25] Whereas a murderous husband narrates Poe's tale, the narrator in Rice's is a woman beset by her affection for the romantic charm of Clint, her lifelong friend and unrequited love, but her outward churlishness makes such an admission impossible. The narrator is not alone in her romantic aspirations for Clint. The narrator humorously recounts her jealousy at the beginning of the story:

[O]ne night I happened to be sitting behind a potted palm, hitching up a stocking that had come loose from its moorings and I saw him. Me and a green-eyed monster that kept whispering in my ear, "Go get a bottle of acid and throw it in May Belle Robertson's face." Kept whispering, that is, until I noticed that Clint was kissing May Belle with his eyes open and slightly crossed because he was watching, with that same attitude of clinical detachment, a caterpillar inching its laborious way up May Belle's scarlet chiffon shoulder strap![26]

Pulp audiences would have been immediately struck by the amusingly modern style and tone on display in this passage, yet they would also have recognized Rice's transmutation of the opening paragraphs of "The Black Cat," where the narrator insists on his humanity and general kindness to animals, into an account of Clint's romantic overtures and bored fascination with the caterpillar. That readers see the narrative unfold from a woman's perspective also opens the door for a critique of male impulsivity, a trait exhibited in the "boys-will-be-boys" tradition. Rice's narrator recognizes but seemingly ignores Clint's antisocial behavior, disguising her romantic attraction as motherly discipline and playing the role of a chaperone who will kindly warn the young man against more dangerous entanglements. She is, in fact, an active participant in his misadventures, and although she ostensibly disapproves of his immaturity, her enthusiasm for his recklessness is revealed early on:

Clint's idea of a swell date is to march six miles cross country over hill and dale and barbed wire fences on a November day that has a bit of frozen dribble running through it—and maybe a peevish bull and an irate farmer with a shotgun and six or seven razor-backed hogs of the ilk that eat babies and paralytic grandfathers, and four or five gods obviously on the prowl for the seat of somebody's pants, and—well, this could go on forever. Clint collects trouble the way a blue serge collects lint.[27]

Clint's adventurous naiveté attracts the unnamed narrator, even as she girds herself against the unfortunate consequences of her attachment. Rice is preparing the reader for the conceit of the story, the comparison of the would-be lovers to the beloved radio pair Fibber and Molly McGee.[28] In their show (running from 1935 to 1959), Fibber was the lovable buffoon who roped his wife Molly, the classic comedy straight woman, into various follies.

Rice employs this core device ironically, reimagining Poe's couple in "The Black Cat" as characters in a screwball comedy. In that idiom, the masculinity of the male character is challenged through a battle of the sexes, during which a woman's display of power over her lover subverts the patriarchal restoration that occurs after the two are united.[29] In "The Black Cat," the presence of the one-eyed feline companion, Pluto, perturbs the narrator, reminding him that he cut out the cat's other eye, but in Rice's story, Clint never feels remorse for his misadventures. Rather, the female narrator's inclination to accompany him in these adventures serves only to exacerbate his willingness, evident from childhood onward, to expose her to further humiliation and cruelty. The game show is the scene that fully exposes Clint's willingness to put the narrator at risk, to forego moderation in their relationship while indulging his own adventurous impulses, and his perversity of character mirrors that of the narrator in "The Black Cat." Rice bases her game show, *Facts or Forfeits*, upon *Truth or Consequences*, a 1940s radio program in which contestants attempted humiliatingly ridiculous tasks such as fishing in a public fountain for prize money.[30] In "The Cats," the task for Clint and the narrator ostensibly is to "haunt" an abandoned house. In truth, they have been set up as trespassers who will be frightened for the twenty-dollar prize, and the narrator presumes she and Clint have been tricked into their own scare, imagining first a man in a Dracula costume and then a police officer arriving just in time to be "shot" with blanks.[31] Mixing the modern medium of radio entertainment with the Gothic setting certainly modernizes the Poe story, but Rice also replaces the characterization of the loving and indulgent wife with the portrait of a woman who has grown tired of her companion's playful, immature nature. Clint either cannot discipline himself or refuses to do so, and the adventure in the "haunted house" suits his impulsive character, the dangers of which he realizes almost too late.

This relational shift is evident when Clint and the narrator stumble into the kitchen in search of the stranger they were sent to "haunt." Frustrated, the narrator awaits the inevitable reveal that puts them on the spot and humiliates them before an amused live radio audience, and she grows exasperated with Clint, who seems unaware of the expected reversal as he obsessively sets about completing their prank in order to win the twenty dollars. In the kitchen, the pair encounter a pack of spectral cats—twenty or more, the narrator speculates—whose appearance provokes her into fearfully describing the animals as "sort of E. A. Poeish."[32] She clarifies for the reader that it was not the cats themselves that called to mind Poe's work but something else, something weird eliciting a shudder:

And it was true. I can't describe it. That scene. If I could stand off somewhere and view it dispassionately, I might. But I can't. I've tried. There's absolutely no dispassionate viewing being done. The minute I get my retrospect set up with the proper lens adjustment and the correct number of metric feet distant from my "subject," the exact lighting to catch the detail, my memory goes *blooie* and I am back in that hallway with all those watchful, luminous eyes in a green circle around us, with a thin trickle of bluish moonlight sifting down the front stairs, and the silence pressing in—thick as black cottonwood—closing in, deadening

Clint's voice and mine slowly, but surely closing in even as those eyes are closing in. Inch by creeping inch. Getting closer . . . and closer . . . and closer . . .
and, about then, me and my memory close up shop and turn on the radio and all
the lights and call up a lot of people we know and ask them won't they come
over and have a drink with us.[33]

This scene evokes the exposition of "The Black Cat," in which the narrator
reveals not only his own questionable objectivity but also his anxiety that he
cannot find a natural explanation for the horrible events he recounts:

For the most wild, yet most homely narrative which I am about to pen, I neither
expect nor solicit belief. Mad indeed would I be to expect it, in a case where my
very senses reject their own evidence. Yet, mad am I not—and very surely do
I not dream. But to-morrow I die, and to-day I would unburthen my soul. My
immediate purpose is to place before the world, plainly, succinctly, and without
comment, a series of mere household events. In their consequence, these events
have terrified—have tortured—have destroyed me. Yet I will not attempt to
expound them. To me, they have presented little but Horror—to many they seem
less terrible than *barroques*. Hereafter, perhaps, some intellect may be found
which will reduce my phantasm to the common-ace—some intellect more calm,
more logical, and far less excitable than my own, which will perceive, in the
circumstances I detail with awe, nothing more than an ordinary succession of
very natural causes and effects.[34]

In both texts, the narrators are wrestling with the unreality of their situations,
the weirdness of the stories they find themselves in, but Rice's narrator is the
"calm intellect," the modern skeptic who would dismiss such peculiar events
as chance or circumstance. Facing the incongruity between perception and
reality that Poe's narrator also experiences pushes her to the point of collapse.
Interestingly, Rice's narrator is going to set her mind straight by inviting
friends over to drink, whereas Poe's narrator loses his self-control because
of alcohol. Frequently, alcohol is the cure in Rice's fiction for the travails of
modern life, and in remixing Poe's tale of intemperance, Rice unapologetically asserts the female narrator's prerogative as a modern woman to imbibe
alcohol to "deal with" men.[35] The extent to which Rice intended this to be a
comment on misogyny is uncertain; however, the promised wedding bliss at
the end of the story complicates whatever message about gender and power
the author may have intended to convey. Furthermore, Rice does not appear
to have made any public remarks on the matter, and her narrators do not consistently subvert patriarchal norms.

Nevertheless, for Rice and the other women pulp writers of the early twentieth century, Poe's fiction marked an entry point where Gothic conventions
could be re-deployed in modern settings and ironized through the conflict

with the Weird, cautiously subverting the more misogynistic characteristics of the pulp narratives such as the menacing of female characters to incite male characters to action, the visible display (and graphic description) of female bodies, and many other tropes. Such a comparison between the Gothic and the modern calls to mind Greye La Spina's serial novel *Invaders from the Dark*, which appeared in the April, May, and June issues of *Weird Tales* in 1925.[36] The story turns on the appointment of a young woman, Portia Delorme, to the home of a reclusive occultist, Mr. Differdale.[37] She becomes enthralled by his work, marries him to keep up appearances (although the relationship remains unconsummated), and carries on his mysterious work after his death. When a Russian werewolf, Princess Tchernova, moves into the neighborhood, Portia, with the help of her aunt, attempts to rescue her would-be suitor, Owen Edwardes, from the monster's clutches. Portia is also saving the United States from the intrusion of evil spiritual powers from the Old World, but the narrative emphasis on saving Owen's soul reverses the classic Weird fiction motif of the endangered female victim saved by a man. Only Portia possesses the knowledge and the moral fortitude to combat the werewolf, setting her apart from the provincial men and women in her small New York neighborhood.

La Spina's work indicates that many women writers were bound by the marketplace demands of pulp fiction but found in the pages of pulp magazines like *Unknown* (also known as *Unknown Worlds*) places where the conventions of horror could be subverted, even repurposed humorously or ironically, to make pointed assertions about fear-based writing. That it was *female* pulp writers who embraced this subversive parodying of the "shudder-coining" of the period should not be too surprising.[38] After all, most of the women authors in *Unknown* were already veteran writers who had been negotiating the popular marketplace for years, suggesting that they were confident in their authorial autonomy. Jane Rice was the only novice, but she had become a favorite of *Unknown*'s editor, the legendary John W. Campbell, almost immediately, and through her work he may have found the fullest expression of his own editorial goals for the magazine.

Even so, Campbell did not at first know what *Unknown*'s generic focus would be. The early issues were an exciting mélange of science fiction, horror, and fantasy, with stories often mixing genres. Campbell's experiment in the pages of *Unknown* was less certain, more responsive to its audience's tastes than other pulps, as the advertisement in the inaugural issue (March 1939) announced:

Street & Smith present herewith a new magazine, dedicated to a new type of entertainment. UNKNOWN is both our title and our only classification; the material we plan to present is to be like none that has ever, anywhere, been presented consistently before.

No terms, then, have been evolved to describe this magazine; as it has never before existed. We will deal with the *Unknown*, but in a manner uniquely and completely different from the stories you have seen in the past.

One rule only we apply as limitation to an author's imagination; that the resultant story must be pure entertainment. Whether it be the chuckle over *Trouble with Water* or the thrill of uncertain discomfort invoked by *Sinister Barrier* to leave you uncertain of your uncertainty that it is pure fiction. Perhaps you're wrong, you know. The facts Russell states *are* facts. A man may well strike truth in what is meant as fiction—

But each month we will bring either a full novel-length story, complete, or two thirty-thousand-word short novels, plus some forty thousand words of short stories and novelettes.

And each month we shall bring you a magazine wherein the authors are bound by but one rule—pure entertainment. Beyond that—read and determine by our offering this month, the quality and the material we cannot otherwise better define.[39]

Campbell asserts that such a magazine "*has never before existed*," despite the availability of other shudder pulps on the market that would have been examples for comparison, and he invokes the same false boasting that inspired the early editors of *Weird Tales*. By the next issue, at least, Campbell had a more definitive idea of what *Unknown* emphatically was not. In the April 1939 issue, he responds to skeptical subscribers:

The general reaction seems to be expressed in one letter asking "Will you keep UNKNOWN on par with this first issue, or will you soon descend to zombies, werewolves, vampires, charnel houses and other rigamarole of current pulps?"

UNKNOWN is a totally different kind of magazine, and it's going to stay different. We are not going to use 19th century ghost stories, with 19th century trimmings. We are not going to begin stories "Had I known what horror faced me that night, never would I have set forth on that fatal journey—" or "They say I am mad, but I am not mad. Just listen to my story, and you shall judge—"[40]

Campbell alludes here to some of Poe's most famous and often imitated stories ("The Fall of the House of Usher" and "The Tell-Tale Heart"), but his assertion that the magazine would not publish "19th century ghost stories, with 19th century trimmings" was also a renunciation of the Poe-obsessed Weird fiction found in *Weird Tales* and elsewhere.

That is not to say that other Poe stories were not useful templates for the more unusual stories featured in the magazine. The selections in *Unknown* were less slavishly imitative of Poe than many pieces in *Weird Tales*, but they were still very much grounded in the same Gothic style. And even when authors elected not to imitate Poe's Gothicism, they found inspiration in his more unusual stories. In the very first short story of the inaugural issue of *Unknown*, "Who Wants Power?," Mona Farnsworth (pseudonym of Muriel Newhall) creates a pastiche of Poe's "Some Words with a Mummy," a satire that exploited antebellum interest in Egyptology.[41] In Poe's story the resurrected mummy debates the merits of modern invention and knowledge with scholars, usually winning most of the arguments but humorously failing to answer the assertion that patent medicines were an example of the modern era's superiority to the ancient past.[42] Farnsworth posits a similar allegory to satirize twentieth-century British technology and imperialism. As the story begins, Cuthbert is overseeing the excavation of a tomb, one that he already rummaged through and from which he retrieved a "thin, elaborately jeweled case."[43] He knows that this case holds some great power, yet it remains unclear whether Cuthbert's constant shivering is a symptom of anxiety about concealing the case's secret. He does withhold the truth about the tomb and its resident from the excavation leader, Dr. Jedediah Gill, saying, "There is nothing in the least unusual to report, sir, about the mummy," and although Cuthbert does not lie directly, Dr. Gill is frustrated all the same.[44] Cuthbert has a tenuous position on the archaeological team, as Dr. Gill reminds him. For example, Cuthbert's vaunted ability to know what the mummies experienced in life is a point of ridicule: "There are even those people, my dear Cuthbert, who have gone so far as to suggest that the reports you send in to us regarding the personal experiences, the individual reactions, so to speak, which these mummies have experienced during life are, in fact, the purest figment of your imagination."[45] Farnsworth credits Cuthbert's ability to a sort of clairvoyance "or a sort of archaeological mind reading," but this extrasensory power is mostly a device to discredit the scientific knowledge of the Egyptologists, who resemble the misguided experts in "Some Words with a Mummy."[46] Through the case's magic, Cuthbert is privy to knowledge that undermines the most astute observations made by the other scholars; he knows that if he should reveal what he knows they would only ignore his claims.

What Cuthbert feels is the terrible burden of the case and its power. He wants to dispose of the artifact as soon as possible. However, he cannot figure out a way to do so that would absolve him of any guilt. Even so, Cuthbert doubts the case's power until he accidentally waves his hand in the air and imagines the pyramids floating off. And they do rise—before, in a terrified voice, he screams for them to stop. Knowing the full power of the case, he debates what to do:

> Throw it away—and not know what became of it? Throw it away and run the risk of having it fall into other hands? Perhaps have someone find it who was malicious or vindictive—or even merely mischievous. Suppose a man given to

practical joking found it and by some accident of thought discovered its power. Cuthbert shuddered and hastily stuffed the thing into his own pocket.[47]

Cuthbert is the reader's conscience, at least that of the reader who would similarly fear the inevitable exploitation of the case. Like Poe's narrator in "Some Words with a Mummy," Cuthbert is deeply misanthropic, fearing other people more than the power of the case itself, and he knows what will happen. Once the secret is revealed, a conversation among the other excavation members sets up the inherent satire of the story. Dr. Gill thinks only of his own glory, and he insists that Cuthbert use the case to lift the sand from the various excavation sites throughout Egypt so that the British explorers need not pay their workers. Cyril Jameson, the blond English representative of the British army, imagines the greatness of the Empire after the successful irrigation of the Sahara through the agency of the case. Meanwhile, Mr. Henderson, the financier, exclaims that the case should be used to remove mountains to enable construction of a lucrative canal through the center of Africa.[48] Finally, Dr. Gill confronts Cuthbert in his bedroom later that evening, waving a revolver. During the ensuing struggle, Cuthbert commands the case to float off into the night. Calm follows: "His whole mind was concentrated upon the glad fact that the case—and the power—was gone, beyond argument and beyond men."[49] In the end, the "light Gothic" mood of the story belies, to some extent, the serious social critique evident in the work. With the case gone, the world is safe from its corrupting power and its misuse by agents of imperialist capitalism.

The female writers of *Unknown* explored similar fantastic themes in the service of satire. Indicating that the supernatural events are part of a cosmic absurdity, a joke gone wrong, the characters in these stories are not punished for reprehensible transgressions, but the audience is invited to laugh at their fates. Campbell asserted as much in his final editorial commentary. Though publication ended in October 1943, Campbell compiled a 1948 anthology of select stories from the magazine titled *From Unknown Worlds*. Within this book, he reflected on the legacy of his magazine and what the authors had achieved:

> The stories contained herein are fantasy, selected from the pages of the magazine "Unknown Worlds"—but a type of fantasy that is decidedly not standard, conventional, or stock stuff. The old "Unknown Worlds" believed that fantasy was intended for fun; it used the familiar creatures of mythology and folklore, but treated them in a most disrespectful fashion. Fantasy—and the Things of fantasy, are, we felt, much more fun than anything else, if you'll just take off those traditional wrappings of the "grim and gharstly."
>
> This, then, is an anthology of the Light Fantastic, in which werewolves get the hotfoot, demons are haunted, and anything goes—provided it's fun.

It's perfectly true that the fantasy chiller has a place; we agree to that, and you'll find them with us, too. But not, please, the gloom and terror spread on with a trowel, driven in with a mallet and staked out with an oak stave through its heart. Horror injected with a sharp and poisoned needle is just as effective as when applied with the blunt-instrument technique of the so-called Gothic Horror tale.[50]

What Campbell meant by "effective" is unclear, though the reference to spreading terror on with a trowel, a nod to Poe's "The Cask of Amontillado," is an ironic allusion to the effusive shudder-coining Lovecraft winced at, so the extent to which such stories could "prick" the audience is not addressed. Although many of the stories have continued to be anthologized in Gothic and horror collections, their lighter and satirical features have not always been acknowledged. Such an omission recalls the popular neglect of Poe's humorously bizarre stories.

When Jane Rice's stories from *Unknown*, especially "The Refugee" and "The Idol of the Flies," have been anthologized, the marketing language used to promote them has focused on the presumed gruesomeness of the characters' deaths rather than the modernist satire embedded within the terror. In "Idol of the Flies" from *Unknown*'s June 1942 issue, the "bratty" Pruitt, a psychopath in the making, flees a swarm of flies and drowns when he becomes entangled, ironically, in the net he had thrown into the water earlier in the story. His subsequent drowning is attended by representatives of the various animals he has tormented.[51] While not laughter-inducing, the tale elicits a grim chuckle, which was certainly Rice's goal.[52] Like the King in Poe's "Hop-Frog," Pruitt's brutality is turned against him in a final reckoning that exposes his moral failings. The King in "Hop-Frog" intends to frighten the women of the court with the clever practical joke of masquerading as ourang-outangs, a jape suggested by the jester Hop-Frog, while in Rice's story the practical joke is the lengthy harassment of Miss Bittner, the tutor and professed "flyophobe," with dead flies.[53] Each story depends on a performance of brutal misogyny that sparks the turn in events. Rice's villain and Poe's meet death by similar means. Although Pruitt is not burned to death like the King, he is nevertheless a victim of his own practical joke; Pruitt is chased into the nearby pond by a swarm of mayflies, and he drowns there, tangled in the net he had thrown into the water while tormenting the handyman Harry.[54] Similarly, the King and his seven councilors, once costumed as ourang-outangs in tar and flax, find themselves entangled in a chandelier's chain. Hop-Frog's revenge is complete when he sets the King and his company aflame, but it is Poe's descriptions of the court jester—with "the agility of a monkey" and "the fang-like teeth of the dwarf"—that unites the two stories, both of which showcase the trope of an animal avenger seeking justice for human cruelty.[55]

Indeed, Poe's macabre humor may have been the feature most frequently imitated by female pulp authors, who often wrote in the "light fantastic" mode Campbell championed in *Unknown*. Referring to the Gothic Horror tale as a "blunt instrument" conveys an underlying criticism of the graphic violence demonstrated in shudder pulps throughout the 1930s, a time before the Comics Code Authority started regulating the content of comic books in 1954. Horror comics would largely replace the shudder pulps, especially those dedicated to the tales of weird menace as defined by Robert Kenneth Jones, but the pulps would continue throughout the 1940s and 1950s, focusing more intently on science fiction and fantasy than horror. The role that violence played in the early years of the shudder pulps diminished, and even the horrifying monsters were substituted for real-life villains or clever twists of fate. Female pulp authors also moved on to television writing, just as their male counterparts had, but some still wrote Gothic or Weird tales for the pulps and the emerging mass market paperbacks. Mary Elizabeth Counselman, for example, was one of the few female writers whose careers bridged the transition between pulps and paperbacks, and her stories feature the twists of fate that became increasingly commonplace. For instance, in her shocking short story "Night Court," a reckless driver, Bob Trask, is brought before a jury of the dead after running down a little girl one night. He has escaped justice so many times before that he cannot muster any sympathy from the victims who confront him within the spectral court. The judgment against him is a "fate worse than death": a bewildering cliché, since the stubbornly unrepentant young man cannot imagine what would be worse than dying. When he returns to the natural world, the twist is revealed when he begins piecing together the events that preceded his supernatural court appearance: the blonde girl he feared he had killed hours earlier is revealed to have been a vision of his future child who would inevitably die under the wheels of his car.[56]

Later women horror writers—Patricia Highsmith, Shirley Jackson, Flannery O'Connor, and Joyce Carol Oates, to name only four—would prefer these tales of cruel fate to Weird fiction, even as these authors continued to tread in the footsteps of Poe. His writing represented a middle way between the Gothic shudder-coinings of sheeted ghosts with their clanging chains and the existential crisis made manifest in the Weird as cosmic horror. In this way, "terror's true source" for the female pulp authors was personal, psychological, and even cathartic in its exorcizing of the insidious and persistent anxiety that plagued the narrators and—by extension, perhaps—the readers. Fate was unkind, even cruel, in its indifference to the human condition, as their stories indicated, and by emphasizing that theme, those works exhibited Poe's literary influence, transforming the grim and bleak reality of the nineteenth-century Gothic into the modernized version displayed in the pulps.

NOTES

1. Among contemporary monographs recommended are Michael Ashley's *The Time Machines: The Story of Science-Fiction Pulp Magazines from the Beginning to 1950* (Liverpool: Liverpool University Press, 2000); Eric Leif Davin's *Partners in Wonder: Women and the Birth of Science Fiction: 1926–1965* (Lanham, MD: Lexington Books, 2005); and Lisa Yaszeck and Patrick B. Sharp's *Sisters of Tomorrow: The First Women of Science Fiction* (Middletown, CT: Wesleyan University Press, 2016), though so many of the recent studies focus exclusively on the emergence of science fiction rather than the whole body of speculative fiction. Notably, however, Lisa Kröger and Melanie R. Anderson's *Monster She Wrote: The Women Who Pioneered Horror and Speculative Fiction* (Philadelphia: Quirk Books, 2019) includes a chapter on women pulp writers, and numerous collections of weird fiction by women have published in recent years, such as Melissa Edmundson's *Women's Weird: Stories by Women, 1890–1940* (London, Handheld Classics, 2019); Melanie R. Anderson's *The Women of Weird Tales* (Richmond: Valancourt Books, 2020); and Lisa Morton's *Weird Women, Vol. II 1840–1925* (New York: Pegasus Books, 2021), among others. Scholarship dedicated to "shudder" pulp magazines does exist, and some important studies are Robert Kenneth Jones's *The Shudder Pulps: A History of the Weird Menace Magazines of the 1930s* (Berkeley Heights: Wildside Press, 1978); Kevin Valliant's thesis for the College of William and Mary, *Fears in Concrete Forms: Modernity and Horror in the United States: 1880–1939* (2015); and Ed Hulse's *Satan Lives for My Love!: Sex and Sadism in Marvel's Horror Pulps, 1938–1940* (Morris Plains: Murania Press, 2019).

2. *Weird Tales* (1923–1954), *Ghost Stories* (1926–1932), *Terror Tales* (1931–1941), *Horror Stories* (1935–1941), and a smattering of other pulp magazines with shorter but still influential runs are included, not to mention those pulps dedicated exclusively to the field of "weird menace" such as *Dime Mystery Magazine* (1930–1949).

3. The United Kingdom had its own version of the pulps and general fiction magazines like *The Strand*, perhaps best known by contemporary readers for featuring Arthur Conan Doyle's Sherlock Holmes stories and Agatha Christie's Hercule Poirot mysteries. During Poe's era, *Blackwood's Magazine* had published similar fare.

4. *Weird Tales*, February 1927, 1.

5. Ibid., 1.

6. Genre categories then and now are problematic, and pulp magazines tended to use the term *fantasy* when referring to Gothic or Weird fiction, with the occasional usage of *horror* denoting the type of fantasy featured. Moreover, branding terms were sometimes coded so that *mystery* might be used to designate a pulp featuring *weird menace* stories (i.e., those featuring supernatural antagonists who would later prove altogether natural), while a pulp titled *Spicy Mystery* would indicate to potential readers a weird menace magazine with light eroticism, usually in the form of the female protagonist, undoubtedly nude or half-dressed at some point, harassed by a villainous brute or cult.

7. See Robert Kenneth Jones, *The Shudder Pulps: A History of the Weird Menace Magazines of the 1930s* (Rockville, MD: Wildside Press, 1978).

8. Eric Leif Davin, *Partners in Wonder: Women and the Birth of Science Fiction, 1926–1965* (Lanham, MD: Lexington Books, 2006), 66.

9. Meredith Davis, "The Accusing Voice," *Weird Tales* (March 1923): 112.

10. Ibid., 117.

11. Ibid., 118.

12. As Jones asserts in *The Shudder Pulps: A History of the Weird Menace Magazines of the 1930s*, three "distinctive elements" set the shudder pulps apart from the magazines that preceded them and accounted for the new type of story that had come into being: "Gothicism, sadism and weird menacism" (7). Among the three, only "weird menacism" might be unfamiliar to contemporary readers, but for pulp readers of the era, that element was the mainstay of the shudder pulps, in which supernatural plot points are revealed to have realistic conclusions—often revealing human villains at work behind the scenes.

13. Although Baird's authorship of the editorial is disputable, he is credited here with representing the overall editorial philosophy of the magazine.

14. Mike Ashley, *The Time Machines*, 41.

15. "Why Weird Tales?," *Weird Tales* (May 1924): 1.

16. Lee Server, *Danger Is My Business: An Illustrated History of the Fabulous Pulp Magazines, 1896–1953* (San Francisco: Chronicle, 1993): 62–65.

17. Kurt Shoemaker, "Scobee's Mountain," *Purple Prose* (November 1998): 12–21.

18. See S. T. Joshi, *The Weird Tale* (Berkeley Heights: Wildside Press, 1990). Joshi includes Bierce among the other founders of the Weird tale: Arthur Machen, Lord Dunsany, Algernon Blackwood, M. R. James, and H. P. Lovecraft. Joshi addresses Edgar Allan Poe's contributions to the history of the Weird in *Unutterable Horror: A History of Supernatural Fiction, from Gilgamesh to the End of the Nineteenth Century*, vol. 1 (New York: Hippocampus Press, 2004) and elsewhere.

19. Baird, 1.

20. Ibid., 2.

21. Ibid., 1–2

22. Ibid., 2.

23. Davin, *Partners in Wonder*, 68.

24. Campbell ceased editing in 1971, but the magazine continues into the present.

25. Rice's story never made it into print during *Unknown*'s initial run, as the last issue was published in October 1943—one month before the story was to appear. Note: the name *Unknown* was later changed to *Unknown Worlds* around the same time that the magazine dispensed with illustrated covers, presumably to save money.

26. Jane Rice, "The Cats," *The Idol of the Flies and Other Stories*, ed. Stefan R. Dziemianowicz and Jim Rockill (Seattle: Midnight House, 2003), 221.

27. Ibid., 221.

28. Ibid., 231.

29. Ken Dancyger and Jeff Rush, *Alternative Scriptwriting* (New York: Focal Press, 2006), 85.

30. The show's popularity led to many other parodies, but a more interesting bit of trivia is that a town in New Mexico renamed itself Truth or Consequences to make its

residents eligible for prizes. For more information, visit the following webpage: https://www.rusc.com/old-time-radio/Truth-Or-Consequences.aspx?s=698.

31. Rice "The Cats," 225.

32. Ibid., 231.

33. Ibid., 231

34. Edgar Allan Poe, "The Black Cat," *The Collected Tales of Edgar Allan Poe*, ed. Thomas Ollive Mabbott, vol. 3 (Cambridge: Harvard University Press), 849–50.

35. Cocktails and alcohol in general appear often in Rice's fiction, but none so humorously as "The Elixir," in which a nauseating mixture of leftover liquors transports the main character to the era of the witch trials and a showdown with the male antagonists who accuse her of witchcraft.

36. Greye La Spina, "Invaders from the Dark," *Weird Tales* (April, May, June 1925): 61–98; 273–98; 431–49.

37. The name "Portia Delorme" may allude to a character in the 1849 version of Poe's "Bridal Ballad," wherein the deceased lover haunting the female speaker is identified as "dead D'Elormie." In her novel, Grey La Spina sets up a similar romantic triangle involving the human Portia Delorme, the werewolf Princess Tchernova, and Owen Edwardes. Both texts also employ the "demon lover" trope from Scottish ballads such as "The House Carpenter" (Child no. 243).

38. *Shudder-coining* was the derisive term employed by H. P. Lovecraft in his essay "Supernatural Horror in Literature." See Lovecraft's *The Annotated Supernatural Horror in Literature*, ed. S. T. Joshi (New York: Hippocampus Press, 2012), 55–56. It is used to describe the predictable Gothic fiction of Poe's era: "Poe's spectres thus acquired a convincing malignity possessed by none of their predecessors, and established a new standard of realism in the annals of literary horror. The impersonal and artistic intent, moreover, was aided by a scientific attitude not often found before; whereby Poe studied the human mind rather than the usages of Gothic fiction, and worked with an analytical knowledge of terror's true sources which doubled the force of his narratives and emancipated him from all the absurdities inherent in merely conventional shudder-coining."

39. "Unknown." *Unknown*. March 1939, 5. The advertisement appears immediately after the table of contents, and the only indicator of authorship is the phrase "The Editor" at the bottom of the page.

40. Ibid., 5.

41. Edgar Allan Poe, "Some Words with a Mummy," *The Collected Tales of Edgar Allan Poe*, ed. Thomas Ollive Mabbott, vol. 3 (Cambridge: Harvard University Press): 1195.

42. For an analysis of this story, see Burton R. Pollin, "Poe's Literary Use of 'Oppodeldoc' and Other Patent Medicines," *Poe Studies* (December 1971): 30–32.

43. "Who Wants Power?" *Unknown* (March 1939): 96.

44. Ibid., 96.

45. Ibid., 97.

46. Ibid., 97.

47. Ibid., 99–100.

48. Ibid., 104–5.

49. Ibid., 106.

50. John W. Campbell Jr., *From Unknown Worlds* (New York: Street and Smith Publications, 1948), 3.

51. See Kevin Knott, "Jane Rice's 'The Idol of the Flies': Evil as Unwelcome Houseguest," *Gothic Animals: Uncanny Otherness and the Animal With-Out*, ed. Ruth Heholt and Melissa Edmundson (New York: Palgrave Macmillan, 2020): 173–86.

52. Similarly, October 1943's "The Refugee" has an American expatriate dilettante furnishing her meager tea offerings to her French neighbors with the processed and cooked body of a werewolf who had arrived on her doorstep.

53. Jane Rice, "The Idol of the Flies," *Unknown Worlds* (June 1942): 91.

54. Ibid., 93.

55. Edgar Allan Poe, "Hop-Frog," *The Collected Tales of Edgar Allan Poe*, vol. 3, ed. Thomas Ollive Mabbott (Cambridge: Harvard University Press), 1353.

56. Mary Elizabeth Counselman, "Night Court," *Weird Tales* (March 1953): 46.

Chapter Eight

Traces of Poe's House of Usher in the Work of Contemporary Women Horror Writers

Melanie R. Anderson

Unlike other notable writers in the American canon, Poe has continued to have a robust academic following *and* a ubiquitous presence in the world of popular culture. Readers of popular genre fiction often are reminded of Poe's phantasmagorically weird and otherworldly settings, his unreliable narrators, his creepy houses, and his characters' crimes, obsessions, and violent actions. Although his imagination was limitless, Poe failed to explore female perspectives as deeply as he could have. For example, Allan Lloyd-Smith identifies the "fear of the feminine" as a common trope of early American Gothic writing, and he points to several of Poe's stories as purveyors of this theme, including "The Fall of the House of Usher."[1] Commenting on similar themes, Renée L. Bergland focuses on the penchant of white nineteenth-century American writers for presenting historically marginalized characters as ghostly figures on the edges of their narratives.[2] Lloyd-Smith's theory of the early Gothic "fear of the feminine" and Bergland's idea of the spectralization of marginalized individuals eerily bring to mind Poe's representation of Madeline Usher as silent and ghostly before she is prematurely buried. Many current authors, especially diverse women writers of horror, are taking up the task of acknowledging the literary legacy of early male writers like Poe yet revising their exclusionary premises by producing vibrant and terrifying works that address problematic parts of the Gothic tradition with an awareness of today's reading audience and contemporary social realities. This chapter explores how ghostly traces of Poe's "The Fall of the House of Usher" haunt the creations of Sarah Waters, Cherie Priest, and Silvia Moreno-Garcia.

The setting of the haunted house, an integral part of Poe's development of the American Gothic, is also a vital characteristic of contemporary domestic horror by these women, all of whom give that trope a feminist twist by emphasizing the experiences of historically marginalized characters who resist patriarchal control and the threat of erasure.

POE AND THE FOUNDATIONAL HOUSE OF USHER

To appreciate these adaptations, one must first examine Poe's own use of the haunted house motif. Moving beyond Gothic conventions inherited from Europe, Poe transformed the haunted house into an important fictional device he used to plumb the depths of psychological terror. One of his most famous tales, "The Fall of the House of Usher," serves as a prime example of the way the haunted house draws attention to the domestic terror of dysfunctional family life.[3] Much of that terror is foreshadowed in the unnamed narrator's first glimpse of the manor:

> I looked upon the scene before me—upon the mere house, and the simple landscape features of the domain—upon the bleak walls—upon the vacant eye-like windows—upon a few rank sedges—and upon a few white trunks of decayed trees—with an utter depression of soul which I can compare to no earthly sensation more properly than to the after-dream of the reveller upon opium—the bitter lapse into everyday life—the hideous dropping off of the veil.[4]

In this moment, the dejected narrator is terrified by the façade of the House of Usher, and he is unable to describe specifically and concretely his horror of this house with its sinister similarities to a human face. Reaching for experiential correlatives, he references opium fantasies, dreams, and hypnagogic trances. He looks at the reflection of the house in the tarn before it, and his depression is unrelieved. There is no clear description of where this home in the fog is, and, when the narrator enters the mansion, the reader has a creeping feeling that he leaves reality for another plane of existence.[5] With its sense of terror and uncertainty, this encounter with a haunted home, or a Bad Place, to use Stephen King's term, is a scene frequently employed by horror authors countless times since Poe.[6]

To be sure, even without a castle for the setting, the Gothic elements in the tale are evident, especially in the House of Usher and the family that lives within its walls. Poe uses themes of traditional Gothic literature, such as isolation, decay, family secrets, dysfunction, and violence, but he connects these terrors to a building that seems malevolent and that reflects the psychological distresses of its inhabitants. It has "eye-like windows," after all. Although the castle is gone, there is still the whiff of aristocracy, a class element that was important to British Gothic tales. For example, the narrator observes that the "peasantry" in the area refer to the family and the house together by the "appellation of the 'House of Usher.'"[7] The family line, however, has dwindled to two individuals, and readers assume the family's bank accounts have decreased as well. Moreover, the "barely perceptible fissure" in the house's face and foundation implies weakness or damage in the house and family, and the manor does literally fall at the end of the story after both of the Usher twins die.[8] Thus, the decay of the house mirrors the disintegration of the family inside. Dale Bailey acknowledges that Poe's story is ambiguous, has psychological implications, and can be a "mirror" for readers' knowledge and experiences, but he points to Poe's description of the house as malevolent as something new in American Gothic fiction.[9] He writes, "And while the House of Usher is in many respects typical of the traditional Gothic setting— a vast, ancient, aristocratic mansion in a vaguely European landscape—Poe attributes to it at least one revolutionary quality that will become central to the haunted house formula: the house is alive. It possesses its own malign will."[10] This house is a Bad Place.

In the story, Roderick is convinced that his house is malevolent by its very nature, and this is clear in his description of the construction of the house and the connections he believes it shares with the surrounding landscape. The narrator attributes Roderick's theory of "the sentience of all vegetable things," his perception of awareness in the plant life and inanimate objects that surround him, to a "disordered fancy":

> The belief, however, was connected . . . with the gray stones of the home of his forefathers. The conditions of the sentience had been here, he imagined, fulfilled in the method of collocation of these stones—in the order of their arrangement, as well as in that of the many *fungi* which overspread them, and of the decayed trees which stood around—above all, in the long undisturbed endurance of this arrangement, and in its reduplication in the still waters of the tarn.[11]

Roderick concludes by noting the weird "atmosphere" that the fungus has created around the home and claims that this unhealthy ambiance has harmed his family for centuries. Roderick connects the house and grounds to the physical and mental maladies that he and his sister have inherited. According to Bailey, Usher's obsession with the design of the house shows that "[a]n obscure conjunction of architecture and geometry has endowed the house with a malign will and intelligence utterly distinct from any merely human revenant."[12] By contrast, the narrator does not believe that the house has supernatural power, dismissing his friend's theories as worthy of "no comment."[13] The narrator does not believe that there could be an uncanny connection between the minds of the Ushers and their house. Indeed, he spends a lot of time during his visit trying to cheer Roderick up with painting, music, and reading (activities he thinks appropriate for an invalid) as well as trying to explain what is happening in the house without resorting to supernatural causes. He fails miserably in both efforts. Even though he prizes his rationality, he fails to see that he and Usher buried Madeline alive. Showing his own unreliability as a narrator in this otherworldly setting, he tells the reader he remembers everything he and Usher did together but admits that he "should fail in any attempt to convey an idea of the exact character of the studies, or of the occupations, in which [Usher] involved" him.[14] And there is the climactic return of the buried Madeline, which happens while the narrator reads a book to calm Roderick. Roderick knows Madeline is coming, but the narrator does not believe the sounds he is hearing are from anything other than the storm outside—until Madeline kills her brother and the narrator flees the collapsing house.

The initial repression of Madeline calls to mind the ghostly representations of women as one of the marginalized groups Bergland identifies and the "fear of the feminine" that Lloyd-Smith detects, but this silencing is also a sign of the family dysfunction within the House of Usher. Readers know neither why Roderick would be willing to bury his sister alive nor why, if he was unaware she was still alive at the burial, he would leave her entombed without responding to the sounds of her attempts to escape, sounds his acute hearing had registered for days. Since the Usher line "lay in the direct line of descent" and "had put forth, at no period, any enduring branch," there is an implication that Roderick tried to destroy the incestuous Usher clan for reasons related to family history or issues of inheritance.[15] Whatever she represents for Roderick as she haunts him, flitting silently through the house in the background or clawing maniacally at the lid of her coffin, Poe does not explain. Madeline's imprisonment, however, makes her an archetype of marginalization that contemporary women horror writers are challenging and revising.

Significantly, Roderick attempts to bury the reasons for his actions within his mind, and this act replicates the entombment of Madeline's body in the family crypt. Repression and "the impossibility of forgetting" are, according to Eric Savoy, the most important aspects of American Gothic haunted house fiction.[16] Riffing on the description of Madeline as a "tenant" in her tomb of live burial (a haunted house within a larger one), Savoy argues that "the entire tradition of American gothic can be conceptualized as the attempt to invoke 'the face of the tenant'—the specter of Otherness that haunts the house of national narrative . . . [through] a double talk that gazes in terror at what it is compelled to bring forward but cannot explain, that writes what it cannot read."[17] Madeline is the silent Other of the text; she is a sign that cannot be explained for Roderick and the narrator. But she cannot be completely forgotten: she erupts in violence and seeks retribution. Roderick hides her, but he cannot forget her.[18]

This trope of the haunted house that Poe relied on in "Usher" is also integral to the work of women writers of horror.[19] Gina Wisker describes the haunted houses of contemporary women's Gothic writing as spaces where history, experience, and perspective are contested. Citing Poe's "Usher" as a "model" of domestic Gothic, Wisker posits: "In contemporary women's domestic Gothic ghost stories, the complex histories of troubled families, the incarceration of the domestic space and domestic roles are expressed and enacted in uncanny returns, in homes which explode or implode."[20] For Wisker, the terrors in these horror narratives are embedded in domestic spaces, and alternative perspectives often haunt from marginal areas like attics and basements.[21] In any era, women writers use the Gothic to address what is ignored or elided, and the supernatural helps bring attention to these hidden narratives. It can subvert the space of the home as well, thereby showing the uncanny possibilities that lie beneath domesticity.

Remodeling the House of Usher in Women's Horror Fiction

The contemporary writer Sarah Waters revisits and revises "The Fall of the House of Usher" in *The Little Stranger* (2009). Set in rural Warwickshire during the early 1950s, this book is clearly influenced by early Gothic writers of the 1700s. The novel also has callbacks to Poe's tale, including a character named Roderick. In *The Little Stranger*, Waters depicts a decrepit large estate, Hundreds Hall, owned by the Ayreses, a once wealthy aristocratic family. Hundreds Hall and the Ayres family are crumbling in post–World War II Britain in the face of a changing socioeconomic system. The remaining family members include Mrs. Ayres and her two surviving adult children. Caroline and Roderick both served in the war, and Roderick has ghastly physical and mental combat wounds, the former from a plane crash and the latter a case of what people would think of today as PTSD. An older daughter, Susan, died at age eight of diphtheria before Caroline and Roderick were born. This was a horrible blow to Mrs. Ayres, who still mourns the loss and feels guilt because her grief created a wedge between her and her other children.

Onto this stage of pain and loss, both past and present, steps Dr. Faraday, the son of a maid who worked at Hundreds Hall when he was a child. Mired in a strange mix of jealousy, entitlement, and resentment, Faraday has always felt a connection to Hundreds. The book begins with Faraday remembering when he was a ten-year-old observing Mr. and Mrs. Ayres and Susan at an Empire Day gathering. During the party, Faraday went inside the house and into a restricted room. He cut an acorn-shaped piece of plaster off of the wall. For Faraday, that defacement and theft were not, however, acts of vandalism. He remembers, "I wasn't a spiteful or destructive boy. It was simply that, in admiring the house, I wanted to possess a piece of it—or rather, as if the admiration itself, which I suspected a more ordinary child would not have felt, entitled me to it."[22] He spends his life obsessed with Hundreds and ultimately will do whatever he can to be in charge of it, even as he denies resenting the family for exploiting his mother.

Dr. Faraday provides descriptions of the decay of Hundreds Hall thirty years after the theft of the plaster acorn, when he is summoned in the place of the family's regular doctor to treat a young servant girl named Betty. His initial sighting of the Hall calls to mind the ruin of the House of Usher. Once Faraday maneuvers his car up the overgrown drive, he sees Hundreds Hall clearly for the first time as an adult:

> What horrified me were the signs of decay. Sections of the lovely weathered edgings seemed to have fallen completely away, so that the house's uncertain Georgian outline was even more tentative than before. Ivy had spread, then patchily died, and hung like tangled rat's-tail hair. The steps leading up to the broad front door were cracked, with weeds growing lushly up through the seams.[23]

The former glory of the house is gone. Rooms are regularly shut when the family cannot pay for the upkeep, and Mrs. Ayres worries about her inability to dress for guests. The family's respected place in the community is a holdover from the past. Even though it is none of his concern, Faraday is horrified to learn that Roderick is in the process of selling parcels of Hundreds Hall's park for affordable council houses. The doctor sees the Hall as occupying a liminal space between what it was and what it seems to be. In his eyes, the past glories haunt the present ruins. He thinks, "I had an impression of the house being held in some sort of balance. One could see so painfully, I thought, both the glorious thing it had recently been, and the ruin it was on the way to becoming."[24]

The Ayreses see the house differently, especially Caroline, who had to return after she began a life separate from the family, and Roderick, who must try to manage a property in inevitable decline. For the siblings, Hundreds is like a prison. Caroline tells the doctor, "'Hundreds is lovely. But it's a sort of lovely monster! It needs to be fed all the time, with money and hard work. And when one feels *them*'—she nodded to the row of sombre portraits— 'at one's shoulder, looking on, it can begin to seem like a frightful burden. . . . It's hardest on Rod, because he has the extra responsibility of being master.'"[25] The monstrous house is tied to the watching ancestors just as present financial concerns depend upon past edicts of inheritance, marriage, and pro-creation. Roderick feels trapped by these strictures as well. He acknowledges that he and Caroline will most likely not marry. Nevertheless, instead of selling the house, he remains trapped in the intense anxiety of trying to save it. He tells Faraday, "If you like the damn house so much, why don't you try running it! I'd like to see you. . . . Don't you know that in every second of every day the whole damn thing's in danger of crashing down, and taking me, and Caroline, and Mother down with it?"[26] This hypothetical crashing end recalls the collapse of Poe's House of Usher, and like his literary namesake, Waters's Roderick is concerned about the sentience of his ancestral manse. Roderick receives numerous injuries from ordinary household objects that have become malevolent. He believes that the thing he wants to save is trying to injure and expel him.

Dr. Faraday, the narrator, is reminiscent of the outsider narrator in "Usher" in his persistent attempts to rationalize the Ayreses' uncanny experiences in their home without fully understanding them. Unlike Poe's narrator, Faraday is desperate to rise in social station, and he does not stop at misinterpreting the family's difficulties and offering ultimately useless and dangerous ratio-nalizations. He believes that his parents worked themselves to death to make him a respectable doctor, and he makes it his mission to move up another rung on the class ladder and acquire Hundreds Hall through marriage to Caroline. Gina Wisker suggests Faraday "believes he is a prince coming to rescue a sleeping beauty," and she writes that he "is caught in a narrative which has women and their homes as prizes, a story in which he can play a role of rescuer with his new medical knowledge."[27] *He* is the threat to the family. When Faraday dismisses Caroline's attempts to explain the supernatural events at Hundreds, she correctly asserts that "we've only had trouble since *you've* been in" the house.[28] After Faraday offers to treat Roderick's leg with electrolysis so he can keep visiting the Hall, the Ayreses' horrors multiply. He is unrelentingly "rational" throughout the novel, denying the family's suspi-cions that something supernatural is going on at Hundreds. He rules Roddy as mentally unstable and has him committed, and he tries to do the same to Mrs. Ayres before she commits suicide. He then pressures Caroline into an engagement to prevent her from leaving Hundreds. He hints of an engage-ment to the other doctors in town before ever asking Caroline to marry him, and he begins planning for a wedding without her knowledge. When Caroline finally accepts his proposal, she is far from enthusiastic: "Yes, if you like. Only let me go to bed! I'm so, so tired."[29] Finally, for a doctor who believes he is completely rational and calm, Faraday has quite an explosion of temper when Caroline stands up to him and extricates herself from their question-able engagement. She plans to sell the estate and go to Canada or America. Faraday denies that his sole interest is gaining Hundreds, but he immediately consults a lawyer to see about having Caroline committed. Faraday spends the time left before Caroline's departure constantly calling and visiting her, demanding that she stay and marry him.

Unfortunately for Caroline, much like Madeline Usher, she does not get to have a life away from Hundreds. On the night before she is to leave, Caroline plunges to her death from the main stairway in Hundreds, and there is an indication that the act was not, as some believed, suicide. The young servant Betty swears she heard Caroline call out, "You," right before she fell, "as if she had seen someone she knew."[30] In spite of that testimony, Faraday speaks at the inquest as an expert about Caroline's mental state and continues his control of the family story. Faraday calls Betty's statement into question as superstitious, and he officially rewrites Caroline's death as a suicide, even though, by all accounts, Caroline was happy to be leaving Hundreds and resuming her independent life. Once the family is gone, Faraday uses his copies of the estate's keys that were unknown to the Ayreses to access the house whenever he wishes. He searches in vain for a ghost, but tellingly, he realizes that "what [he is] looking at is only a cracked window-pane, and that the face gazing distortedly from it, baffled and longing, is [his] own."[31] Faraday has his own moment of seeing his identity in the home that he desired above all else. This recognition suggests that Faraday was the poltergeist (or "The Little Stranger," as he and his colleague Dr. Seely called it) tormenting the family, and that he was the presence Caroline saw and spoke to before her fall. Every time something terrible happens at Hundreds, Faraday simultaneously experiences intense emotion that he cannot comprehend. During various incidents, Faraday is angry and rageful; he has strange nightmares; or he describes experiencing a fugue state in which he enters the grounds and the house and does things he cannot remember clearly. Faraday's obsession with owning Hundreds, trapping Caroline in a marriage socially advantageous to himself, and displacing the Ayres family, gives him, an outsider, control over the inheritance and the secrets the house still holds. Faraday's usurpations may reflect the shifting class relations of post–World War II Britain, but the Ayreses are trapped in the past, unable to adapt to the changes. Caroline, as a marriageable woman called back home to take care of her brother and mother, ultimately cannot escape ancestral expectations (represented by those family portraits) and social pressures that she marry and keep up Hundreds Hall. Faraday manipulates the situation for his own purposes, but his motives are not questioned by the other doctors and people in town. Caroline's independent behavior makes her a puzzle to the surrounding society, so it is not difficult for them to accept the doctor's interpretation of her death. Wisker writes, "[T]his novel exposes the limitations of established roles for women—mothers, wives, daughters, servants, nurturers—and problematises and questions both the security of women's 'place'—the home—and the narratives in which women find themselves constructed and constrained, which reinforce domesticity and the domestic."[32] Caroline's options as a woman of her social station are still limited, even after her taste of freedom during the war. While Caroline's story is "buried" in Hundreds by the outsider Faraday rather than her brother Roderick, Caroline's fate resembles the ends of previous Gothic heroines, and it is reminiscent of the imprisonment and death of Madeline in Poe's nineteenth-century domestic ghost story.[33]

If "Gothic plots are family plots," then Cherie Priest's *The Family Plot* (2016) emblazons its Gothic pedigree in its title.[34] Moreover, the novel includes different types of "plots." There is the story of the dysfunctional Withrow family with a continuing spectral struggle over the family narrative between a brother and sister, but there are also two burial grounds, one the official Withrow plot at the town cemetery in Chattanooga, Tennessee, and the other a fake Halloween decoration plot, in which murder victims and family pariahs were buried and some nasty family secrets repressed. *The Family Plot* incorporates the idea of inheritance with a descendant, Augusta Withrow, who wants nothing to do with the family house or its memories, and the family estate becomes commodified in salvage. Pieces of the house (and possibly its haunting) will be sold to other families to use in restoration projects. Augusta wants the property razed and the land donated to the local Civil War park, but she is selling everything, including the house, outbuildings, and all they contain, to Music City Salvage. The owner, Chuck Dutton, cannot believe his luck at acquiring the estate. Although it is a risk with his lack of present capital, the purchase could pay off grandly, thereby guaranteeing the security of his family business. Chuck needs to pick over and sell the Withrow belongings to make money, but his crew, led by his recently divorced daughter Dahlia, ends up picking at secret Withrow wounds.

Augusta, like most inheritors of a Bad Place, hates her family's house. She tells Dahlia that she left it as soon as she could, and she refuses to enter it when Dahlia wants to show her a photo album that the crew found on the property. She says, "I wish you and your crew the best. But goddamn this house, and this land, and everything left upon it. When you're finished here, the devil can take that, too."[35] By contrast, Dahlia loves the Withrow home, and she explores the house alone before the rest of the crew arrives. Inside, she introduces herself and apologizes for the teardown: "I'd save you if I could, but I can't—so I'll save what pieces I can. In that way, you'll live on someplace else. That's all I can offer. But I promise, I will take you apart with love . . . and I'll never forget you."[36] Immediately, strange things occur: she hears the house speak to her; she realizes that she could not hear her team calling to her from outside the house, even with its broken windows; and she finds the front door that she had left open closed and bolted. She tries to rationalize these events away, but the menace within the house is clear from the words she hears spoken in it: "*an angry thing*," "*unloved*," and "*lost*."[37]

Dahlia's feelings about the Withrow house are complicated, and they end up marking her as the chosen victim of the house's angry ghost, Abigail. Dahlia acknowledges that she feels a deeper connection to the Withrow house than she experienced during past salvage jobs, and she sees the other ghosts on the property, Buddy and Hazel, more often than her coworkers do. As she does with all the houses she must demolish, she wishes she could save the Withrow house, thinking of all the things she could fix and restore. Her desire to save the house goes deeper than her love of restoration work, though. While looking at the Withrow house, she recalls her former home, a place taken from her in a contentious divorce. Similar to inheritance squabbles in Gothic novels, divorce separates family members, and it disconnects people from homes. Dahlia's anger over the loss of money, time, and love put into the home she lost bubbles up as the Withrow house speaks to her. Dahlia remembers that *she* was the one who had chosen her home, saved for the down payment and mortgage, and invested in all the restoration work she completed with her own hands. Then, her ex-husband, Andy, "[took] it away just because he knew she loved it."[38] In addition, the end of her marriage not only resulted in the loss of her home, but it also strained the family business by damaging her relationship with her cousin Bobby, a member of the crew working at the Withrow house. The two quarrel incessantly, but Dahlia remembers how close they were as kids. She blames Andy for taking her friend from her. At the end of the novel, Augusta speculates that Abigail tried to kill Dahlia either because she was the only woman on the crew or "because [she was] alone and angry."[39] Dahlia denies being angry, but she does spend a lot of time during the job trying to discover the past of the Withrow family. Perhaps the desire to solve the mystery of the Withrows' past and understand their secrets is a way to tamp down and ignore her own secret anger, pain, and loss. Unfortunately, her raw emotions over the divorce and loss of her home are still there, whether or not she admits the fact. And her investigation into the family's past allows Abigail to target her as a fellow sufferer of loss at the hands of men. When Dahlia is trapped alone in the house after her nephew Gabe's horrible injury forces the rest of the crew out into a storm to try to get help, Abigail forces Dahlia to relive the Withrows' past from Abigail's perspective. But Abigail adds to the torment by making Dahlia ruminate on her feelings about Andy and the divorce.

Beyond her repressed anger over the loss of her home, marriage, and possibly her closest childhood friend, Dahlia is a victim of a domestic haunting because of the way she idealizes homes instead of focusing on destroying houses, which is her profession. Whereas her father and the men on her crew think of wrecking the house as a job to do so they can sell salvageable parts,

Dahlia is ambivalent about the work. She sees its financial necessity, but as she tells Brad, "I *always* want to save the house. . . . Except for the one time when I bought the place myself, it's never worked out. But this one, this Withrow house . . . it's a hot mess, but I really love it. It speaks to me."[40] When she admits to Brad that the house says it is "unhappy" and "angry," he asks if she is really describing herself. She tosses back, "Can't it be both of us?"[41] As in other domestic Gothic ghost stories, the love of a home and its possibilities as a beautiful and nostalgic location are connected to loss, anger, and finances. The house has always held opposites inside of it such as life and death, hope and loss, love and anger, as well as a sense of belonging and the pain of exclusion, and Dahlia is receptive to this mix. When Dahlia finds a photo album, she still offers it to Augusta, even though Augusta's only interest in the estate is its destruction. Dahlia cannot imagine throwing out a piece of her family history, and she eagerly keeps the album for herself—almost as if she wants a connection to the Withrow house. She accepts that houses can be haunted because they are intimate family spaces where people live and die. She sees houses as vessels of the past, but she verges on romanticizing them. The Withrow house's past is, of course, traumatic and violent. It is enigmatic because there are no indisputable records of what happened to its inhabitants. To understand the family history, Dahlia relies on the perspectives of the ghosts, speculation (hers and her crew's), and documents written by a single observer. On the one hand, unlike Faraday in *The Little Stranger*, Dahlia may believe in the supernatural, but on the other hand, like his efforts, her quest to understand the Withrow family's past and the haunting is doomed to fail since there is no clear evidence of what happened. Similar to Poe's narrator and Faraday, Dahlia sees herself in the Withrow estate, and her pain and loss merge with the house's. That identification is most likely why the ghosts of the sisters Hazel and Abigail both communicate with her.

The center of the Withrow family mystery is the burial of Abigail's story, and bits of it are unearthed throughout the novel by Dahlia and her crew—at one point they actually dig up a body in the fake Halloween cemetery. Augusta's Aunt Abigail is Hazel and Buddy's sister. She is the first ghost seen by the crew, and then they see the specter of her suitor, a soldier she murdered. Even though Buddy died when he was an adult, his ghost appears as a child traumatized by Abigail's homicidal actions. Fearing their abusive father, Hazel, during her life, hid in her room from the other family members, and her ghost occasionally lingers there. Wisker notes that versions of the past creep around haunted houses "to reveal alternative readings of history, identity and ways of seeing the world," and in *The Family Plot*, each specter is tied to a location in the Withrow house associated with personal trauma.[42] Buddy haunts the outbuildings and the attic, where he witnessed the murder. Hazel haunts her bedroom and can appear in reflective surfaces when Dahlia looks at them—another hint that Dahlia may see her own fractured family life in the house. Abigail, through visceral and terrifying manifestations, haunts the bathrooms, in particular the one attached to her old room where she gave birth to a baby who may or may not have been stillborn.

Augusta tells Dahlia that she and Hazel believed that "spinsterhood was the only way a woman might get out [of the family/house] alive," and when Dahlia witnesses episodes of the past through the hauntings, she learns why.[43] Judson Withrow was intent on making good matches for his children to carry on the property and the Withrow name, and he was so obsessed with appearances that he participated in concealing evidence of the soldier's murder by hiding the body in the fake cemetery. The family covered up Abigail's loss of the baby, after she buried it in the fake plot, by sending her to a mental hospital where she was treated harshly, and then her father tried to arrange her marriage into an illustrious family. When Abigail committed suicide, the family disowned her by refusing to bury her in the official family plot; she was interred in the fake plot instead. The Withrows' goals for Abigail were marrying well, having children, and honoring the family name. As a rejected ghost, exiled from her family's story, Abigail rages within the house, reliving her traumatic moments and looking for a woman with similar anger to manipulate.

Abigail sees Dahlia as the perfect victim. As previously mentioned, during Dahlia's final, chaotic night in the Withrow house, Abigail recreates the past of the Withrow family for Dahlia to observe Abigail's version of events. Then Abigail tries to connect her anger to Dahlia's. When Dahlia points out that Abigail is not completely innocent because she killed her lover, Abigail responds, "But you understand. You wanted to hurt yours. You *still* want to hurt him."[44] Dahlia protests that she did not want to hurt her ex-husband and that she barely fought for the house since she knew Andy came from money and could "take it anyhow."[45] Abigail presses Dahlia to accept her anger: "You loved that house, and he didn't even care about it. It was just spiteful, what he did."[46] The ghost goes so far as to tell Dahlia that her husband had a girlfriend before the divorce was finalized and may have been cheating on her before the end of their relationship. Abigail tells Dahlia, "Men don't care. Even when they know what they've done, and what it means—they don't care. They just leave us behind to clean up their messes."[47] Moved by Abigail's justified anger, Dahlia, suspecting that Andy had cheated on her, calls his cell. Her worst fears are confirmed: a woman answers the phone and does not know who is calling. Dahlia thinks, "If the woman who answered didn't see her name on the incoming call display, then Andy had removed her from his contacts, too."[48] Still, Dahlia protests against her anger, but Abigail is relentless. She tells Dahlia that she is haunting the house not to be part of the Withrow family but to show that she has outlasted them and their attempts to elide her. Abigail says she committed suicide so they would not "send me away again," adding, "I won't let you send me away, either."[49] In a scene described like a possession by Abigail, Dahlia slices her wrists on broken glass, and Abigail triumphantly declares, "Now you have to stay."[50] Dahlia believes that Abigail was trying to prevent the crew from expelling her and to keep Dahlia with her as a companion. Her family and doctor wonder if she might have attempted suicide because of her strange phone call to Andy. Although she protests that it was an accident, the cause is unclear.

The final tap of the shovel in the burial of Abigail's past is delivered by her brother Buddy, whose power over his sister's story is reminiscent of the control Roderick exercised over Madeline in Poe's tale. Dahlia learns that Abigail is enraged that Buddy's narrative of what happened has superseded her own, and she retells her account of the past while Buddy's ghost repeats his version. Buddy had, however, the advantage of living longer than Abigail, and he eventually committed his story to paper. One of the pieces of Withrow property put up for sale is the murder ballad that Buddy wrote about his sister titled "The Family Plot." This poem is a condemnation of "wicked women" like his sister, who, according to Buddy, seduced and murdered a young man named Gregory, murdered her baby born of the union, seduced another man, made a pact with the Devil, and committed suicide. The end of the ballad specifically warns innocent men to avoid women like his sister.[51] Dahlia learns that Abigail's discredited—but most likely true—version of events is different. In that account, Abigail killed Gregory for promising marriage and then abandoning her with a baby. When she asked if he was at least sorry for what he had done to her, he dismissed her, asking, "Sorry for what?"[52] Then she gave birth to a stillborn baby and subsequently suffered in a mental hospital. When she returned and prepared to marry, Buddy revealed the story of the baby at the wedding. In so doing, he dashed her hopes of escaping from her past and her father's control. Buddy, as the succeeding patriarch of the family, controlled the narration of Abigail's story. Rather than admitting the roles his father and Gregory played in Abigail's suffering, he twisted the story to make her seem evil and aberrant for trying to make her own choices. Abigail's anger at having her story repressed and revised is formidable, but her only outlet is to haunt the home where the dysfunction and violence took place. At the end of the novel, Dahlia has a flash of Abigail's violence when she goes back to work among pieces of the Withrow estate. The scene is ambiguous. While Dahlia changes the bandages on her arms in the salvage company's bathroom, she feels a chill in the air, perceives smells and sounds that she experienced at the Withrow house, and, in the mirror, sees a fleeting image of Abigail standing close behind her. The lightbulb in the room explodes, and Dahlia is left in darkness. Readers are left unsure whether Dahlia survives the attack. Whatever the outcome, the haunting is not over just because the

Withrow house has been torn down. Like Madeline Usher's, Abigail's anger is so violent and connected to the pieces of the house—and perhaps unfortunately to Dahlia, who has not fully faced up to her own past and anger—that it outlasts her family and overflows from the domestic space that held her contested story.

Although Mexican-Canadian author Silvia Moreno-Garcia was influenced by past writers of horror, the protagonist of her 2020 novel *Mexican Gothic* is a woman of color who would have been marginalized in earlier fiction. Moreno-Garcia also emphasizes the racism at the heart of European colonialism and white aristocratic incest. There are a few nods to Poe in this novel, from the house High Place and its connection with a particular family, to the premature burial of women who later unleash their wrath. The moment when the protagonist, Noemí Taboada, first sees Howard Doyle's mansion High Place is reminiscent of the narrator's first glimpse of the House of Usher:

> Then, all of a sudden, they were there, emerging into a clearing, and the house seemed to leap out of the mist to greet them with eager arms. It was so odd! It looked absolutely Victorian in construction, with its broken shingles, elaborate ornamentation, and dirty bay windows. She'd never seen anything like it in real life. . . . The house loomed over them like a great, quiet gargoyle. It might have been foreboding, evoking images of ghosts and haunted places, if it had not seemed so tired.[53]

Noemí has come to this house on a mission for her father to investigate the condition of her cousin, Catalina, whose name suggests "catalepsy." Catalina spends much of her married life in a drug-induced haze. She had married Virgil Doyle suddenly, with little explanation of his origins to her family. After her move to High Place, she sends home strange letters claiming Virgil is poisoning her. Most disturbingly, Catalina asserts that she is losing time and that ghosts come out of the walls of her room to watch her while she wastes away.

What Noemí finds upon her arrival is a weird British Gothic invasion of the small Mexican mountain mining town of El Triunfo. The patriarch Howard Doyle, who is Virgil's father, forbids anyone to leave High Place unless they need to find an heir or heiress with the right bloodlines to marry. Howard abhors the Spanish language and the Mexican people. Virgil's cousin Francis tells Noemí that High Place is "a little piece of England" and that the very soil around the house was imported from Europe to grow gardens identical to those the Doyles left behind.[54] Like Dracula invading England from the periphery of the Empire and bringing along his coffin of Transylvanian soil, the imperial Doyles invade Mexico with their postage stamp of English earth. Obsessed with eugenics and racial purity, Howard insults Noemí with comments about her skin color and heritage at dinner. His purposes for coming to Mexico many years ago (too many for him to still be alive naturally) were to practice his English ways in a new place and to exploit local workers while avoiding any intermingling with those he deemed cultural others. As Noemí unravels the horrific history of the Doyles, she learns that, like the Ushers in Poe's story, Howard had insisted on incest to keep the family tree "pure" and to hold his connection to the fungus that keeps his consciousness alive. Everyone who came into contact with High Place was exposed to the fungus that grew within its walls, in its catacombs, and all over the English cemetery on the property. When the laborers died of exposure or because of mining accidents, their bodies were added as "mulch" to keep the psychotropic fungus growing.[55] Howard discovered long ago that this fungus had healing properties that could be used to prolong his life, as long as a willing body was available for the transfer of his consciousness when his own body wore out.[56]

This fungus presents another interesting correlation to Poe's tale. Roderick believed the Usher house was infected with a sentient, phosphorescent fungus that made it a Bad Place and possibly infected the Usher family. High Place's weird, glowing fungus is similarly uncanny. It does not simply prolong life abnormally. The fungus also infects the people within, at times making them sick like Catalina, who is useless to Howard's plan. At other times, the fungal infection prepares them for incorporation into the family. Noemí is not physically sickened by the fungus, but it does affect her consciousness and invade her dreams. The Doyles believe she is compatible with them, despite her ethnicity, because of her strength. She becomes part of the psychic web linking the family members, the house, and the mushrooms. Francis tells Noemí, "The fungus, it runs under the house, all the way to the cemetery and back. It's in the walls. Like a giant spider's web. In that web we can preserve memories, thoughts, caught like the flies that wander into a real web. We call that repository of our thoughts, of our memories, *the gloom.*"[57] The house is a liminal space that holds the living physical family and their possessions, and for those dosed by the fungus who survive, High Place is a dreamy, psychic space subsumed in the family's memories. Once she is sufficiently infected by the fungus by Howard through a particularly gruesome initiation rite, Noemí, in her dreams, perceives the house as a pulsing wound, and she learns about the Doyles' past from observing memories in the gloom. She tries to speak to two of the women Howard sacrificed to spread the fungus: Agnes, one of his many previous wives, who is buried in the cemetery; and Ruth, Howard's daughter, who tried to kill her entire family to stop what she saw as cruel madness. Howard and Virgil use the gloom to manipulate and abuse Noemí, psychologically and physically, as they try to break her will. After she is tested to see whether she can withstand the fungus, Howard decides to transfer his mind to Virgil, and then, as Virgil, to marry Noemí, thus reinvigorating the family's bloodline and financial power while continuing this horror. Reminiscent of the Gothic "fear of the feminine," Howard's investment in patriarchy and eugenics is clear when Francis tells Noemí that Howard has always refused to transfer his mind into a woman's body.[58] He thinks of women as objects to collect for his lust and for the continuation of his family. Women bear the children that carry on the line or are sacrificed to keep the fungus growing.

By the end of the novel, Noemí makes a striking discovery about the gloom and its connection to Howard's violence against women. In the catacombs beneath High Place, she discovers the mummified body of Howard's previous wife Agnes. Frozen in a scream, Agnes's body may be dead, but her mind, connected to the fungus, has created the space for the gloom. She is, in a sense, to borrow a *Star Trek* metaphor, the Hive Queen of this collective, except that she is a hostage to Howard's overweening hubris. Noemí deduces that while the mushrooms had healing powers, the only way to use them to achieve immortality would be to meld them to a human mind. She thinks, "The fungus needed a human mind that could serve as a vessel for memories, that could offer control. The fungus and the proper human mind, fused together, were like wax, and Howard was like a seal, and he imprinted himself upon new bodies like a seal on paper."[59] Forced to look at Agnes while inside the gloom, Noemí realizes that the tormented woman was infected with the fungus and buried alive. She experiences Agnes's final emotions while the victim, still alive in her coffin, "screamed and screamed but nobody came."[60] Agnes is, Noemí acknowledges, the horrific secret at the heart of High Place. She was imprisoned for Howard's fiendish purposes, both in her unhappy and fearful marriage and in her live burial. With this insight, Noemí describes the gloom as "[t]he creation of an afterlife, furnished with the marrow and the bones and the neurons of a woman, made of stems and spores."[61] Agnes may have been used as mushroom mulch like the other victims, but her mind was the material used to create the gloom.

Like Madeline Usher, she turns out, however, not to be a quiet victim, although it takes her longer to retaliate. During a fraught scene in the catacombs in which escape seems impossible, Virgil threatens Noemí and Catalina and tortures Francis. Noemí suddenly realizes that the buzzing sound in the gloom is actually Agnes's rage, and it is building:

[T]he frightening and twisted gloom that surrounded them was the manifestation of all the suffering that had been inflicted on this woman. Agnes. Driven to madness, driven to anger, driven to despair, and even now a sliver of that woman remained, and that sliver was still screaming in agony. . . . The buzzing was her voice. She could not communicate properly any longer but could still scream of unspeakable horrors inflicted on her, of ruin and pain. Even when coherent memory and thought had been scraped away, this searing rage remained, burning the minds of any who wandered near it.[62]

In a flash, Noemí understands that the repeated imperative she kept hearing in the gloom, *"open your eyes,"* is Agnes's wish for someone to look at her and wake her from this sleepwalking nightmare.[63] Noemí sets Agnes's body on fire. Fed by the combustible fungus, the flames spread throughout the house and grounds, destroying High Place and finishing off the Doyles. Howard, who has been physically injured multiple times, loses his psychic link and burns; Virgil and Francis are thrown into seizures as their uncanny bonds to the fungus are damaged. Francis barely survives to escape with Noemí and Catalina.

Similar to Agnes, Catalina finds her strength, surprising Howard and Virgil, who think the poisoning from the fungus has left her a torpid shell to be used for their pleasure. Throughout most of the novel, Catalina is in a stupor. When she has moments of lucidity, what she tells Noemí about High Place is disturbing and makes Noemí question the woman's sanity, until she too experiences the gloom. In a situation recalling Madeline Usher's catalepsy, Catalina seems to be docile, bedridden much of the time, and under the control of the men. Nevertheless, she has anger inside, and she acts on that anger during the escape. When Howard is attempting to transfer, Catalina stabs him in the eye, and as Moreno-Garcia writes, "Noemí wasn't aware that Catalina could be capable of such rage. It was naked hatred, it made Noemí gasp."[64] Later, in the catacombs, Catalina dispatches Virgil when he is incapacitated by the destruction of the gloom. For Howard Doyle, the women in *Mexican Gothic* are necessary sacrifices for his racist grand plans. They are merely objects in his plot to gain immortality, and they are pawns in his bid to resuscitate his dying aristocratic roots. For Howard, women become wives who bring dowries and mothers who produce children to keep his whole monstrous affair going. However, he clearly underestimates them. In the past, his daughter had almost killed him when she tried to stop him, leaving him injured and wary, and in the novel's present, the rage of Catalina and Agnes is unleashed. These two repressed characters explosively retaliate, bringing it all, house and family, down. Doyle's predatory colonial and patriarchal schemes fall to ashes.

Poe contributed to the development of the haunted house, but contemporary women writers of horror, like Sarah Waters, Cherie Priest, and Silvia Moreno-Garcia, continue to update it. These authors adopt the broken and dangerous family home with its connections to dysfunction, violence, inheritance, secrets, repression, and imprisonment, but they focus on historically marginalized characters. All of the women in these novels are aware of the restrictions with which family and society bind them, and they all attempt to rebel. In these recent novels, women investigate the mysteries of competing narratives of the past, raging against being buried, controlled, and silenced. These narratives renovate the House of Usher by openly revealing repressed terrors similar to traumas that Poe buries with the silenced Madeline and the Usher family's foreclosed past.

NOTES

1. Allan Lloyd-Smith, *American Gothic Fiction: An Introduction* (New York: Continuum, 2004), 58.

2. Renée L. Bergland, *The National Uncanny: Indian Ghosts and American Subjects* (Hanover: University Press of New England, 2000), 7.

3. Lloyd-Smith notes that Poe was pivotal in moving the Gothic from England and Germany of the eighteenth and nineteenth centuries to America. He cites the complaints of writers like James Fenimore Cooper and Nathaniel Hawthorne that America lacked the centuries-long dark past of a place like Europe (26–27). But America had its own fodder for Gothic horror. Early settlers feared the forests, the isolation, the indigenous population, and the Devil. Furthermore, America has a history of oppression of women and people of color that often haunts American Gothic fiction. Poe also set much of his horror fiction within houses, and it is not surprising that families and homes figure prominently in American horror fiction, as they go back to the roots of Gothic fiction in England. In the British Gothic tradition, family inheritances tied to castles often drive the plots. Estates are intimately connected to the people who inhabit them. Furthermore, even if the American iteration of the domestic home replaced the aristocratic castle, the transplanted inhabitants still could not escape the terrors of isolation, history, and family. Traditional Gothic castles as well as American homes hide within their walls secrets of violence, neglect, and patriarchal control. For a discussion of the importance of family in traditional Gothic fiction, see Anne Williams, *Art of Darkness: The Poetics of Gothic* (Chicago: University of Chicago Press, 1995), 22.

4. Edgar Allan Poe, "The Fall of the House of Usher," in *Edgar Allan Poe: Poetry, Tales, and Selected Essays*, ed. Patrick F. Quinn and G. R. Thompson (New York: Library of America, 1996), 317.

5. For an important allegorical reading of this scene, see Richard Wilbur's "The House of Poe," rpt. in *The Recognition of Edgar Allan Poe*, ed. Eric W. Carlson (Ann Arbor: Michigan UP, 1966), 264–67.

6. See Stephen King, *Danse Macabre* (1981; repr., New York: Gallery Books, 2010).

7. Poe, 319.

8. Ibid., 320.

9. Dale Bailey, *American Nightmares: The Haunted House Formula in American Popular Fiction* (Bowling Green: Bowling Green State University Popular Press, 1999), 20.

10. Ibid., 21–22.

11. Poe, 327.

12. Bailey, 22. Significantly, Bailey draws a line from this moment to Shirley Jackson's description of her Bad Place in *The Haunting of Hill House* (1959).

13. Poe, 328.

14. Ibid., 324.

15. Ibid., 318.

16. Eric Savoy, "The Face of the Tenant: A Theory of American Gothic," in *American Gothic: New Interventions in a National Narrative*, ed. Robert K. Martin and Eric Savoy (Iowa City: University of Iowa Press, 1998), 9.

17. Ibid., 13–14.

18. For further discussion of how fictional haunted houses enact uncanny returns of the past, see Rebecca Janicker, *The Literary Haunted House: Lovecraft, Matheson, King and the Horror in Between* (Jefferson, NC: McFarland & Co., Inc., Publishers, 2015), 19.

19. For a discussion of the history of violence against women within domestic spaces in traditional Gothic novels, see Kate Ferguson Ellis, *The Contested Castle: Gothic Novels and the Subversion of Domestic Ideology* (Urbana: University of Illinois Press, 1989).

20. Gina Wisker, *Contemporary Women's Gothic Fiction: Carnival, Hauntings, and Vampire Kisses* (London: Palgrave [Springer Nature], 2016), 208.

21. Ibid., 14.

22. Sarah Waters, *The Little Stranger* (New York: Riverhead Books, 2009), 3.

23. Ibid., 5.

24. Ibid., 53.

25. Ibid., 69.

26. Ibid., 157.

27. Gina Wisker, "The Feminist Gothic in *The Little Stranger*: Troubling Narratives of Continuity and Change," in *Sarah Waters and Contemporary Feminisms*, ed. Adele Jones and Claire O'Callaghan (London: Palgrave, 2016), 104.

28. Waters, 374.

29. Ibid., 447.

30. Ibid., 494.

31. Ibid., 510.

32. Wisker, "The Feminist Gothic," 103.

33. Ibid., 97.

34. Williams, 22.

35. Cherie Priest, *The Family Plot* (New York: Tor, 2016), 152.

36. Ibid., 43.

37. Ibid., 45, 46, 54.

38. Ibid., 46.

39. Ibid., 349.

40. Ibid., 168.

41. Ibid., 168.

42. Wisker, *Contemporary Women's Gothic Fiction*, 14.

43. Priest, 149.

44. Ibid., 322.

45. Ibid., 322.

46. Ibid., 322.

47. Ibid., 323.

48. Ibid., 324.

49. Ibid., 329.

50. Ibid., 331.

51. Ibid., 356–60.

52. Ibid., 318.

53. Silvia Moreno-Garcia, *Mexican Gothic* (New York: Del Rey, 2020), 20.

54. Ibid., 18.

55. Ibid., 236.

56. In addition to the "Usher" allusions, there are shades of Poe's "Ligeia" in *Mexican Gothic*, including the idea of a monstrous will to live, the poisoning of a beautiful young woman, and the claustrophobic atmosphere.

57. Moreno-Garcia, 211.

58. Lloyd-Smith, 58; Moreno-Garcia, 249.

59. Ibid., 283.

60. Ibid., 282.

61. Ibid., 284.

62. Ibid., 289.

63. Ibid., 290.

64. Ibid., 270–71.

Afterword

Maureen Cobb Mabbott and The Collected Works of Edgar Allan Poe

Travis Montgomery

For many scholars, Thomas Ollive Mabbott is a household name associated with *The Collected Works of Edgar Allan Poe* (hereafter *Collected Works*), a carefully edited and annotated three-volume set of Poe's writings issued by Harvard University Press and known to specialists as the Mabbott edition. This scholarly milestone is the product of a career dedicated to the study of Poe, a professional pursuit during which Thomas identified literary sources, tracked down reprintings, and consulted manuscripts. Individual volumes of *Collected Works* display the fruits of that labor. Each book features detailed headnotes and annotations for every Poe piece, and the pages of edited text contain lists of variants, information that illuminates Poe's revising practices. Furthermore, the three volumes, taken together, offer a reliable canon of Poe's poetry and tales. Published before the 1980s, the Mabbott edition remains, despite its age, indispensable, its continuing relevance most evident in the frequency with which critics reference it. Such broad usage keeps Thomas's name alive.

The name of his wife, Maureen Cobb Mabbott, is, however, less familiar, even though she played a key role in the publication of *Collected Works*, and this afterword serves as an appropriate conclusion to *Women and Poe*, a collection that highlights the importance of women as shapers of Poe reception. The primary reason why Maureen's contributions to Poe studies have not received the attention they deserve is that she worked outside the academy, an institution that, especially so in her time, promoted and supported the scholarly achievements of male professors—the people who made up the majority of its members. As the wife of a professor, Maureen spent much of her time at home, performing the sort of household duties expected of many women during the mid-twentieth century, and separated from the public spaces of university life, she did not, as a scholar, have the visibility of a conventional academic. Her case underscores a problem with attempts to account for meaningful scholarly labor by focusing on colleges. Emphasizing work performed by faculty members and editors at university presses can render the contributions of others invisible. Lives like Maureen's are, however, reminders that important scholarship happens beyond the institutional confines of higher education.

On more than one occasion, Maureen "claimed she was no Poe scholar," and although she did not pursue a professorial career, her intellectual credentials were impressive.[1] She had a master's degree in English, but unlike Thomas, who had a long career in academe, Maureen taught at the university level for only one year. She did, however, do some scholarly writing, the life and works of Leonardo da Vinci being her chosen subject, and in 1936, her *Catalogue of the Lieb Memorial Collection of Vinciana* saw print.[2] Nevertheless, her primary interests took her outside the world of scholarship. Maureen "wrote poetry almost every day," publishing some of her work, and she was an art connoisseur, volunteering at the Metropolitan Museum of Art and supporting the Whitney Museum of American Art.[3] These activities Maureen performed while keeping house and raising her daughter Jane. Busy as she was, she *did* make time for Poe scholarship. In fact, her name graced the title pages of volumes two and three of *Collected Works*, both of which appeared long after the death of her husband, and according to those pages, Maureen provided "assistance" for the project.[4] Although Harvard University Press acknowledged some of her contributions to the Mabbott edition, those efforts as well as her support for fellow scholars have not been widely recognized. By the time she joined the team working on that project, Maureen had a wealth of experience that qualified her for the job. With her unique training and talents, she was, in fact, the *ideal* candidate to help Harvard University Press publish *Collected Works*.

Her rural upbringing provided a firm foundation for that undertaking. Known as "Mernie" to friends and family, Maureen grew up on a farm in a squarish piece of northern Missouri called Carroll County, and she described her early life in *Shannondale*, a short memoir peppered with evocative poetry. Carroll County is west of Hannibal, the river town where Mark Twain spent his boyhood years and found inspiration for *The Adventures of Huckleberry Finn*, a book that Maureen studied in school.[5] Like Twain, she delighted in her childhood home. Born in 1899, she lived nearly a decade in a house without gas lighting and running water, but her mind flourished in the country. Nearby lived her two grandfathers, who were Civil War veterans, their battle yarns feeding her interest in things past.[6] Natural wonders provided other delights. Each summer, meadowlarks made "silver music" that thrilled her. Another source of joy was her favorite Maiden Blush tree, which she recalled in lyrical prose:

> Its apples, when ripe, had a golden tone with a faint, rosy blush, depending on how they had caught the sun. The first branches of the tree were strong and low. A little higher was a comfortable place for reading or dreaming. There, sheltered by leaves, . . . I was within calling distance but far away. Up still higher, my arms around a slender bough, my cheek pressed against its bark, I would stand and watch the cloud castles form and reform in the blue immensity above me.[7]

Full of sensory pleasures, the Cobb homeplace furnished ample resources for her creative growth, her imaginative ripening; the aesthetic sensitivity that Maureen developed during childhood helped her become a splendid writer, an astute admirer of art, and a careful reader. For a healthy child like Maureen, life on a self-sustaining farm had additional value. There was always plenty of work to do, and everyone, including children, had to pitch in. While "watering chickens, washing dishes, tending babies, pumping water, churning butter" and performing other chores, she learned the value of hard work, building habits of self-reliance and industry that made her a diligent editor.[8]

Such household labor was surely demanding, but it neither dampened her spirits nor dulled her faculties, as her voracious reading demonstrated. From an early age, Maureen loved the printed word. In her memoir, she recalled finding unfamiliar "words in magazines and newspapers" and asking adults for pronunciation help. Constant questioning of that sort, she insisted, made her "a nuisance to all grown-ups."[9] Soon enough, she could read independently. In grade school, Maureen delved into Norse mythology, and the grand cadences of the King James Bible, a book that she read at home, appealed to her poetic sensibility. Her schoolhouse had a single room, in which she often listened to the teacher work with older students, gathering any crumbs of knowledge she might add to her ever-increasing store.[10]

So compelling was her love of literature that Maureen decided to go to college, where she could read and study deeply. Although this ambition seemed peculiar to her farmer father, he supported Maureen's dream, pledging that "if she could earn the money for the first year, he would find a way to pay for the rest."[11] To cover her share, Maureen moved to Oklahoma, where she did secretarial work for a lawyer and boarded with family members. Two years later, Northwestern University awarded her a scholarship, and for a year, she attended classes there before tragedy upset her educational plans. In late spring, Maureen unexpectedly lost her father. She then left Illinois for Missouri, where she became a teacher. This arrangement did not, however,

please her relatives, who "would not let [Maureen] sacrifice herself."[12] Her
cleverness, her fascination with books, and her intellectual promise must
have profoundly impressed them. Supported by family, Maureen considered
her options, discovering that she could finish her degree at the University of
Chicago, where the quarter system was in place. The only problem was that
the spring quarter began *before* the school year for her students ended. To this
dilemma Maureen found a brilliant solution. She proposed meeting for class
six days each week instead of five so she could close the school in March and
travel to Chicago before the spring term started. The school board backed the
plan, and Maureen enrolled in college courses. Studying English, she earned
her bachelor's degree in 1924. Three years later, the University of Chicago
granted her a master's degree in the same subject.[13] "After graduate school,"
Maureen moved to Ohio, where she taught "at Western College . . . for a year
before her marriage."[14]

Love of reading and art brought Maureen and Thomas together. They
came, however, from different worlds. A native of New York City, Thomas
was the child of privilege, and he knew little of farm life. Nevertheless,
the two met in 1923 in the Windy City, where he taught at Northwestern
University while she studied English at the University of Chicago.[15] To some
extent, their courtship was epistolary, and the letters they exchanged during
the 1920s often touched on literary themes, Elizabethan poetry and Poe being
frequent discussion topics.[16] Thomas's enthusiasm for Poe exceeded hers, but
Maureen did enjoy the writer's popular tales and poems—especially the latter, which she, a poet herself, found interesting for their artistry.[17] Admiration
of fine paintings and sculptures was another delight Thomas and Maureen
shared. During a 1927 visit to London, he wrote her a letter expressing the
awe that he felt while gazing at classical statuary in the British Museum.
Those remnants of Grecian glory were, Thomas averred, transcendently
beautiful, and dashes scattered throughout the missive conveyed his breathless wonder.[18] Touching in its affective candor, that letter revealed a powerful
intimacy between writer and recipient, a deep trust based on mutual respect.
Their partnership lasted for decades. Married in 1928, the Mabbotts spent
the majority of their years together in New York City, relishing its libraries,
bookstores, and museums.[19] Thomas taught at Hunter College and combed
through library collections while Maureen pursued her own aesthetic interests and worked as a homemaker. Different as their individual lives were, the
Mabbotts had an intellectual companionship rare for its time.[20]

During his Hunter years, Thomas devoted much of his time to research,
planning a complete set of Poe's writings that would supersede the edition
prepared by James A. Harrison, and "Maureen . . . who served as an assistant to her husband during the many years of his research," had an intimate
knowledge of the work he was doing.[21] That work came to a temporary halt in

Fig. A.1. Thomas and Maureen Mabbott, 1936. Reproduced by kind permission of Jane Mabbott Austrian.

1968, the year that Thomas died of bone cancer. According to his colleagues Clarence Gohdes and Rollo Silver, Thomas had, by that time, essentially completed the first volume of his Poe edition:

> The printer's copy for the texts of the poems and for the accompanying apparatus had been read and approved by [Thomas]. He had completed recent revisions of the preface and the introduction to the poems, of all the appendixes, and of the "Annals," as he called his outline of Poe's biography and career as a writer. He had also corrected ninety-five galleys—more than half—of the proofs of the poems and commentary.[22]

Apparently, the text was not as near completion as that account implied. A recent study of the Mabbott Papers at the University of Iowa has revealed that Maureen's "hand appears throughout the file on 'The Raven,'" indicating that her contributions to the *Poems* volume involved more than copyediting.[23] Polishing of that sort certainly consumed much of her time. Eleanor D. Kewer, a Harvard University Press editor, and Maureen checked the remaining proofs and put the final touches on the book, which was published in 1969.[24]

More substantial was the work Maureen did for the next two volumes of the Mabbott edition. Although Thomas "had empowered [Gohdes and Silver] to look after the interests of the edition if he could not," the two men did little to prepare the remaining volumes for publication.[25] Those scholars did, however, provide counsel on textual matters while Maureen and Kewer sorted through typescripts that Thomas had left "in rough form."[26] That arrangement was ideal. Assisted by the seasoned editor Kewer, Maureen was, indeed, her husband's natural successor, for despite their academic credentials, Gohdes and Silver simply knew less about the project than Maureen did. Reflecting on the matter after publication, she acknowledged that personal experience gave her special insights into Thomas's work: "I had not done scholarship on Poe, but I had lived in the house with him for forty years. My husband was a man of many interests, and in a way Poe was a *background* figure in our lives, but he was always there." She added, "I was familiar with the Mabbott aims for the edition, with its problems and materials, and with the personalities in Poe scholarship. . . ."[27] Such familiarity ensured quality control. Organizing material for the *Tales & Sketches* volumes, Maureen used the *Poems* book as a model. For that publication Thomas had prepared exhaustive variant lists for the poems, and before his death, he had compiled similar lists for Poe's short fictional works. Knowing how much Thomas cared about giving scholars easy access to textual variants, Maureen took recording that material for the *Tales & Sketches* volumes seriously.[28] This task, which was her primary undertaking, presented some challenges. Following discussions between Maureen and editors at Harvard University Press, a superscript system for documenting variants in the prose texts was adopted, but that system was not original with Thomas. Thus Maureen—aided by Patricia Edwards Clyne, one of Thomas's former students—spent "long hours . . . comparing and reviewing all the original texts—and visiting manuscripts again because . . . so-called facsimiles . . . could not be trusted."[29] She even accounted for misprints.[30]

In addition, Maureen weighed in on the annotations. While working on the *Tales & Sketches* volumes, she made notes indicating that she checked and modified material originally prepared by Thomas. The Mabbott Papers offer the evidence. For example, one document shows that Maureen rejected what she considered a gratuitous note about minor terminological blunders in Poe's "The Murders in the Rue Morgue" identified by researchers.[31] Additional evidence of her involvement in annotation appears on a photocopy of an 1827 source for Poe's "The Premature Burial," a document that contains what seem to be Maureen's handwritten remarks about French names from Poe's tale. Those comments were probably used to modify note 5 on page 970 of the second volume.[32] Both of these items suggest that Maureen tried to keep *all* the material in the Mabbott edition current, useful, and accurate.

Her nearly decade-long labor was Herculean, but with the help of Clyne and the supervision of Kewer, Maureen finished the job, giving scholars an indispensable tool for understanding the writing habits of a great American author. A perfectionist in matters of literary craft, Poe frequently revisited his published works and made textual changes, some of which were considerable. The Mabbott edition presented what was, in the late 1970s, the most comprehensive record of those changes, a variant archive revealing how Poe's writings evolved throughout his career. Maureen's work made that archive available for general use.

The year 1978 was when the *Tales & Sketches* volumes, to which Maureen had dedicated untold hours, were published. At that time, Thomas was long dead, and critics familiar with his Poe edition were eager for additional installments. Greeted by accolades, the new offerings from Harvard University Press did not disappoint. For David B. Kesterton, the appearance of those books ensured that *Collected Works* "will undoubtedly stand for years as the major scholarly edition of the poems and short prose works" of Poe.[33] Not all of the reviews were, however, laudatory. In a lengthy piece for *Poe Studies*, Joseph J. Moldenhauer declared the editing process that shaped the *Tales & Sketches* volumes unsound because Thomas, its architect, did not follow the "set of concrete procedures for recapturing authorial intention" established by Sir Walter Wilson Greg. Moldenhauer nevertheless conceded that the Mabbott volumes had "fringe benefits of immense value to scholars and critics," attributing those benefits to the hard work of Thomas.[34] That assertion was partially true. Brimming with annotations and information about variants, the *Tales & Sketches* texts *were* quite useful for Poe research. Those books were not, however, the handiwork of one laborer. According to Blake Bronson-Bartlett, those texts were part of "an editorial project perhaps directed by [Thomas], but not completely attributable to him in any of the three volumes."[35] The latter two especially bore out that claim. Editorial collaboration brought those books into existence, and without Maureen, the *Tales & Sketches* volumes probably would not have seen the light of day.

Her contributions to Poe studies did not end with the printing of those texts. For the rest of her life, she supported other editors and researchers. Shortly after the final volumes of the Mabbott edition were published, Maureen donated a set of *Tales & Sketches* to the Poe Foundation, which maintained the Poe Shrine (now Poe Museum) in Richmond. The group's president at the time, Bruce V. English, thanked her for the books, noting that they would make a nice addition to the organization's library, which was an important resource for scholars within and without the United States.[36] To provide additional material for researchers, Maureen offered the Poe Foundation a copy of her husband's "Observations on Poets and Poetry."[37] Another beneficiary of her assistance was Burton R. Pollin, who set out to finish the comprehensive edition of Poe's writings that Thomas had planned. That project was never completed, but Pollin did publish five volumes in a series titled *The Collected Writings of Edgar Allan Poe*.[38] While preparing those books, he relied on sources from Thomas's collection that Maureen graciously provided, and Pollin acknowledged her help in the first two volumes.[39] In addition, he expressed sincere admiration for Maureen and Kewer, whose "painstaking methods of editing" inspired his own efforts.[40] Maureen's editorial prowess also caught the attention of Benjamin F. Fisher, another notable figure in the Poe world. In fact, in his dedication to *Poe at Work: Seven Textual Studies*, Fisher included her name in a list of "Three Distinguished Editors."[41] Her reputation preceding her, Maureen was invited to address "the Poe group of the Modern Languages Association" at the 1978 convention, and in 1980, she published an essay about her husband's Poe scholarship, a piece that Jay Hubbell of Duke University had solicited and that the Edgar Allan Poe Society of Baltimore printed in cooperation with the Enoch Pratt Free Library and the Library of the University of Baltimore.[42] Maureen also extended personal hospitality to Poe specialists in her Lexington Avenue apartment. Such largesse impressed Fisher, who, remembering years of friendship with her, judged her "a great human being, one who encompassed, within a compact frame much intellectuality, aesthetic awareness and sensitivity, and a gracious social presence."[43] After she left Manhattan for Medford Lees, a retirement home, Maureen maintained relationships within the Poe world, corresponding with Fisher and others until her death in 1993.[44]

Poe studies simply would not be what it is without Maureen, a brilliant woman whose name should be more familiar than it is. In addition to mentoring many scholars in the field, she generously dedicated a large portion of her time to finishing books that her husband started but never lived to see in print. Eager to give Thomas credit for his scholarship, Maureen understated hers, never calling herself a Poe specialist. Such a title has, however, limited value for anyone trying to appreciate the ways in which Maureen influenced the study of Poe and his writings. Her editorial achievements and collegial spirit are the credentials by which "she showed," as Fisher has said, "that she *was* a Poe scholar."[45] The best reminder of that truth is perhaps the Mabbott edition itself, the name emblazoned on its covers shared by *two* notable editors, Thomas and Maureen.

NOTE FROM THE AUTHOR

Travis Montgomery thanks the Special Collections staff at the Main Library of the University of Iowa for their assistance, which involved searching for materials in the Mabbott Papers and finding contact information for the

Fig. A.2. The Mabbotts with their granddaughter Gabrielle, c. 1965. Reproduced by kind permission of Jane Mabbott Austrian.

Mabbott legatee. Denise K. Anderson, Lindsay Moen, Micaela R. Terronez, and Zoe Webb were especially helpful. Blake Bronson-Bartlett, who created the university's "Mabbott Poe" site, pointed out some relevant materials. A personal friend of Maureen Cobb Mabbott, Benjamin F. Fisher kindly sat for an interview and lent the author printed materials relevant to this project. The curator of The Poe Museum, Christopher P. Semtner, provided scanned images of letters from the museum's correspondence files. Jeffrey Savoye, the secretary of the Edgar Allan Poe Society of Baltimore, answered queries about Maureen's connections to that organization. Those responses helped the author avoid some factual errors. Maureen's daughter Jane Mabbott Austrian shared important information about her mother's college years, and with the help of her daughter Gabrielle Albans Hirschfeld, Austrian provided family photos of Thomas and Maureen. For the generosity of Austrian and Hirschfeld, the author is most grateful.

NOTES

1. Travis Montgomery, interview with Benjamin F. Fisher, Oxford, Mississippi, March 19, 2018. The words quoted are Fisher's. Unless otherwise indicated, this interview is the source of biographical information mentioned in this paragraph.

2. Mabbott, Maureen Cobb. *Catalogue of the Lieb Memorial Collection of Vinciana* (Hoboken: Stevens Institute of Technology, 1936).

3. Montgomery, interview with Benjamin F. Fisher. The words quoted are Fisher's.

4. See Thomas Ollive Mabbott, ed., *The Collected Works of Edgar Allan Poe,* vols. 2 and 3 (Cambridge: Harvard University Press, 1978).

5. Maureen Cobb Mabbott, *Shannondale* (Solon: Maecenas Press, 1984), 39–40. For additional information about Maureen's childhood, see *Shannondale: Epilogue* (Solon: Maecenas Press, 1988).

6. Mabbott, *Shannondale*, untitled preface (n.p.), 40.

7. Ibid., 7, 45–46.

8. Ibid., 45.

9. Ibid., 21.

10. Ibid., 23, 22.

11. Jane Mabbott Austrian, email message to author June 20, 2019, 9:38 a.m.

12. Ibid.

13. Jane Mabbott Austrian, email message to author October 31, 2021, 6:19 p.m.

14. Austrian, email message to author, June 20, 2019, 9:38 a.m. Unless otherwise indicated, the factual material in this paragraph derives from this message.

15. Austrian, email message to author, November 1, 2021, 10:30 a.m.

16. See Thomas Ollive Mabbott, "Observations on Poets and Poetry," *Books at Iowa* 29 (November 1978): 14–35. This article, which appeared after Thomas's death, contains excerpts from his letters to Maureen. The selections are hers, and an unsigned introduction precedes those excerpts. For additional excerpts from Thomas's letters to Maureen, see Maureen Cobb Mabbott, *Mabbott as Poe Scholar: The Early Years* (Baltimore: The Enoch Pratt Free Library, the Edgar Allan Poe Society of Baltimore, and the Library of the University of Baltimore, 1980), 10–19.

17. Montgomery, interview with Benjamin F. Fisher.

18. A facsimile of the letter appears on page 30 of Mabbott's "Observations on Poets and Poetry."

19. Austrian, email message to author, November 1, 2021, 10:30 a.m.

20. Thomas's respect for his wife's intellect reflects his attitudes toward women with academic ambitions. According to Hunter alumna Patricia Edwards Clyne, Thomas "considered women to be equal to men in all respects" at a time when the university where he taught rarely allowed women to wear trousers on campus. "Thomas O. Mabbott as Teacher," *Books at Iowa* 34 (April 1981): 31, 34.

21. Clarence Gohdes and Rollo Silver, "Acknowledgments," *The Collected Works of Edgar Allan Poe,* ed. Thomas Ollive Mabbott, vol. 1 (Cambridge: Harvard University Press, 1969), viii.

22. Ibid.

23. Blake Bronson-Bartlett, "About," Mabbott Poe, https://mabbottpoe.org/about.

24. Gohdes and Silver, "Acknowledgements," viii.

25. Mabbott, *Mabbott as Poe Scholar*, 29.

26. Ibid. Maureen did seek advice from other Poe scholars, whom she and Kewer identify in the "Acknowledgements" for vol. 2 of *Collected Works*. See pp. v–vi. The

information in the second half of the sentence derives from the author's interview with Benjamin F. Fisher, and the words quoted are Fisher's.

27. Mabbott, *Mabbott as Poe Scholar*, 27.

28. Ibid., 30.

29. Ibid.

30. Ibid., 31.

31. Blake Bronson-Bartlett described this document and posted an image of it on the Mabbott Poe site. See "other people's fun," "The Murders in the Rue Morgue," "Mabbott's Research Files," Mabbott Poe, http://mabbottpoe.org/items/show/319.

32. See "'Philadelphia The Casket. September 1827,' 6 Images," "The Premature Burial," "Mabbott's Research Files," Mabbott Poe, http://mabbottpoe.org/items/show /346. Bronson-Bartlett posted the images, providing commentary on the material.

33. David B. Kesterton, "Review: New Resources for Poe Studies," *The Southern Literary Journal* 15, no. 2 (Spring 1983): 103.

34. Joseph J. Moldenhauer, "Mabbott's Poe and the Question of Copy-Text," *Poe Studies* 11, no. 2 (1978): 42, 46.

35. Bronson-Bartlett, "About."

36. Maureen Cobb Mabbott, *Maureen Cobb Mabbott to Bruce V. English, March 10, 1978.* Letter. Poe Museum, *Correspondence Files*; Bruce V. English, *Bruce V. English to Maureen Cobb Mabbott, April 9, 1978.* Letter. Poe Museum (Richmond, VA), *Correspondence Files*.

37. Bruce V. English, *Bruce V. English to Maureen Cobb Mabbott, March 4, 1979.* Letter. Poe Museum (Richmond, VA), *Correspondence Files*.

38. For the fifth volume, J. V. Ridgely served as Pollin's coeditor.

39. Burton R. Pollin, ed., *The Collected Writings of Edgar Allan Poe,* vol. 1 (Boston: Twayne, 1981), v; Burton R. Pollin, ed., *The Collected Writings of Edgar Allan Poe,* vol. 2 (New York: Gordian Press, 1985), vi.

40. Pollin, ed., *Collected Writings,* vol. 1.

41. Benjamin F. Fisher, ed., *Poe at Work: Seven Textual Studies* (Baltimore: The Edgar Allan Poe Society of Baltimore, 1978).

42. Mabbott, *Mabbott as Poe Scholar*, 25. For a brief account of the preparation and publication of that essay, see "Acknowledgements" in *Mabbott as Poe Scholar*.

43. Benjamin F. Fisher, "Maureen Cobb Mabbott," *PSA Newsletter* 21, no. 2 (Fall 1993): 5.

44. The factual material presented in the second half of this paragraph derives from the interview with Benjamin F. Fisher.

45. Montgomery, interview with Benjamin F. Fisher.

Index

"The Accusing Voice" (Davis), 134
adaptations of Poe's writings (comics),
109, 111, 112–14, 117. *See also* "The
Black Cat" (Moore and Reppion);
The Masque of the Red Death (Pini);
"Ligeia" (Pollack and Geary); *Poe*
series (Asala); *Poe: Stories and
Poems: A Graphic Novel Adaptation*
(Hinds); *Ravenous* (Brown); *Spirits
of the Dead* (Corben); *The Surreal
Adventures of Edgar Allan Poo*
(MacPherson and Boatwright);
"The System of Doctor Tarr and
Professor Fether" (Despeyroux and
Serratosa); "The Tell-Tale Heart"
(Slater and Duke)
adaptations of Poe's writings (film),
92, 93, 100, 101–2, 105n8. *See also*
Argento, Dario; *Berenice* (Latosh);
The Black Cat (Gordon); Corman,
Roger; *Edgar Allan Poe's "Morella"*
(Ferrell); Green, Rob; McTeigue,
James; Wynorski, Jim
Adventure, 135
affective spiritualism, 22, 23, 26–28, 31,
36, 37, 38. *See also* "The Colloquy
of Monos and Una" (Poe); *Eureka*
(Poe); "Mesmeric Revelation" (Poe);
Philothea (Child)

Akutagawa, Ryūnosuke, 76
"Al Aaraaf" (Poe), 30
Allan, Frances, 10–11
Allan, John, 1, 6–7, 8, 10, 11
Allen, Hervey, 12
Alterton, Margaret, 59
*American Transcendental
Quarterly* (*ATQ*), 63
Amper, Susan, 57
Anderson, Gayle Denington, 58
Anderson, Melanie R., 147n1
"Annabel Lee" (Hinds), 114–15, *115.
See also Poe: Stories and Poems: A
Graphic Novel Adaptation* (Hinds)
"Annabel Lee" (Poe), 61, 80, 114–15
*An Appeal in Favor of That Class of
Americans Called Africans* (Child),
27, 39, 42n27, 47n75. *See also* Child,
Lydia Maria
Appignanesi, Lisa, 18n53
Argento, Dario, 100, 101–2, 105n8
Argersinger, Jana, 56, 63,
67n53, 73n125
Argosy, 135
Aristotle, 23, 36
Armiento, Amy Branam, 54, 58, 70n100
Asala, Jason, 118. *See also Poe*
series (Asala)
Ashley, Michael, 147n1

About the Editors and Contributors

Melanie R. Anderson is associate professor of English at Delta State University in Cleveland, Mississippi. She is the coauthor of the award-winning book *Monster, She Wrote: The Women Who Pioneered Horror and Speculative Fiction* (2019) and the author of *Spectrality in the Novels of Toni Morrison* (2013). She has coedited three collections of essays, the most recent of which is *Shirley Jackson and Domesticity: Beyond the Haunted House* (2020). She also cohosts two podcasts about horror: *The Know Fear Cast* and the *Monster, She Wrote Podcast.*

Amy Branam Armiento is professor of English at Frostburg State University, and she is immediate past president of the Poe Studies Association. Many of her publications and invited lectures focus on the treatment of women in nineteenth-century short stories and poems, including her book chapter "Mother Goddess Manifestations in Poe's 'Morella' and 'Catholic Hymn'" in *Perspectives on Poe: Deciphering Poe* (Lehigh University Press/Rowman & Littlefield, 2013).

Adam C. Bradford is professor of English at Idaho State University. His scholarship and teaching focus on nineteenth-century American literature and culture. He has published several articles and essays on Poe, including a monograph titled *Communities of Death: Whitman, Poe and the Nineteenth-Century American Culture of Mourning* (2014). He is the 2018 winner of the James W. Gargano Award for his essay "'Any Peculiar Taste of Prepossession'?: Poe and the Antebellum Registers of Authorial Interpretation," which appeared in *Poe Studies: History, Theory, Interpretation.*

Kevin Knott is associate professor of English at Frostburg State University, where he teaches advanced composition, Restoration and eighteenth-century British literature, and survey courses on the Gothic and Shirley Jackson. His recent research includes comprehensive studies of the conte cruel in the nineteenth and twentieth centuries (especially as written by Shirley Jackson), as well as examining the marketing and evolution of horror in early twentieth-century pulp magazines.

John Edward Martin is a scholarly communication librarian at the University of North Texas and an adjunct instructor in the Department of Information Sciences. He is also the organizer of the Comics Studies at UNT outreach initiative. He serves as Book Review Editor of *The Edgar Allan Poe Review* and has published previous chapters on Poe's works in *Perspectives on Poe: Deciphering Poe* (Lehigh University Press/Rowman & Littlefield, 2013) and in *Fear and Learning: Essays on the Pedagogy of Horror* (2013). He holds a PhD in American literature from Northwestern University and an MS in library science from the University of North Texas.

Travis Montgomery is associate professor of English at Oklahoma Christian University. He serves on the advisory board for *Poe Studies*, and one of his essays recently appeared in *Anthologizing Poe: Editions, Translations, and (Trans)National Canons* (Lehigh University Press/Rowman & Littlefield, 2020). His work has also been published in *The Cambridge Companion to American Gothic* as well as in journals such as *Gothic Studies* and *American Literary Realism*.

Clara Petino received her PhD from the University of Cologne, Germany, with a dissertation on the Salem witch trials and their legacy in American literature. Her book *Salem—A Literary Profile: Themes and Motifs in the Depiction of Colonial and Contemporary Salem* was published in 2021.

Alexandra Reuber is senior professor of practice of French at Tulane University. Her research interests are Gothic and horror fiction, popular culture studies, and second language acquisition. Her recent publications include the following: "Lost in the Supermarket: When 'The Mist' Fogs Our Mind . . . When Basic Emotions Transform into Monstrous Acts," in *Violence in the Films of Stephen King* (Lexington Books, 2021); "Gothic Recall: Stephen King's Uncanny Revival of the Frankenstein Myth," in *The Modern Stephen King Canon: Beyond Horror* (Rowman & Littlefield, 2018); and "Identity Crisis and Personality Disorders in Edgar Allan Poe's 'William Wilson' (1839), David Fincher's *Fight Club* (1999), and James Mangold's *Identity* (2003)" in *Adapting Poe: Re-Imaginings in International and Popular Culture* (2012).

Sandra Tomc is professor of English Language and Literatures at the University of British Columbia, Vancouver. Specializing in nineteenth-century

U.S. print culture, she is the author of *Industry and the Creative Mind: The Eccentric Writer in American Literature and Entertainment, 1790–1860* (2012) and *Fashion Nation: Picturing the United States in the Long Nineteenth Century* (2021). Her articles on Poe and other nineteenth-century U.S. writers have appeared in *The Oxford Handbook of Edgar Allan Poe*, *ELH, American Literature*, and *Representations*.